Heidegger's *Being and Time*
and the Possibility of Political Philosophy

HEIDEGGER'S
Being and Time
and the Possibility of Political Philosophy

MARK BLITZ

PAUL DRY BOOKS
Philadelphia 2017

First Paul Dry Books edition, 2017

Paul Dry Books
Philadelphia, Pennsylvania
www.pauldrybooks.com

Printed in the United States

ISBN 978-1-58988-117-4

To Ellen;
Daniel, Lisa, and Caterina;
and Adam, Erin, Evan, Grant, and Lia

Acknowledgments

Several colleagues have helped me with this book. Among them I wish to mention Werner Dannhauser.

Harvey Mansfield, Jr., first attracted me to the study of political philosophy, and remains my model as both teacher and scholar.

I am pleased to acknowledge the skill of my editors at Cornell and the patience of my family. My parents transmitted a love of learning; for that, and for much else, I will always be grateful.

I would like to thank Paul Dry for suggesting and undertaking a new edition of the book.

Contents

For this new edition of *Heidegger's* Being and Time *and the Possibility of Political Philosophy* I have left the text unchanged. I believe that the book remains an accurate summary and analysis of the major topics of *Being and Time* and of its implications for political philosophy. In the Afterword I describe my book's genesis, reiterate and amplify my discussion of several of Heidegger's themes, and examine what the material from his lectures and seminars published during the past thirty-five years teaches us about his politics.

Introduction

This book explores the implications for political philosophy of Heidegger's *Being and Time*. My method is to summarize and explicate Heidegger's analyses and then to comment on them. The explications vary in length, depending upon the amount of detail needed to clarify Heidegger's argument or to illustrate problems and issues raised in Heidegger's text or in my discussion. My aim is to help the reader understand Heidegger's analysis of Being and man's Being in general and the meaning of his discussion for moral and political philosophy in particular. I will attempt to clarify what appears to be obscure, but I will not attempt easy clarity at the expense of accuracy. Moreover, I will attempt throughout to keep the difficulties and uncertainties of Heidegger's enterprise in full view. Consequently, my remarks will sometimes raise questions that I do not answer definitively.

It is customary for citizens in modern democracies to rely on scholars and intellectuals to discover the ways and means that sustain the political community. This reliance has grown continuously as the effects of scientific research have spread. Indeed, institutions have arisen that have claimed public policy as a field of scientific study, and the government has come increasingly to be managed by those with technical training. At the same time, there has been a growing mistrust of politics—an increasing dislike for political conflict and increasing forgetfulness of the place of honor, glory, and pride in the political community.

Our habitual reliance on scholarly guidance, however, is today accompanied by an unsteady faith in the ability of scientists and intellectuals successfully to manage political affairs. In fact, the spread of the scientific approach may itself have caused our contemporary belief in the difficulty of accurate political judgment and effective government. Who now claims confidently that more technically "rational" control of men and affairs is appropriate when technology takes the lead both in shattering traditional mores and in threatening ungodly destruction?

More important, few today believe truly that scholars and intellectuals can correctly understand the root purposes of politics. For we now hear incessantly from the scholars themselves that political goals arise from values that are seen from perspectives that cannot be defended objectively. Indeed, attempts to discuss the purpose of politics, justice, are called "philosophical" precisely because we think them ultimately empty: what we now call philosophy seems to be the area within what we previously called philosophy that has been unable to convert itself into science. Philosophy as a pursuit appears doomed to labor within presupposition and assumption.

Yet, science cannot honestly assert this limitation of philosophy, because to do so, and even to distinguish rigorously between science and philosophy, would require science to speak to areas beyond its competence. It seems that neither philosophy nor science can explain or justify itself as a rational activity and choiceworthy human pursuit, whatever its relation to politics. For how could such a discussion be carried on if philosophy is finally meaningless and if the rationality of science cannot justify human activity?

But if scholars are not to guide us, who is? It can hardly be political men in an age when politics has uncertain status and substance and increasingly relinquishes authority to rational administrators and technical advisers. We must therefore conclude that if the purposes and possibilities of politics and philosophy are to be assessed correctly, the meaning and justification of practical and theoretical activity must be reconsidered, and the entire relationship between politics and philosophy must be rethought. But precisely if the situation is as we have outlined, who can begin to engage in such a consideration, and what could be the concepts of such a rethinking? Are we not in the midst of the paralysis that has become popularly known as the crisis of the West? I suggest that the reconsideration must return to the original phenomena from which the meaning of politics, philosophy, and science are first understood; that it must put into question its own attempt to know; and that it must be ready to surrender the conceptions and distinctions with which it begins.

Any of several scholarly possibilities would offer a proper entrance to this effort—among them, to explore the origin of philosophy and especially political philosophy in the Greeks; to study the origin of modern philosophy and especially political philosophy among Machiavelli and his followers; to examine the unmasking of philosophy and morality in Nietzsche; or to analyze the radical questioning of what and how things are, of "being," which animates the work of Heidegger. From among these possibilities, I choose the last.

Heidegger's work attempts to uncover the ontological sources of the practical and theoretical, the everyday and scientific understanding of what is. Readers partially familiar with his writings may think that his inquiry into "being" does not touch on the concerns of political philosophy. They are wrong. In the course of his works Heidegger thematically discusses the distinction between theory and practice; what is common and what is whole; the meaning of the "public;" science and technology; the meaning of ends and purposes; what is "good"; justice; courage; leadership; moral regulations; "guilt"; values; and tradition and history as well. It is true that Heidegger nowhere engages in traditional political philosophy, but neither are the traditional philosophy of art, knowledge, science, or history found in his books, even when he devotes a full essay to a particular domain.

In any event, what I seek in Heidegger is not political philosophy or political science as such, but an examination of the conditions that make these enterprises possible. I am neither trying to find an "ideal" state or moral code in Heidegger nor trying to build one directly upon his analysis; and I am not attempting to erect upon his foundation a "phenomenological" social science to replace or supplement the current orthodoxies. Rather, I am seeking to assess the underlying meaning, possibility, and intelligibility of the concepts and distinctions—for example, theory and practice, wholes and parts, ends and means—that ultimately control the range and precision with which politics and morality can be understood.

I have chosen to analyze *Being and Time,* rather than Heidegger's other works, for three reasons. First, the topics I have mentioned are discussed in *Being and Time.* Second, Heidegger's other writings are fully accessible only after *Being and Time,* his first major work and still his fundamental one, has been analyzed. Whether there is an essential difference between early and late Heidegger, or among the Heideggers of the 1920s, 1930s, 1940s, 1950s, and 1960s, cannot be discussed intelligently unless we first have grasped *Being and Time.* (I must say, however, that the more carefully I study *Being and Time,* the less transparent are the scholarly descriptions of the different Heideggers, let alone their grounds.) Above all, I am not concerned with "Heidegger," but with what he thinks about. Within this concern, the question of the connections between Heidegger's works can indeed be legitimate, if our understanding of these works is sufficient.

Whatever the use of *Being and Time* for understanding politics and morality—and I believe it is great—these topics are not Heidegger's focus. Consequently, I will sometimes need to explore areas that Heidegger discusses only partially or tangentially, although this exploration is fruitful only in conjunction with the effort to understand *Being and Time's* developed arguments. In particular, I often will consider more than does Heidegger whether the entities supposedly made possible by a Heideggerian mode of Being—for example, human existence— are in fact made possible by it; the murky relations among the various areas of entities and, consequently, among their modes of Being; and the place of entities not obviously "released" by a Heideggerian mode of Being.[1] But these considerations, in

---

[1] In Chapter 5 I will also consider a recently published series of lectures, *The Fundamental Problems of Phenomenology,* delivered in 1927, in which Heidegger develops certain issues left incomplete in *Being and Time.*

turn, both force and enable me to illuminate the issues of Being and human Being that Heidegger is directly concerned with.

While I will present and clarify Heidegger's discussions as carefully as I can, I do not intend simply to agree with them. On the contrary, I will often question and criticize his remarks. But because my own arguments may illuminate my concerns less than do Heidegger's, I will attempt to present Heidegger clearly at the level on which he intends to be understood. Moreover, my criticisms of Heidegger will have force only as they are based on a detailed exegesis and analysis of his arguments.

The ground for my critical understanding of Heidegger's conception of Being and man is precisely my attempt to bring Heidegger's discussion of Being to bear on the question of the possible subject matter and study of politics. In general, I will explore the possibility that Plato and Aristotle's understanding of man, rethought in light of the issues raised by Heidegger, properly accounts for the phenomena he discusses while illuminating areas he leaves in the dark. My criticism will be exploratory, not dogmatic, both because it will seek a full understanding of Heidegger himself and because it will not pretend to be conclusive where it is only tentative.

A critical approach is obviously necessary to deal theoretically with the issues an author raises. Beyond this, there are special reasons why Heidegger's discussions must be questioned as well as clarified. For *Being and Time* may be not only an attempt to return to the original ground from which political purpose, morality, and theory arose but also part of the very crisis I have outlined. *Being and Time* projects an understanding of man as essentially "finite," "temporal," "historical." Does not this view enforce the relativism that is fundamental to the problems of our time? The precise meaning of history and temporality in Heidegger's work, and whether his understanding adequately defends or can adequately be criticized on the basis of its temporality and historicality once these are properly understood, depends on the substance of my study of his book. Readers inclined to dismiss out of hand anyone they have heard is a "relativist" should therefore relax their prejudice. But the surface connection of Heidegger's book to the uncovering of the "truth" of relativism reminds us of the possibly questionable character of his own rethinking.

The peculiar need to analyze *Being and Time* critically is even more obvious when we remember that Heidegger collaborated with the Nazi regime in the first year of its power. Many argue that Heidegger's "politics" is completely irrelevant for understanding his thought. This argument initially is useful because indignation seriously interferes with understanding. Ultimately, however, this dismissal of Heidegger's politics is both philosophically ridiculous and politically dangerous. The precise nature of the connection between a thinker's thought and his practical speeches and deeds is a difficult and revealing subject, hardly to be dismissed with the prejudice that no connection is relevant. It would be both philosophically strange and politically frightening to discover that the thought of the deepest thinkers does not—in several views, cannot—inform their serious practical concerns. This entire subject is a central *problem* for the political philosopher, for the precise nature of the connection is not obvious. For this reason, those who believe they know in advance exactly the form this connection must take are mistaken. The exact relation between *Being and Time* and Heidegger's support of the Nazis—indeed, just what this support was—is difficult to discern. Those who wish to understand must therefore moderate their otherwise understandable outrage and open themselves to Heidegger's arguments.

I will discuss the circumstances and implications of Heidegger's connection with the Nazis in Chapter 6. Here I mention it to emphasize the necessity of attempting to understand Heidegger critically.

My book is addressed primarily to students of political and moral thought. Because of this intended readership and in order to keep Heidegger's arguments directly before us, I summarize material from *Being and Time* that is already well known to Heidegger scholars. I hope that my book will nevertheless also interest Heideggerians, for they too should be concerned with the issues I discuss of moral and political philosophy. And along the way, I take up many issues beyond the immediate concerns of politics.

Heidegger's language in *Being and Time* is notoriously difficult. But his odd constructions, repetitive phrases, and unique coinages are necessary to the precision of his argument. My exegesis and analysis cannot stray too far from his language if they are to be accurate and useful. Consequently, some of what follows, particularly the sections where I explicate Heidegger, is unfortunately but necessarily clumsy. I have tried to correct this somewhat, and stay within the worthy conventions of academic prose, by using synonyms. Thus, I normally use some terms interchangeably—man and *Dasein,* problem and question, understanding and comprehending, "ontic" and concrete. Strange terms and central distinctions such as ontic versus ontological, existent*ial* versus existent*iell* and Being versus entities are discussed in footnotes or in Chapter 1. Of course, to grasp these terms and distinctions fully is to understand *Being and Time* fully.

I have differentiated exposition from analysis and commentary by using headings within each chapter, and I have keyed the exposition to the relevant paragraph in *Being and Time.* Because Heidegger discusses important subjects more than once, my analysis, which follows the order of his argument, also discusses several issues more than once. Most analyses are taken up to a point, dropped, then developed further on when Heidegger turns to them again. This gives some of my analyses an inconclusive or even dialectical quality that may annoy some readers. But we are dealing here with arguments and evidence, not "positions," and the arguments are built from interrelated discussions that modify each other. In any event, I do reach several conclusions, both along the way and in my "conclusion."

The questioning nature of my analysis may seem most obtrusive as I discuss Heidegger's introduction; the majority of the analyses there will not be directly relevant to political philosophy. Furthermore, the first several pages of Chapter 2 will primarily contain explication. Readers will therefore be urged more than once to wait patiently for more obviously pertinent inquiries.

1. *Man and Being: Preliminary Characterization, Preliminary Problems*

Discussions of *Being and Time* usually begin by setting it within the philosophical context of the fifty years preceding it. After all, *Being and Time* develops Kierkegaard's understanding of death and anxiety, Nietzsche's concern with fate and history, Dilthey's examination of history and life, and Husserl's analyses of temporality and the transcendental subject. And Heidegger's own teachings seem to demand that he be understood within his immediate philosophical environment.

But the relevant context for discussing *Being and Time* is as much the twenty-five hundred as the fifty years preceding the book. Heidegger also develops Aristotle's discussion of means and ends, the medieval analysis of being's transcendence, and Kant's understanding of "conditions of possibility." To illuminate such an environment sufficiently would require a work far beyond the present one. Even a compressed discussion—say, "from Hegel to Heidegger"—would likely be distorted. And if it were possible to illuminate properly at least the immediate philosophic environment, placing Heidegger too securely within it would be misleading. Reducing Heidegger's thought to secure and familiar categories would betray Heidegger's own sense of the radical nature of his enterprise.

For this reason, let us begin the study of *Being and Time* with Heidegger's own introduction to his theme. As we proceed, however, I will often attempt to clarify particular arguments by contrasting them with those of other thinkers, and I will address Heidegger's own understanding of the importance of history and the history of philosophy.

[1]

The question that Heidegger considers in *Being and Time* is the question of Being, a subject obviously remote from concrete political concerns and seemingly remote from political philosophy. But if we are to understand Heidegger's work we must follow the problem that explicitly guides it, and this problem is especially prominent in the introduction. In due course, we will arrive at Heidegger's discussion of man and matters more obviously relevant to political thought.

If Being is to be investigated, some definite question must be asked.[1] Heidegger asks: What is the *meaning* of Being? a question that is neither inevitable nor obvious. One could also ask: How did it come about that there is Being rather than nothing? For what reason is there Being? From what is Being composed? What is its structure? How does it look or sound or taste? Yet, several of these questions seem inappropriate. In what way, for example, could Being have a characteristic sound or shape? That this seems unanswerable suggests that Being is already grasped as it is investigated; indeed, Being could hardly be questioned were it not in some sense already intelligible. An investigation of Being, therefore, examines precisely this vague meaning that is taken for granted whenever what "is" is dealt with or discussed. This examination is necessary if presuppositions about Being are not to distort all inquiry into it. The bulk of *Being and Time* is guided by just this problem: the meaning of Being is presupposed in the very search for the meaning of Being. What is the nature of this presupposition? How is Being grasped in advance? How can Being be questioned thematically or philosophically? The characteristics of Being that Heidegger discusses emerge in his attempt to understand what Being is and how it offers itself to our understanding.

Before Heidegger begins his detailed analysis, he must give a preliminary characterization of these very issues. Consequently, his introduction begins with a discussion of the necessity of the

---

[1]"Being" translates *Sein;* "entities" translates *Seindes* and is used interchangeably with "beings." An entity is any thing which is, but no entity is Being, or "To Be," as such. The precise meaning of Being, and the precise relation of Being to entities, is the subject of *Being and Time* as a whole.

question of Being, the structure of questioning in general, the philosophical priority of the question, and its ordinary, or everyday, priority. Heidegger can discuss these themes only by indicating enough about the meaning of Being to elucidate the necessity and possibility of explicit inquiry into it. Consequently, my analysis of this material will be concerned primarily with the preliminary characterization of Being that makes Heidegger's discussion intelligible. I will attempt to clarify this characterization and to introduce several of the problems that will guide us in our study.

Why Being Is Not Self-Evident: Exposition

(§1) The question of Being must be raised explicitly because it has been forgotten. It has been forgotten because of three presuppositions: Being is considered (a) the most universal and, therefore, emptiest, concept; (b) impossible to define precisely because of its universality; and (c) self-evident because one uses it with sufficient intelligibility whenever one says "is" or "am." The presumed universality of Being, however, appears most peculiar once one suspects, as Aristotle and Thomas suspected, that Being is not a genus or class but transcends such unity, or is a unity by analogy. For what precisely is this transcendence? And the impossibility of defining Being is, in fact, only the impossibility of defining it in any of the ways in which entities are defined. This shows that Being is not an entity; it does not show that "Being" is empty or meaningless. Finally, the ordinary intelligibility of Being is perhaps its most mysterious characteristic: all behavior occurs within an ordinary understanding of "is," but in and for this average understanding the precise meaning of Being is still obscure.——

Why Being Is Not Self-Evident: Analysis

We can discern several characteristics of Being in Heidegger's discussion. The first is that Being can sink into oblivion, that we grasp it clearly neither in the average everyday nor in philosophical understanding. Indeed, the philosophical understanding of Being has in a sense declined from Aristotle, for whom Being was a problem, to Hegel, for whom the issue of the unity of Being is no longer a problem. The question therefore arises: What is the connection between the forgetting of Being in the philosophic tradition and the obscurity of the concept in the average understanding? What enables Heidegger to overcome this forgetfulness, if he overcomes it?

The second leading characteristic of Being suggested in Heidegger's discussion is that Being is radically different from everything else. It is not an entity and, therefore, cannot be the highest entity. It is not a genus or species and, therefore, cannot be the most general entity or the most general concept. It is not a category, such as quality or quantity. It cannot even be all the categories added together because, according to Heidegger, the problem of Being for Aristotle was precisely the *problem* of the unity of the categories. Being is a unity, but the nature of the unity that it is is unclear. To speak of Being's transcendence or analogical unity is, therefore, to express its peculiarity. Heidegger does not go on at this point to develop the positive meaning of transcendence and analogy, but whatever this meaning, it cannot be the sameness of a typical analogy among entities or the transcendence of a rarified entity.

Not only does Being's difference from all other things suggest that Being is unclear in itself, it also suggests that its relationship to entities is unclear. Indeed, this unclarity extends to the connection between Being and the categories, the genera, and the species, for some or all of these may themselves merely be entities. But whatever the obscurities, we may say that because Being is not an ordinary unity, its connection to entities cannot be the kind of connection entities have to one another, nor the kind of connection genera and species have to the entities within them. Being, therefore, could not cause entities in the manner of a general law or supreme end. Indeed, if Being is radically different from any entity, then all the theoretical terms we use to designate the unity of Being—for example, cause, result, product, law, participation, whole, part—must be questioned. Nothing is more crucial in understanding Heidegger than keeping sight of this radical split between Heidegger's Being and the functions, powers, and possibilities that belong to what is said to *be,* in the emphatic sense, in the philosophic tradition. This split, in turn, makes especially difficult the task of considering the possibilities of political philosophy in the light of Heidegger's enterprise, for we are forced to consider what is even more remote from politics than is metaphysics itself. Even the familiar terms we use to discuss the connection between the possibilities of political action and knowledge and the fullest theoretical possibilities may be misleading.

The Structure of Questions: Exposition

(§2) Heidegger further develops his preliminary understanding of Being in the next section of the Introduction, a discussion of the structure of questions. All questions, he argues, are guided in advance by what is sought: they are about something, in this case Being; have something they intend to uncover, in this case the *meaning* of Being; and interrogate something to reach their end, in this case entities, in particular, man. What, therefore is the preliminary understanding of Being and its meaning that guides Heidegger's inquiry? Being is that which "determines entities as entities"; Being is that wherein entities are already understood; Being is the meaning of entities; Being is "always" the Being of entities; Being is not itself some "possible entity," and, therefore, entities *as* entities cannot be defined by tracing their genesis from another entity.[2] Moreover, because Heidegger asks about Being explicitly, the "Being" uncovered through his inquiry must be determined and conceptualized, an "available concept." Such a conceptualization, he argues, exists neither in the average understanding of Being nor in previous philosophical inquiry. Finally, it belongs to the "ownmost meaning" of the question of Being, that Being is essentially related to inquiry into it; and this inquiry belongs to man's mode of Being.

[2]Martin Heidegger, *Sein und Zeit,* 11th ed. (Tubingen; Max Niemayer Verlag, 1967), p. 6. I have, for the most part, followed the translation *Being and Time* by John Macquarrie and Edward Robinson (New York: Harper & Row, 1962), but I have made some changes. The pagination of the English translation has been correlated with that of the eighth German edition. I cite the German. *Sein und Zeit* was published first in 1927.

The Structure of Questions: Analysis

The precise meaning of Being's "determining" entities as entities is necessarily unclear at this stage. We can see, however, that such determining cannot be the causal determination effected by one entity upon another. Moreover, Being—that which determines entities as such—is also said to be that on the basis of which entities are understood. This suggests that the intelligibility of entities may be equivalent to their Being: to "determine" an entity as an entity is to be the ground of its intelligibility when we cannot understand such grounding in a manner, such as efficient causality, that equates Being with an entity. But this suggestion points to a peculiarly close connection between Being and intelligibility, between Being and what is usually a characteristic necessary for human use or activity. This connection is strengthened by Heidegger's remark that there is an essential relationship between Being and inquiry about it, that is, that the connection is not accidental. Such a connection might seem to imply that the whole question of the meaning of Being is circular, or that Being *is* only as it enters man's subjective view. But Heidegger argues that the study of Being is not viciously circular: it is not debilitating that Being is in some sense presupposed in an inquiry into it and that the human Being of the inquirer is essentially connected to Being. Rather, these considerations are the leading clues to uncovering the problem. The justification and implications of this claim will become clearer when we discuss Heidegger's preliminary characterization of man in his introduction and his developed understanding in the book as a whole. Here, the decisive point is that if man is not a "subject," Being cannot be an "object" for this subject: just as other traditional conceptions of Being are not what Heidegger intends, so too Being as the most objective thing of all objective things is not what he intends. Consequently, Heidegger's claim that there is an essential connection between Being and human understanding is not intended to be a claim that what and how things are is subjective.

We may continue to develop the precursory understanding of

Being found in Heidegger's introduction and begin to explore the clarity of his presentation by analyzing his understanding of inquiry.

To what evidence does Heidegger point in elucidating the structures of questioning? He does not appeal to verbal definition, to inductive proof, to psychological evidence. Nor does he suggest that he has told us the essence of inquiry in the sense of a universal definition applicable to all questions. Indeed, it is unclear what kind of universality these structures have that "belong[s] to a question in general."[3] Moreover, it is difficult to see why and how, say, a technical, a theoretical, and a simple everyday question have but one structure. More important, the structures themselves are not obviously complete: the mystery, riddle, contradiction, or uncertainty that spurs questioning, and that has appeared so far to be a leading characteristic of Being itself, is not mentioned by Heidegger in his formal account of inquiry. But the leading issue we face here is this: How can the question of Being, which is no entity, have the same characteristic structure as questions concerning entities? In particular, if Being and entities are radically different, why should the solution to the problem of Being be in the form of a determinate concept, as is the case with the theoretical understanding of entities; why should, or how can, Being offer itself to explicit understanding conceptually? Precisely because Heidegger contends that the question of Being is radically different from questions about entities, the identity—or mere similarity—of the structures is peculiar. Our arguments do not require that Being could not offer itself as a determinate concept, but they raise the possibility that Heidegger's enterprise is guided in advance by an understanding of theoretical inquiry into Being inappropriate to the radical difference he proposes between Being and entities. Indeed, the precise status of explicit inquiry into matters such as "Being," when these inquiries are measured against other human activities, is the central question of political philosophy from its

[3] *Sein und Zeit*, p. 5. My translation.

inception with Socrates. We will discuss this problem thematically in Chapters 5 and 6.

The Importance of the Question of Being: Exposition

Heidegger advances his preliminary discussion of Being in the next section of his introduction. Here, he attempts to show the importance for the sciences of ontological knowledge and the importance for both traditional ontology and the sciences of his own inquiry.

(§3) The totality of entities, he argues, can be split into several subject matters, and these can become themes for the various sciences—for example, physics, mathematics, and historiology. The way in which a science has delimited its subject can be seen in its basic concepts. But we have not grounded sufficiently either a science's basic concepts or the area they mark off until we have clarified the distinctive mode of Being of the entities in the subject area. For an area's entities have always been split in advance in accordance with the various domains of Being, and this advance or "prescientific" understanding of the mode of Being of the group of entities is the understanding from which a science's basic concepts arise. Precisely because this comprehension on which the sciences are based is normally naïve and prescientific, we cannot fully ground these concepts until we interpret them by means of an *explicit* understanding of the relevant domain of Being.

Even the explicit "ontological" understanding of a domain of Being, however, is not the most original one. For both the explicit and the naïve comprehension of a domain are grounded in a naïve understanding of Being-as-such. Therefore, we need to investigate Being in order fully to bring about the aim of the sciences and the aim of the ontological elucidation of Being's domains. We can thus understand Being as such and in general as that which gives the a priori conditions for the possibility of the ontologies, which themselves provide the a priori conditions for the possibility of the sciences. Only when we fully understand Being itself can we—through a "nondeductive" genealogy of its different "possible ways"—fully understand Being's domains.

The Importance of the Question of Being: Analysis

Because this passage considers Being thematically, we will discuss the problems it raises rather than reiterate what Heidegger says. The leading notion is that the question of Being ascertains conditions of "possibility." Both the meaning of possibility and the reason that it is the decisive term are unclear; clarification depends upon Heidegger's developed argument. But here we already wonder whether Being makes understanding possible by making entities intelligible or whether our understanding of Being makes science possible simply because of the exigencies of the act of human comprehension, without essential connection to Being as the ground of the intelligibility of what is understood. It is difficult to discuss this issue without considering Being as the object of the subject's understanding, and, indeed, without considering Being as both the cause of entities, which can therefore be understood, and the cause of the subject's powers of comprehension. But such objectivity and causality are not elements of what Heidegger calls Being. Therefore, we are once more directed to the problems of the connection between intelligibility and Being. Indeed, in order to indicate the importance of Being, Heidegger gives five examples of how crises in basic concepts—which are based on Being—are the genuine "movement" of the sciences. In all, the crisis is a "tottering" of the relationship between what is investigated and the investigation itself.

The second issue here concerns the relationship between Being and its domains, and entities and their areas. They seem to have a similar structure: Being has domains investigated by "ontologies," and the ontologies project, in advance, an understanding of Being-as-such; the totality of entities has areas investigated by the sciences, and the sciences project, in advance, an understanding of a domain of Being. But, first, is there a master science that inquires into the totality of entities and, therefore, more directly or immediately must understand Being-as-such? Second, are entities always understood only within a domain or can they be understood directly in terms of Being as such? Third, can entities have a hierarchical or deductive relationship *among* their areas or is their relationship equivalent to that of the "nondeductive genealogical" relations of domains of Being to Being?

We may emphasize these questions by drawing together Heidegger's various remarks about entities. He distinguishes between the sciences' merely "ontic" inquiry into entities and the explicit or implicit ontology on which such inquiry depends. Yet, this concrete scientific inquiry into entities, this "ontic" inquiry, considers what entities *are* and even the mere fact that they *are;* and Being is always the meaning of *entities.* Furthermore, everything toward which we behave in any way, including ourselves, is an entity, and the entities can be located in the various domains of Being. How, then, can we strictly distinguish "ontic" activity—activity dealing with entities—from ontological activity—activity dealing with domains of Being—given that Heidegger offers no explicit distinguishing statement? They cannot be distinguished on the basis of whether an activity has projected an explicit ontology nor on the basis of whether an activity is explicitly theoretical. For we always have some average understanding of Being, and the theoretical sciences themselves are not explicitly ontological.

I suggest that "ontic" inquiry into entities considers their characteristics once they have come to light in a certain domain of Being. Thus, for example, technically measuring an object's weight deals with it as an entity; discussing the object's weight in units of gravity deals with it as an entity; and discovering the fundamental physical laws and causes is "ontic" inquiry about entities. That is, even the most general truths about natural things are not, as such, ontological; but general inquiry is possible only because naturally objective entities have been discovered in their structure of Being. In this sense, explicit or implicit understanding of the structure is "ontological," and treatment of entities within the structure is "ontic." A domain of Being makes entities possible, and "ontic" inquiry considers the characteristics of entities once they have been discovered in this possibility.

Heidegger also speaks of, but does not explicitly separate, a third activity, namely, interpreting entities *as* entities of such and such a type. Such understanding directly considers neither the domain of Being nor entities' concrete characteristics. According to Heidegger, for example, Kant disclosed the structure of Being of nature, the a priori characteristics of nature. Let us call this structure the objectivity of an object. If this is ontological inquiry, and if physics discusses the concrete characteristics and laws of matter, what of the activity that explicitly or implicitly interprets entities *as* natural objects? Heidegger treats this activity as part of the ontological understanding (indeed, he seems almost to equate the two), but it does not seem equivalent to understanding the domain of Being-as-such. In any event, a domain of Being is not the *cause* of entities within it, and every entity within a structure "is" equally with any other, whatever the causal relationships among them as entities. Beyond this, however, we remain unclear about the sense and degree of Being's making possible entities within a domain. How, if at all, does Being make possible every characteristic and relation among entities?

The problem of the connection between entities, domains of Being, and Being as such can be specified by further considering Heidegger's reference to Kant. Heidegger argues that Kant helped to disclose the structure of Nature. He also says here that Plato and Aristotle ran ahead of the sciences by explicitly disclosing entities in their Being. Yet, we wonder about the relationship between the ancients and Kant. For it is unclear that the entities discussed by modern physics and the entities understood by the ancients as making up nature can both *be*, and it is unclear that the virtuous activities interpreted by Aristotle and the moral activities interpreted by Kant can both *be*. Can both Kantian moral imperatives and Aristotelian prudential judgments truly "*be*" when they are concretely incompatible as entities? Or are they, in fact, compatible entities within the same domain, or different entities within different domains? Although we need not, we may conceive of this issue as a "historical" question; Heidegger himself considers historical entities to be an authentic area of entities. But a similar problem arises concerning the entities within other areas that Heidegger mentions—living entities, spatial entities, the entities experienced in theology. Indeed, the implications of Heidegger's understanding of Being for the relations among the sciences, and for the question of the relation between a science and the prescientific experience of the entities with which it deals, will become central in my analysis. For I will argue, in Chapter 6, that these implications are decisively tied to the judgments concerning the relations between a "people" and its scholars that enabled Heidegger to support the Third Reich.

Whatever the difficulty of these problems, we might say that there is a sense in which the *function* of "Being," for Heidegger, has become clear. For the sake of knowledge of entities, these entities must be grasped explicitly in what determines them as entities of such and such a type: they must be grasped in their Being. And for the sake of knowledge of the domains of Being, the domains must be grasped in their Being-as-such. In this sense, the "meaning" of Being is to determine entities. But we must remember that this characterization of Being has served to justify Heidegger's inquiry in terms of the sciences. It therefore partially misleads us concerning his basic intention. First, it is unclear why the problem of Being-as-such should have been always obscure and presently forgotten. Heidegger is able to demonstrate its importance to us convincingly in a very few steps; why did Plato and Kant fail? Second, the "ontological" knowledge allowed by Heidegger to previous philosophers often appears to focus precisely on entities as entities, on any entity simply in its determination as entity. How else should one understand Plato's *Sophist*, for example? But Heidegger's book opens with a quotation from that very work. Nothing in this section clarifies the gulf between Heidegger's enterprise and the previous ones; several of our questions are the questions we might ask of any "metaphysics." Whatever the specific differences between Being as a general concept and highest cause, and Being as the determiner of entities that makes them and understanding them possible, the structure and order of the relation of Being to entities, the kind of "thing" Being itself is, is difficult to distinguish. But Heidegger intends such a distinction, as we have seen in analyzing the earliest sections. Beyond the normal difficulties of these questions lies the fact that it is from Being as such that the terms of these problems—incompatibility, similarity, difference—first intelligibly derive. I conclude, therefore, that nothing short of Heidegger's full exploration of the meaning of Being will enable us to answer our questions.

[2]

The first task of the first chapter of Heidegger's introduction is to offer his preliminary understanding of the problem of Being. The second task is to indicate that man is the entity to be interrogated in this question.

Why Man Is the Entity Who Must Be Interrogated: Exposition

(§4) Heidegger has already indicated the importance of man in his investigation by suggesting the connection between Being and the understanding of Being. He further clarifies man's importance in the section before us now, which concerns the "ontical" priority of the question of Being. Man, according to Heidegger, is the distinctive *entity* because man alone understands Being. This means, first, that men, as entities, have Being as one of their concrete affairs: man alone is "ontically" characterized by a relation to Being. The Being to which he is related is his own Being, for which Heidegger uses the term "existence." Each and every man understands himself through the possibilities he has chosen or grown up in, and in taking hold of or neglecting these possibilities he decides his own existence. This decision (and this understanding) has nothing to do with theory or philosophy: it is meant to characterize what happens to everyone every day. Man, therefore, understands his own Being in his everyday affairs as an entity: in his concrete decisions as an entity, in what Heidegger calls his *existentiell* decisions, he understands his existence. But this implies that a man's existent*iell* understanding of his Being must be a structural characteristic of all human Being. Otherwise it could not be possible. The theoretical *analysis* of the structures of human Being, the theoretical analysis of existence, constitutes "existent*ial*" understanding; Heidegger calls the structures themselves the "existentials."

But, we may object—and despite our interest in man—that although an analysis of the existentials would be significant, it is unclear how this analysis can lead to a theoretical or "thematic" understanding of Being as such. It is also unclear why an analysis of the Being of other entities might not be equally revealing. The answer to the first objection is that the understanding of the existentials as states of *Being* must itself include an understanding of Being as such: the existential analytic, therefore, ultimately depends upon understanding the meaning of this Being. The answer to the second objection, according to Heidegger, is that man's Being is always "Being-in-a-world." Consequently, man's comprehension of his own Being contains an understanding both of the Being of the "world" and the Being of entities accessible within the world. It therefore includes comprehension of the Being of what is other than man. But this also means that any thematic exploration that begins from nonhuman Being is motivated by, and based on, the understanding of Being which first belongs to man. For these reasons, man is the entity Heidegger will interrogate: he now uses the term *Dasein* rather than "man" in order to keep in view the fact that he is discussing man in relation to his Being.

Why Man Is the Entity Who Must Be Interrogated: Analysis

Let us first bring out what is unique in Heidegger's characterization of man's Being as "existence." Existence, here, does not mean reality, or actuality, or mere "thatness," as it does when one asks, say, whether or not a particular building still exists, whatever its nature or function. Rather, Heidegger identifies existence with possibility. But this also suggests that the "essence" related to this "existence" cannot be the nature, or class character, or "whatness" of a subject that has possible members who may or may not be actual. Therefore, Heidegger can say that the "essence" of man is that he has his existence to be: man cannot have his essence in the manner in which other entities possess theirs. Moreover, man cannot have his existence as an accident: existence is what each man has as his own, as his most proper characteristic, as his distinctive characteristic. Man exists *as* his possibilities, his essence, and *is* his possibilities, his essence, in his existence. To clarify further the meaning of human existence and possibility we must await Heidegger's substantive discussions in the course of *Being and Time*.

This is also true of Heidegger's statement concerning man's "Being-in-the-world," which I will discuss substantively in the next chapter. But note here that to state that understanding the Being of other entities belongs to man's Being is to suggest that a relationship to these entities is essential, not accidental; therefore, the epistemological problem of how man could ever know or deal with other entities must also be put on new footing.

The kind of Being toward other entities that Heidegger mentions here is science; man's priority for first understanding the Being projected by the sciences in advance of their activity indicates the priority of man, in Heidegger's investigation, over the entities discovered by the sciences. But science is hardly the only manner in which we deal with entities; the understanding of Being that belongs to all human existence is related to all worldly entities. This suggests that human activities other than science may be equally revealing, perhaps more revealing, in uncovering human and nonhuman Being. Indeed, this proves to be the case as the book progresses. For, whatever the causal relationship of the entities discovered by science to the things dealt with in ordinary life, the *Being* of all these entities first becomes accessible only through man's understanding.

But what is the relationship of this understanding to Being itself? Heidegger does not suggest that man's Being is equivalent to Being as such, only that the understanding of Being is made possible by man's Being. Because no other entity has such an understanding, we may say that it is in man's Being that Being makes possible its own understanding. Consequently, Being is not a subjective creation of man, and the fact that nonhuman Being comes to light within human existence cannot mean that the "totality of entities" has been "viciously subjectivized." But some questions remain: Is Being as it can be understood all that Being is or can mean? And what is the significance, for human Being and Being as such, of the fact that man's Being, his possibilities, must be *"decided"*? Such deciding would appear at first glance to make any genuine, nonarbitrary, understanding impossible; but, for Heidegger, it proves essential to the way in which Being can have any meaning at all.

These issues also come to the fore when we attempt further to explore Heidegger's justification for his enterprise. This justification has told us that Heidegger's "fundamental ontology" is necessary for the sciences and for basic ontologies, and that we must find the source of fundamental ontology in the existential analysis of man. But this justification is hardly absolute. For in what manner, if any, does Being *itself* require that it be explicitly understood? We begin to grasp the peculiarity of Heidegger's analysis when we see that this question could hardly be answered in any ordinary way: Being, for Heidegger, is not an entity, even the highest entity, neither the philosopher's god nor a God of faith. It does not attract us nor seek obedience from us. Moreover, even if we say that Being and its possibilities of being understood are identical, that Being "is" only in its being understood, it is unclear why Being need be at all. But if we could clarify this necessity, we would then be forced to explain how a Being that "is" only in its being understood could be so obscure, even to the philosophers. The difficulty of such a task is indicated by our need to state it in terms such as "explain," whose ordinary meanings are inappropriate when addressed to Being.

We can see even more clearly the difficulty in justifying Heidegger's task if we ask: In what way does the average, nontheoretical understanding of Being demand explicit clarification? This question points to several answers—true knowledge demands explicit understanding of Being and truth is necessary to satisfy human purposes or to choose the proper practical end. And finally, the theoretical life, complete theoretical understanding, is the fullest expression of what man is. But Heidegger's justification stops short with the sciences. He does say that his fundamental ontology radicalizes man's essential tendency—to understand Being. But he does not show why this tendency ought to be, let alone be radicalized. Indeed, although he shows how the sciences depend on ontology and how ontology depends on explicitly grasping Being as such, he does not even argue that the average unscientific existence that projects the original comprehension of Being is insufficient for itself.

Nonetheless, Heidegger does claim that "only if the inquiry of philosophical research is itself grasped existentielly as a possibility of Being of each existing *Dasein,*" is it possible to disclose the existentials and thereby to grasp a sufficiently "founded" ontological "problematic."[4] Indeed, with this the "ontic priority" of the question of Being "becomes clear." But he does not tell us whether or how this choice can be justified. If the justification consists merely of the arguments that have gone before, the justification is insufficient; if the justification is in terms of Being, it has not yet been offered. But we might suspect that wherever the attempt at justification ultimately leads, it could not lead down ordinary paths. For what is the meaning, or possibility, of the question of justification for the entity, man, whose essence is to be his own existence? If we considered man solely as an entity, we might attempt to offer justifications for human ways by means of other entities. Indeed, because Heidegger does not claim that man is the highest *entity,* the "justification" would have to be by way of another entity—say, god or justice. But such a justification would be difficult to square with man's unique Being as the entity who is "transcendent" by understanding Being. For, if *Being* cannot be derived from entities, then *man,* understood as the comprehender of Being, cannot be so derived. Consequently, the call explicitly to comprehend Heideggerian Being *cannot* be justified by reference to a higher entity. Does man's transcendence, then, point to a mode of justification similar in structure to Kant's transcendental morality? But, according to Heidegger, Kant no more asked the question of Being as such than did the other philosophers. I conclude, therefore, that the question of the justification of human activities is particularly problematic within Heidegger's understanding, precisely if man is always ontological in Heidegger's sense, that is, precisely if man is always related to Being. This is most evident for Heidegger's own activity, but, in a sense, it is true for all activities because man, according to Heidegger, is *always* on-

---

[4] *Sein und Zeit,* p. 13. My translation.

tological. Heidegger suggests that properly comprehending man as "existing" is the condition of the possibility for understanding the meaning of "values," "ends," and the other concepts central to "justification." But if man's Being is existence, I have argued, it is difficult to say how any kind of perfectly "secure" justification could be possible. This unique turmoil into which Heidegger draws any attempt to justify human action—here, the turmoil into which he draws any attempt to justify philosophy or ontology as *the* human action—is his first outstanding result for practical thought. This problem is always before Heidegger himself, but it takes the form primarily of his *distinguishing* the existentials from moral categories, so that we will not confuse his existential analyses with moral judgments.

[3]

First Division: Exposition

(§5, pp. 15-17) We turn now to the second chapter of Heidegger's introduction. Here, Heidegger discusses the design and method of his work. Because man must be interrogated, the first task is to analyze *Dasein* existentially. This analysis might be thought unnecessary, for its goal is to understand Being; but if we always understand Being in some way, do we not need only to bring to light this ordinary understanding? Moreover, several disciplines—ethics, political science, anthropology—have studied man's capacities, powers, and possibilities. If explicit analysis is necessary, why not merely appropriate their discoveries? Heidegger's answer is that both the scientist and the ordinary man take for granted an improper understanding of human Being. Man tends to interpret himself as having the same Being as the nonhuman entities that he encounters within the world. Indeed, it is precisely the ordinary ideas of the Being or "actuality" of entities that are most misleading when applied to man—that he is "in" space, for example. Yet, these ideas are those we usually take for granted, particularly in scientific or scholarly inquiry. Consequently, we cannot use the sciences' results as central clues in understanding man's Being, because the degree to which an adequate understanding of human Being is salvageable from their discoveries awaits the uncovering of such an understanding. Therefore, an explicit existential analysis is necessary.

This difficulty with the sciences suggests that the necessary analysis of *Dasein* may go astray if it attempts to uncover the structure of human Being by focusing on what makes possible some particular activity. Rather, to uncover man's Being we must show man as he is "in himself and from himself," at first and for the most part. That is, we must show him in his average everydayness.——

First Division: Analysis

Because "everydayness" is the theme of the entire first part of *Being and Time* we will defer our questions about it, as Heidegger defers his analysis of it, and discuss, instead, the more general problems concerning human Being that arise in this section. In the course of discussing the sciences, Heidegger remarks that *Dasein's* understanding of Being "develops or decays" with whatever type of Being he may possess. Yet, Heidegger claims that the existential analysis seeks to exhibit "not optional and accidental structures, but essential ones which remain determinative in every type of Being" of *Dasein*.[5] What does Heidegger intend by suggesting that there are developing and decaying understandings of Being, coordinated with a variety of types of human Being, all determined by essential structures of Being?

By a type, or kind, of Being that man possesses, Heidegger means a human activity that we understand in terms of the manner and degree to which it *discloses* Being, particularly the possibilities of human existence. A type is a concrete existent*iell* activity that we examine in terms of the "Being" it naïvely understands, and in terms of the modifications of *Dasein's* structure that make it possible. Different types disclose Being in different degrees, depending on the manner in which the activity must disclose Being in order to be what it is. Consequently, for example, man's Being has in *some* way been understood in all scientific

[5] *Sein und Zeit*, pp. 16-17. My translation.

activities, but the capacities, powers, and possibilities discussed by ethics or "Politik" have emerged from genuine disclosure only in varying degrees.[6] Moreover, a particular existent*iell* understanding may be "primordial" without thereby being existentially primordial. A work of scholarship, for example, may be drawn from a genuine implicit understanding of man's Being and yet be misleading when its discussion of its results is explicitly ontological.

Now, we cannot yet tell whether Heidegger believes there is a precise number and order of the kinds of human Being, nor whether some activities always disclose Being more fundamentally than others. But, in any event, the structures of human Being that Heidegger is about to unfold determine man's disclosure of Being in all its kinds. Whatever the type of human Being, whatever the understanding of Being, it is determined by these structures and their modifications. Still, I must stress that the structures of human Being do not determine man by giving a single inevitable understanding of Being, nor do they make genuine existent*iell* understanding depend on philosophy. Indeed, everyday understanding *is* as much as any other understanding. Otherwise, it could not reveal the all-determining structures. Therefore, whatever the modifications in kinds of Being, "Being" is not a term of distinction. Man's Being, for Heidegger, does not have the character of a Platonic "idea." Nor can it even have the character of a natural law, because Being, unlike a natural law, is not a causal generality.

The difficult implications of this argument are especially apparent if we ask how a human entity *could* be determined by the determiner (Being), if *not* as an image of an idea or effect of a cause. For, in Heidegger's understanding, each man "has" his Being as his *own*. This suggests, when taken in conjunction with

[6]At this stage in the discussion I use "to disclose" (*erschliessen*) and "to understand" synonymously. This enables us to be aware that existential understanding primarily refers to a process of bringing things into the open and laying them out in the open, and not to explaining, deducing, and the like. As the discussion progresses through Chapter 3, I will show that understanding is the decisive element in man's disclosing of Being, but that disclosing (bringing into the open) is broader than understanding, and characterizes all the structures of human Being.

the previous arguments, that each man is "determined" by the essential structures of his Being only in his self-determination. Each man is or "has" his Being only in his disclosure of Being. And this understanding normally mistakes his Being. Man is his Being, his structure of disclosing, in each possibility he understands, but only in his concrete existent*iell* activity *is* he this structure. Man is always his Being, and, at root, there is nothing accidental about him. But we might also say that his Being can in no way be separated from any individual—that, at root, everything is accidental about him.

Second Division: Exposition

(§5, pp. 17-19) Heidegger proceeds next to preview the sections that will follow the chapters of the first division. We might suspect that Heidegger, after uncovering man's Being through analyzing everydayness, will turn to his primary topic—Being, or the meaning of Being, in general. Rather, he suggests that the first division will be provisional because it will merely bring out man's Being, but not interpret the *meaning* of this Being. It will bring to light the meaning of the entity, man, without uncovering how this meaning, or Being, is itself intelligible. The six chapters of the second division, therefore, will attempt to show that the meaning of *Dasein*'s Being is "temporality" (*Zeitlichkeit*). Heidegger will therefore reinterpret his findings in terms of "temporality." This temporal interpretation of human Being is not yet equivalent to answering the question of the meaning of Being "in general," but it "prepares the ground" for such an answer, because time proves to be the *horizon* for *all Dasein*'s comprehension of Being. Now, we ordinarily understand that there are entities in time (for example, historical and natural processes), entities not in time (for example, numerical relationships), and eternal entities beyond time. But how and with what right does time have this function of distinguishing realms of entities and realms of Being? Heidegger will argue that time has "authentic" ontological relevance; to see this, however, we must first genuinely explicate time as the horizon for understanding Being. But genuinely explicating time requires that it be analyzed in terms of "temporality," because temporality is the meaning of man's Being. The concept of time we will then obtain will be different from time as ordinarily understood, or as it has been philosophically understood from Aristotle to Bergson. Beyond this, to see that Being and its modes become intelligible with regard to time is to see Being itself in *its* Temporal character. Indeed, the meaning of Being and its modes is "determined primordially" in terms of time. To interpret the meaning of Being, therefore, is to work out its temporality.

But does this mean that "Being" is temporal in the sense that it is an entity *in* time, a time-bound entity? It could not, for Being is not an entity. Moreover, if Being is temporally determined, then the eternal and nontemporal entities must also be temporal in their Being. The Temporality (*Temporalität*) of Being, therefore, is not the time-boundedness of an entity, and its explication requires the new concept of temporality.——

Second Division: Analysis

To discuss Heidegger's understanding of the temporal meaning of man's Being before presenting his analysis of that Being would be fruitless. I thus defer a discussion of the issues raised here until Chapter 8.[7]

[4]

The final section of Heidegger's introduction is his attempt to describe the method of the work, "phenomenology." The same considerations that call into question traditional ontology, and the very peculiarity of man's relation to Being, make it necessary to discuss explicitly an appropriate method for interrogating man's Being.

---

[7] I will also defer until Chapter 7 an exposition and analysis of the next section of the introduction, Heidegger's projection of the unpublished second part of *Being and Time*, the "destruction of the History of Ontology with the Problematic of Temporality as our clue." But lest it seem that the problems of history and temporality are irrelevant for politics, I will merely point to the essential connection between moral or value relativism and these problems. Are goods, or values, or moral standards "absolute" or "relative," eternal or time-bound? In accord with what kind of Being *are* values and goods? I will discuss these issues thematically, on the basis of *Being and Time*, in the ensuing chapters.

Phenomenology: Exposition

(§7) "Phenomenology" is a compound of phenomenon and "logos": it is to let that which shows itself be seen from itself in the very way in which it shows itself from itself—whatever is discussed phenomenologically must be exhibited directly. A phenomenon in the primary sense is anything that shows itself, for example, a ruddy complexion. This self-showing *then* enables it to be a semblance of something else, or an indication of something else, for example, good health. The semblance or indication is a "mere" phenomenon, a phenomenon in the secondary sense. Now, if this consideration holds for any phenomenon, what are the specific phenomena, the specific things to be displayed, in thematic phenomenlogy? Phenomenology is explicit exhibition and, therefore, makes thematic what usually lies hidden. This is the *Being* of entities, which entities usually do show themselves, and the meaning and modifications of this Being. The "logos," the *letting* be seen, is interpretation, or "hermeneutics." Heidegger later discusses this in detail, but here he suggests that a "logos" of phenomena is *Dasein*'s making known to his own understanding the meaning of Being and of his own Being. This "making known" is interpretation, the working out of the possibilities, the meaning, wherein intelligibility lies. From this we see that phenomenology, fundamental ontology, and "hermeneutics," the three terms Heidegger uses to describe his enterprise, are identical when understood properly. But this mention of hermeneutics tells us no more than does the discussion of phenomenology about the *techniques* to be used in letting Being be seen. These techniques resemble Husserl's phenomenological techniques or the techniques of "hermeneutics" understood as the methodology of historiology, but they are not equivalent. How Heidegger goes about discovering a structure of Being is best shown in his concrete descriptions.

Phenomenology: Analysis

Here, the central issues relevant to Being and man concern Being's hiddenness: Heidegger's discussion of Being and its Being hidden, covered up, or disguised, indicates once more the importance of this characteristic. But Heidegger does not yet develop this Being covered as belonging to Being itself. Rather, its hiddenness appears to belong to man's understanding and communication. It is not simply accidental, but how, or whether, it can be conceived *prior* to the exigencies of human comprehension is unclear. Also unclear is the connection between the letting be seen of an entity and the letting be seen of Being. If Being "lies beyond any possible character an entity may possess," why is the discussion of phenomenology "formally equivalent" whether the phenomena are entities or Being, and whether the "logos" lets entities or Being be seen?[8] How can Being's entering into unhiddenness be so similar to entities' entering unhiddenness?

In general, then, Heidegger's introduction presents the basic orientation toward man and Being that guides his discussion. But it presents many questions as well. How can his enterprise be justified? What is the relation between "Being" and entities? What is the relation between Being and understanding? We will develop this orientation and pursue these questions as we proceed with our discussion.[9]

[8]*Sein und Zeit*, p. 38. For the Heideggerian connection of truth and method, see Hans Georg Gadamer, *Wahrheit und Methode* (Tubingen: J. C. B. Mohr, 1960).

[9]For a discussion of the introduction consider, among others, Otto Poggeler, *Der Denkweg Martin Heideggers* (Pfullingen: Verlag Gunter Neske, 1963). For a recent translation of the Introduction, consult Martin Heidegger, *Basic Writings*, edited by David Farrell Krell (New York: Harper & Row, 1977); the translation is by Joan Stambaugh in collaboration with J. Glenn Gray and the editor. The purpose of my footnote references to the Heidegger literature is to point to works which are particularly illuminating on some specific topic. I will resist the almost irresistible temptation to engage in scholarly disputation. Such disputation would lengthen the book excessively and detract from its chief aims.

2. *Political Possibilities and Everyday Entities*

The first part of *Being and Time* consists of Heidegger's "preparatory" analysis of human Being. I will summarize the six chapters of this analysis, clarify and question what is summarized, and bring out its implication for political philosophy. Before we begin, note that the key to understanding Heidegger's discussion is to remember that the heart of man's Being is his openness to a Being-as-such that is not an entity of any sort. This means that what Heidegger says about man is not a discussion of human "nature" or the human essence as traditionally understood. Such a discussion would comprehend man on the basis of a "being" that, according to Heidegger, erroneously views man as the highest, most general, or most powerful entity. But Heidegger's "existential analytic" is not existentialism as understood after Sartre, for existentialism is a counter to (and so remains within the ambit of) the usual understanding that what is essential is prior to what exists contingently or accidentally. Heidegger's discussion is, nonetheless, an analysis of the most decisive human things and thus of the traditional subject of political philosophy. The connection between traditional analyses and the structures he uncovers is among the problems with which we will deal.

[1]

Existential Analysis and Ordinary Inquiry: Exposition

(§9-11) Heidegger's opening chapter repeats his preliminary characterization of human Being, distinguishes existential analysis from other inquiry into man, and clarifies the propriety of beginning with a discussion of "everydayness." Man, according to Heidegger, is the entity who comports himself to his own Being, which is always an issue for him. Man's Being is *existence,* and all his characteristics must therefore be understood as possible ways to be, not as the properties of a thing. Man is also the entity whose Being is in each case "mine." This means that I am not merely an instance of a class, an instance incapable of having my Being as an issue. Rather, because "mineness" belongs to existence, I am always mine in one way or another. Therefore, I always have myself as something to *decide,* and have always made some decision. In particular, I can be myself authentically, I can be my own, or I can be myself inauthentically. Whatever the precise meaning of authenticity (and Heidegger discusses this later), authenticity *is* no more than inauthenticity: when I am authentic I *am* not more fully than when I am inauthentic.

If Heidegger's task is to uncover the "structure of existentiality [that] lies *a priori*" in all kinds of existence, which kind should he analyze?[1] For the reasons mentioned in Chapter 1, Heidegger believes that his analysis begins best by considering the undifferentiated existence he calls average everydayness. We must not confuse such everydayness with primitive existence, for we find it in highly developed cultures. Indeed, the primitive has both a specific everydayness of its own and possibilities of Being that are not of the everyday variety.

Heidegger's analysis of everydayness is intended to reveal the "existentials," the structures of existence. We must distinguish existentials from categories, which are the structures of things: indeed, categories and existentials are the two basic possibilities or modes of Being. The reason that existential analysis must be differentiated from anthropology, psychology, or biology, and the reason that Heidegger claims distinction from analyses such as Scheler's or Dilthey's centering on "life" or the "person," is precisely that all these approaches fail to clarify the distinctive *Being* of man. Most analyses objectify man: they consider him as if he were a thing. Several analyses at least consider man to be a "subject," but the being of this subject is still preconceived as the

[1] *Sein und Zeit,* p. 44.

simple presence-at-hand that belongs to things. Some analyses attempt to distinguish man from any thing or subject: they dispute the reification of "consciousness" and center upon "spirit" or "personality" or life. But these analyses then fail to clarify the *Being* of spirit, personality, and life. Indeed, even if one could clarify the Being of the "subject," the Being of man then conceived as a union of body, soul, and spirit could not be found by adding together the separate findings because "some idea of the Being of the whole" must be presupposed in such a finding. But it is this idea that is left unclarified.[2]

The ground of these failures to elucidate the distinctive character of man's Being, according to Heidegger, is the continued dominance of the traditional perspective of Christianity and the ancient world. The ancients, Heidegger argues, defined man in a manner we interpret as "rational animal," "something living that has reason."[3] But the Being of the animal is understood as occurrence and presence-at-hand, and the Being of both reason and the compound is left unclear. Indeed, the ancients understood Being in terms of nonhuman entities within the world: this Being, the categories, is what reason (*logos*) allows to come to view as what is already in every entity we can encounter. Christianity adds the idea of man's having transcendence beyond intelligence, but it understands man to be an entity created in God's image. The Being of God, of "creating," and of the finite created entity are then interpreted through ancient ontology. The result is that man traditionally is interpreted to have the presence-at-hand of things, and discussions of his essential properties as an entity are carried out within this erroneous understanding.——

Existential Analysis and Ordinary Inquiry: Analysis

Heidegger's discussion raises the same issues of the meaning of possibility and of the understanding of Being that I outlined earlier. I will develop them here by discussing everydayness. The decisive character of everydayness is that it is "preontological"—that it is not conditioned by a definite *idea* of exis-

[2] *Sein und Zeit*, p. 48.
[3] *Sein und Zeit*, p. 48.

tence. It is for this reason that Heidegger faces the problem of distinguishing it from the primitive. But his discussion of the primitive raises its own questions. What differentiates primitive and modern everydayness? It seemingly could not be the existential structures, because these always belong to *Dasein*. Is it, then, the specific concrete content of everyday life, or is it the nonhuman modes of Being, and the other entities in these modes, that happen to be disclosed, discovered, and developed in the average everyday way? I believe Heidegger intends this second possibility, but whatever the case, this problem suggests the core of what Heidegger means by everydayness and the difficulties in grasping it. Everydayness refers to a specific existent*iell* understanding of Being and, in particular, to a specific existent*iell* understanding of, and holding of, man's Being, which Heidegger then analyzes to uncover its a priori structures. In general, when Heidegger analyzes any human possibility, he analyzes it as a possibility of human Being. This means that he analyzes it in terms of how it belongs to *"Dasein*'s" disclosing of Being and his discovery of entities in their Being. But precisely because man is ontological in each of his concrete "ontic" affairs, it is sometimes difficult to see clearly in any given instance whether Heidegger is analyzing within the ontological horizon. Heidegger's analysis is particularly problematic with "everydayness," which refers both to concrete everyday indifference and concern and to the mode of Being a priori in this concern, the mode usually governing all our possibilities including everydayness in the concrete sense. This difficulty is exacerbated by Heidegger's argument that man exists always and only as possible and is possible always and only as existent. The *Being* of a man's "capacities" is the combined structure that permits these capacities to disclose Being, including his own Being; only through this structure are his capacities freed at all. At any time, a man is capable of disclosing Being, including his own Being. And his own Being is the very structure of these disclosive capabilities. They *are* only insofar as they disclose, and they are themselves grasped in a disclosure. Any capacities or potentialities, therefore, are always grasped *as* modes of my Being, as possibilities, and they *are* those potentialities in their very disclosure of possibilities, including themselves as possibilities.

Whether I "have" myself "authentically" or "inauthentically" depends on whether I disclose my own Being as it is and maintain myself in this possibility in all my disclosure. But disclosing myself as I am not is equally grounded on the a priori structures of disclosure; I therefore *am* no less when I am myself inauthentically.

To elucidate the elements of this disclosing of Being as they lie in everydayness is Heidegger's task in this division. Moreover, because man's Being is in his disclosing Being, *every* mode or kind of concrete disclosure is a mode of *Dasein*'s Being: The "limits" to these concrete or "ontic" modes are precisely the existential structures that lie in each *as* disclosure. But this raises again the question of how man's structures are "always" or lie a priori if these structures, this Being, are *possibilities* to be. Precisely because the "possibilities" of existence can no longer be understood as counter to the actuality of things, and precisely because Temporality is the meaning of, or condition for the intelligibility of, Being, reinterpreting the concepts of possibility and the a priori must be a goal of Heidegger's analysis.

Let us conclude our discussion of this section by pointing to what more it has to say about Being-as-such. In general, it reinforces the following themes and questions: Being is essentially related to man or "logos"; the relationship is not an accident of human interest. An understanding of Being runs ahead of the sciences and philosophical anthropology, but this Being does not *cause* the entities under discussion. The question of human Being is answered at the *level* of the categories; the answer enables us to conceive "consciousness," lived experience, the person, reason, the body in a manner that does not see them as quantities, qualities, or the motions of quantities. But the precise meaning of presence-at-hand—the mode of Being of things—is as unclear at this juncture as the precise meaning of existence.

[2]

The World and Its Worldhood: Exposition

(§12–13) After this opening, Heidegger begins to discuss the basic state of everydayness, which he calls "Being-in-the-world."

Although we must understand Being-in-the-world as a whole, we can bring to light each of its constituent structures separately. These structures are the worldhood of world, "Being-in," and the self who is in the world. Heidegger starts by distinguishing man's "Being-in" from the enclosedness of a spatial thing. Whatever the precise meaning of human spatiality, and whatever the concrete elements of "Being-in," man cannot be in the world the way, say, a book is in a bookcase, because man does not have the categorial structure of a thing. We must understand the possibility and intelligibility of human dwelling and human residing in a manner adequate to human existence. But this understanding does not give positive direction: how is the analysis to proceed? We could attempt to describe a particular human relationship toward the "world." Indeed, we could discuss what always appears primary to the philosophers, "knowing" the "world," knowing nature. But Heidegger claims that knowing entities is not primary, because any entity, even the totality of Nature, must first show itself within a world before we can know it in any particular way. Knowledge is "founded on" "Being-in-the-world" and cannot exist unless it exists together with "Being-in-the-world." Moreover, explicit knowing is not primary because knowing is an activity that may or may not happen to occur; but "Being-in" is a structure of man's Being. We must therefore discuss "Being-in-the-world" in terms of this world in which we always are and by means of how we are always in it.

Now, we always experience "Being-in-the-world" in some way, but ordinarily we think of a relation between the entity "man" and another entity. Indeed, one chief characteristic of "Being-in-the-world" is that we disclose it in a way that leads us to misinterpret ourselves and the world as entities *within* the world. It is this experience of "Being-in-the-world" as man's knowledge of other entities that leads to the misleading conception of man as one more present-at-hand thing. This misconception, in turn, gives rise to the whole series of epistemological problems that seek to clarify how a subject can get outside himself in order to know. But these problems only arise because man always transcends himself, always has already disclosed some world, is always alongside entities within the world. Thus, the so-called problems of epistemology themselves reveal that knowing is founded upon man's prior Being-in-the-world.——

Heidegger's preliminary characterization of world indicates that "world" is not an entity, but, rather, a horizon within which entities are. But might we not investigate this world by considering the horizon which allows theoretical entities to be known? For Heidegger this procedure is inadequate because the entities that are known by theory are freed by the world in their pure presence-at-hand, in their pure look, in their *eidos*. But we first encounter entities as things to be dealt with and used; looking at things theoretically arises as a modification of practical concern. Consequently, the Being of world, its "worldhood," must first be understood in connection with the things of practice. But by indicating this, Heidegger is not suggesting that practice causes theory or that theory reduces to practice. Nor does he mean that man's capacities are more completely fulfilled in practice than in theory. For man's Being and his Being-in-the-world are, as such, neither theoretical nor practical. To clarify this we must proceed with our exposition of Heidegger's analysis.

The clue to the Being of world is found by examining the entities we use and produce in everyday concerns; the fundamental truth about world is that its Being belongs to *Dasein*, not to things. "World" traditionally functions as both an ontic and an ontological term. Ontically, it can mean the totality of present-at-hand entities, or that "wherein" (*woraufhin*) a man lives, the domestic or public environment. Ontologically, it can mean the Being of present-at-hand entities or "The ontologic-existential concept of *worldhood*," the a priori character of worldhood in general.[4] The world to which Heidegger's discussion of Being-in-the-world refers is the domestic environment or public world; "worldhood" is the Being of this world. Only man is worldly in this sense: other entities are said to be *within* the world. Now, if man's world is first the domestic one, we can begin to understand the meaning of world by considering the Being of the entities first encountered domestically. These entities are entities

---

[4] *Sein und Zeit*, p. 65.

that are used, a tool such as a hammer, or a quarry of rock: they are equipment. But, as equipment, they belong to a whole of equipment, for any tool is discovered as a tool only within an entire structure in which things *are* in order to do this or that, in which they are *assigned* to other things, in which they are discovered as service*able,* us*able,* or manipul*able* for others.

Our everyday discovery of equipment is not theoretical, nor is it an explicit grasping of things as equipment. Rather, according to Heidegger, we discover tools in the activity itself and in the circumspection, the looking around, characteristic of everyday concern: we know the hammer as a hammer in the hammering. Even here, however, practical attention is paid to the work *for which* the tool is appropriate, and the work itself is for the sake of one or another human possibility. Now, when we discover equipment as such, we discover it in its "readiness to hand" (*zuhanden*); its readiness-to-hand, its availability, is what Heidegger calls its "involvement" or "destination" (*Bewandtnis*). The Being of any tool is such that *with* it is that toward which it is destined, and with *this* is that for which it is usable: such an involvement is made ontically concrete by a specific service or use. Nothing can be freed as a tool, nothing is able to be involved, unless it is discovered and encountered out of a wholeness of involvements. This totality ultimately terminates in something for the sake of which all the involvements are.

That for the sake of which involvements are is a possibility of human Being. Man is not himself a tool who is involved but he for the sake of whom involvements are freed. Indeed, according to Heidegger, it is only in *Dasein*'s seizing of possibilities that there can be a wholeness of assignments in the context of which the ready-to-hand *is.* This means that worlds are constituted ultimately by man's understanding: for a "world" to exist, *Dasein* must understand a wholeness of assignments in terms of his own possibilities. Such comprehension is not optional. Rather, when a man understands a possibility he also has understood a totality of assignments. *Dasein,* according to Heidegger, always assigns himself *from* that "for the sake of which" he is *to* that which is "in order to" achieve this end. This means that a man's understanding always is submitted to a world with which he is familiar in

HEIDEGGER'S *BEING AND TIME*

advance and from which other entities are allowed to become involved. Heidegger calls *Dasein*'s "already Being familiar" his signifying: the worldhood of any world is "significance." Significance is the wholeness of this signifying: it is *Dasein*'s advance familiarity with the "in order to" and with the "toward this," "in which," and "with which" prescribed by this "in order to." Worldhood, therefore, is an existential component of *Dasein*, and it is the ontological possibility of any particular significations. On these, in turn, all language and words are founded. Moreover, because there are no worlds without *Dasein*, nothing ready-to-hand can be discovered without *Dasein:* man, in his familiarity with significance, is the condition for the possibility of discovering entities "encountered in a world with the type of Being of involvment (readiness-to-hand)."[5]

The Priority of "Readiness-to-Hand" to "Presence-at-Hand": Discussion

Before we attempt fully to analyze this discussion in the final section of this chapter, we must notice two more points in Heidegger's remarks. One might consider his analysis reasonable but ontologically trivial because it discusses entities, such as usable and serviceable tools, that ultimately have no real Being. Rather, what is real are the properties on which these tools are based: hammers have a certain measurable size and weight, coats can warm because of their material structure, man's "possibilities" are biological necessities. Heidegger meets this objection by arguing that the Being disclosed in theoretical observation—presence-at-hand—can be disclosed only by specifically modifying the usual discovery of ready-to-hand entities. This modification can occur when the usual practical looking around within the work world comes across something conspicuously broken, obstrusively missing, or obstinately in the way. Here circumspection is disturbed, and something ready-to-hand is discovered in its presence-at-hand. But this presence-at-hand is still the presence-at-hand of something essentially ready-to-hand. Entities in their *pure* presence-at-hand can become theoretically thematic when the moods belonging to man's con-

---

[5] *Sein und Zeit*, p. 87 (italics omitted).

cern give way to a mere tarrying alongside present-at-hand entities. Then it becomes possible to discover things in their neutral "properties." The theoretical discovery that enables us to assign a weight to a hammer as a purely measurable thing is, therefore, ontologically secondary to discovering the appropriate and inappropriate, the too heavy and too light of ordinary activity. Indeed, nature itself is first revealed as ready-to-hand environmentally: first the quarry is uncovered and only then the static mountain, let alone the physical laws. Moreover, concerned dealing with ready-to-hand entities can itself find the difference between entities that need to be produced and those that produce themselves, just as it can discover a public environment beyond its immediate domestic world, an environment that includes publicly available entities and stable entities, such as the rising and setting sun. For uncovering such entities belongs to the producing and using characteristic of everyday activity.

The result of this discussion is that the Being of present-at-hand entities is no "more" than the Being of ready-to-hand entities: the "properties" of the ready-to-hand are discovered as such and are not subjective valuations placed upon the truth of the present-at-hand.[6] The meaning, or Being, of the heaviness of a hammer or of the location of a hammer in use is its involvement in a world; and this involvement is freed as such for a wholeness of assignments that cannot be reduced to present-at-hand properties. An immensely heavy thing may be too light for a particular task because the "in which" and "with which" of involvements are different from the categories of presence-at-hand. Most fundamentally, what is ready-to-hand is freed within a structure of significance belonging to *Dasein* himself, and for *Dasein* the Being of the ready-to-hand is freed before that of the present-at-hand. Indeed, precisely because the present-at-hand first comes to light in experiences that modify ordinary concern, and precisely because theoretical contemplation of the present-at-hand requires a modified mood and understanding, we can

[6]For the problem of "values" in *Being and Time,* consider Ann Kuhn, "Das Wertproblem in den Fruhwerken Martin Heidegger's und *Sein und Zeit,*" part 4 (dissertation, Munich, 1968).

see that the discovery of the present-at-hand occurs only within *Dasein*'s world. The Being of man, here, the possibility of world-hood, is prior *ontologically* to anything present-at-hand. And as Heidegger has argued throughout, man himself cannot be understood as present-at-hand.

My references to ontological priority are intended to keep in view the limits of Heidegger's arguments. When Heidegger describes the transition from practice to theory, he intends an ontological discussion. This means that he is not offering a causal or historical explanation of how practice—either in general or at the decisive moment among the Greeks—becomes theory. Rather, he is suggesting how human concern as a discovery of entities in their *Being* can be modified to discover present-at-hand entities. This is, concretely, an attempt to suggest that the worldhood of the world allows or frees present-at-hand entities when *Dasein*'s disclosure is modified in certain ways. This new disclosing can be seized concretely and become the condition for explicit theoretical activity. What "causes" it to be explicitly seized, however, is beyond the ontological inquiry and subordinate to it insofar as only this inquiry can tell us what makes theory and the entities it discovers possible in their Being.

Heidegger completes his thematic discussion of the transition from practice to theory only after he shows that time is the meaning of worldhood. But must we not assert even here that present-at-hand properties are there before anything ready-to-hand, if only as material "stuff," and that the ready-to-hand is only a subjective aspect? Heidegger rejects this argument. What is there before a particular ready-to-hand entity are other ready-to-hand entities. Whenever there is man, the ready-to-hand is irreducible to the present-at-hand. But where man is not, it is unclear that there can be a present-at-hand, an independent material stuff, at all. Indeed, it is unclear that there can be "Being" without man. Heidegger does admit, however, that once we discover certain present-at-hand entities, we can then see that they have existed always. It therefore seems that they must in some way be the cause of the entities that become ready-to-hand. But perhaps they cause these entities without in any way causing their Being? Yet, if Being is not identical to causality, how are we to understand the apparently evident connections between, say, the suitability of beef for man and beef's chemical structure, or the discovery of uranium and the consequent discovery of its suitability? I raise these questions now in order to help bring out the peculiarity of Heidegger's analysis, but we cannot discuss them more completely until we consider more fully Heidegger's discussion of theory and practice. We will therefore return to them and proceed now with the explication of Being-in-the-world.[7]

The Everyday Self: Exposition

In discussing "world" I referred to man's understanding of his possibilities, to his having moods, and to the possibility of discourse. These are the three elements of "Being-in." Before analyzing these, however, Heidegger attempts to clarify "who" is in the world, a clarification that sheds light on both the public world and man's Being toward other men. Heidegger discusses this question by considering who man is when he is fascinated by and absorbed in the world; what Heidegger attempts is to *existentially* characterize the everyday self that we are. This means both that the everyday self, whom Heidegger will call the "they self," is to be discussed in his ways of Being and not in his concrete properties, and that the self, the "I," must not be misinterpreted as a present-at-hand substance. As obvious as it may seem to say that the everyday self who experiences things is the constant "I," the ontological meaning of the self is obscure.

(§25-27) The first way to approach everyday selfhood is to understand properly the ontological structure of the giveness of others. We encounter others within a context of equipment; we meet them as those for whom a work—say a house—is destined and as those who produce or supply material poorly or well. I

---

[7]For the problem of world and involvement consider, among others, J. L. Mehta, *The Philosophy of Martin Heidegger* (Varanasi: Banares Hindu University Press, 1967), pp. 136-40; and Walter Biemel, *Martin Heidegger* (New York: Harcourt Brace Jovanovich, 1976), pp. 39-44, translated by J. L. Mehta from *Martin Heidegger in Selbstzeugnissen und Bilddokumenten*. This book also lists the various bibliographies and discussions relating to Heidegger's work and contains an extensive bibliography itself. Also see Richard Schmitt, *Martin Heidegger on Being Human* (Gloucester, Mass.: Peter Smith, 1976), chs. 2, 6.

am not an isolated subject who then discerns other present-at-hand subjects only to wonder theoretically how I can ever know other minds. Rather, I first free and encounter others within a world that is mine also. Others are freed as entities who are like me, entities who are "in" the world and not merely things within it. Indeed, I am there with them too: I encounter my own *Dasein* in the world and I encounter it only when I look away from the ready-to-hand things with which I am absorbed and concerned. For every man, therefore, Being-in-the-world is always "Being-with" others; others are freed in the world as "*Dasein*-with" and I myself am encountered by others as "*Dasein*-with" them. It is my previous understanding of Being-with that ontologically lets others be encountered in a world. Indeed, even when I am alone, I am alone as Being-in-the-world with others; Being alone is a deficient mode of Being-with, not a disproof of it, for I can be alone even when many others are concretely there, namely, when I encounter them as alien and indifferent.

Heidegger has called our circumspective dealing with ready-to-hand entities our "concern." Being-with also deals with entities encountered in the world but, because these entities are themselves human, he calls them matters of solicitude, not concern. But solicitude is never separated from concern because our Being-with others is also a concernful Being-alongside nonhuman entities encountered within the world. Usually, solicitude for others maintains itself in what Heidegger calls the deficient or indifferent modes of not mattering, of passing one another by, and of Being against. I encounter others as "with" me in inconspicuous and obvious ways. But solicitude can also free others in two "positive" modes with numerous mixtures. One mode of solicitude steps in for another and takes over that with which he is to concern himself. Here I take the other's Being, his "care," from him so that he becomes dependent: I deal with the things with which he is concerned but ignore his Being. The second, rarer, possibility leaps ahead of the other in order to help him become free for his care, his Being. This gives the other his care authentically.

The purpose of Heidegger's analysis of others is to illuminate who "I" am "at first and for the most part"; the purpose has not yet been satisfied, Heidegger argues, but the discussion has moved toward its satisfaction. I usually encounter my *own Dasein* in the context of the world in which I am absorbed; both I and the others are what we do, and we are therefore not ourselves. In my concern, moreover, I constantly care about the way I differ from these others whom I am for or against: am I prior to them, or do I need to catch up to them? This means that man is always with others such that he is subjected to them, and others govern his Being and its possibilities. But who are these others? They are no group in particular: they are merely what "one" does, what "we" say, what "they" decide. Indeed I think of the others as *other* in order to hide from myself that I also belong to this "they," and the "dictatorship" of "they" comes to fruition as "they" become more and more inconspicuous and less and less explicit. Those who are usually there with me and he who I am usually myself, are nothing but this "they-self." Every one is like the other when he uses the ready-to-hand public environment of transportation and information; every one enjoys himself, judges, and shrinks back from the "great mass" as "they" shrink back.

The concern with difference and distance from others is one existential characteristic of the "they." Even more fundamentally, the "they" is existentially characterized by a concern with averageness. The Being that I usually project and disclose, the Being for the sake of which I am, is the *averageness* of all possibilities. Consequently, any man ordinarily maintains himself only in average possibilities; these prescribe what can be ventured, what grants success, what is valid. This, in turn, suggests that everything exceptional is reduced to what one can manipulate or has always known. These three characteristics—distantiality, averageness, and leveling—constitute "publicness": the "they's" way of Being is the public way, and it controls all ways in which we interpret man and the world. But this means that primordial matters are passed over, that there is no experience of what is genuine, that everything is obscured and covered up. Moreover, the "they" unburdens any particular man of his responsibility because "they" are responsible; but "they" can take responsibility precisely because "they" are no one in particular. Who, then, is everyday *Dasein?* He is the nobody-in-particular to whom every man has already surrendered; in the everyday no one is himself. Indeed, to say that "they" prescribe my possibilities is to say that man is for the sake of himself as they-self, and that it is the "they" that interprets the world and "articulates the assignment-context of significance."[8] Entities are freed for a wholeness of involvements with which "they" are familiar, within the limits of the "they's" averageness. Everyday, "I" am in a world with others whom I have discovered in an average way; I therefore give myself to myself as "they-self," as "one" who pursues possibilities in the ordinary manner.

My disclosing myself to myself as "one" means that I have not grasped myself in my own way. In fact, in my ordinary projection of human Being I do not even understand the self as *existing.* Rather, preontologically, and, at first, even in explicit ontology, we interpret ourselves as present-at-hand subjects among other present-at-hand subjects and things. We pass over both world and existing because we are usually in the world by Being absorbed in the world's things. Nonetheless, the "they-self" can be distinguished from the authentic self. If a *Dasein* discovers the world in his own way, he discloses his own Being, his authenticity, and is for the sake of that Being. Heidegger does not yet demonstrate the genuine possibility and meaning of such authenticity, but says here that authentic disclosure is always, if not exclusively, a clearing away of the "they's" obscurities. It is an existent*iell* modification of the "they," which is an essential existential structure.

The Ready-to-Hand, the Everyday Self, and Politics: Analysis

We may begin our detailed analysis of the sections on readiness-to-hand and the everyday self by bringing out the understanding of Being that guides them, insofar as that understanding is not evident from Heidegger's explicit remarks. Readiness-to-hand does not cause any entity to be or to become ready-to-hand. Rather, it expresses the ability of an entity to be discovered as involved within a significant horizon. The charac-

---

[8] *Sein und Zeit,* p. 129. My translation.

teristics of readiness-to-hand are not efficient or final causes that produce ready-to-hand things. They are not the material component of any and every ready-to-hand thing nor a form that can be seen in everything ready-to-hand. They do not comprise the most perfect ready-to-hand thing, the most perfectly useful thing in which the ready-to-hand things participate by degrees down to the simply useless or fully detrimental. They are not the laws to which any ready-to-hand thing conforms, nor necessary structures of our practical intelligence. Rather, the characteristics of readiness-to-hand make the ready-to-hand things possible by rendering them capable of Being discovered as involved in worlds. Every ready-to-hand thing is equally ready-to-hand and can be understood in its genuine readiness-to-hand, but this does not mean that each is identical in its concrete usefulness or detrimentality. The Being of the ready-to-hand thus has the character of a field or backdrop against which and out of which ready-to-hand entities can be understood.

I can illustrate this by tracing the manner in which a tool is freed as a tool. For this to occur, the tool must be freed from an equipmental whole that has already been understood. For such a whole of "in order to" to be understood, the possibility of readiness-to-hand must be preconceptually comprehended. And for this possibility to be comprehended, the assignment of the "in order to" toward this work, and the destiny of the work for a possibility of *Dasein,* must be understood; that is, significance must be understood. Significance, in turn, is disclosed when *Dasein,* here *Dasein* as they-self, projects himself in his possibility and assigns himself to the order of assignments in which he thus finds himself. For a thing to be usable, therefore, these contexts must be a priori, not in the sense that one deduces a particular usefulness from them, nor in the sense that involvement and worldhood cause useful things, but because these things can come to light as what they are only if the Being of the tool, and *Dasein*'s Being as worldhood, has already been disclosed. Man's Being does not cause the possibility of involvement, and, even more obviously, neither *Dasein*'s Being nor involvement itself causes the way in which something us*able* or service*able* becomes concrete as more or less fitting for the particular work. Precisely *as* involved, many—indeed, all—of the entities discovered may be completely useless for any concrete task, whatever our will or wish.

I can also illuminate this discussion of readiness-to-hand by considering it as constituting Heidegger's analysis of the genuine Being of things commonly believed to have value, things as appropriate, fitting, useful, harmful, beautiful, and ugly. In one sense, because the fundamental constituent of world is *Dasein*'s possibility, I must clarify the Being of man's possibilities before I can complete this analysis. But although something can be ready-to-hand only if world is, and world is an existential component of man, readiness-to-hand itself is not an existential structure of *Dasein*. In particular, the Being of the ready-to-hand is intended to replace the traditional understanding, stemming from Descartes, whereby, in order to make sense of the everyday world, certain qualities, later called value predicates, are added to the real entities that are present-at-hand. Heidegger's argument is both that understanding such qualities as values robs them of their dignity and that this understanding neglects the ontological priority, or at least equality, of readiness-to-hand to presence-at-hand. Readiness-to-hand is the genuinely independent Being of what is useful and appropriate. The present-at-hand entities and, consequently, the leading Cartesian ontological characteristics of extension in pure space can be discovered only on the basis of world in its worldhood. But the world frees ready-to-hand entities first of all, and, more significantly, frees them on the basis of a Being irreducible to presence-at-hand.

We might consider here that Heidegger attempts to recapture the independence of practice and the things of practice—the pragmatic—in the ancient and particularly the Aristotelian sense. This suggestion is strengthened by the structure of "in order to" and "for the sake of," which is clearly reminiscent of Aristotle's *Ethics* and *Politics*.[9] It is further strengthened by

[9]On the importance of the *Ethics* for Heidegger, especially for his understanding of truth, which we will consider in Chapter 3, consider Krell's introduction to the *Basic Writings*, various recollections by his students, particularly Gadamer, and Gadamer's own discussion of Aristotle in *Wahrheit und Methode*.

Heidegger's discussion of deliberation as the decisive element in circumspective concern. And it appears to be confirmed by Heidegger's references to the *Ethics* and the *Rhetoric* in his forthcoming discussions of truth and everyday moods. But this suggestion is misleading. Heidegger does attempt to recapture or "repeat" possibilities for the discovery of practical things that emerge primarily in Aristotle. But he argues that ancient ontology itself was oriented toward the presence-at-hand of Nature. And he claims that all ontology, not merely Cartesian ontology, has missed the phenomenon of world that he is describing. The ancient understanding of Being and of human Being was guided by the "logos" of the animal-with-logos, the rational animal, who observes the entities that are simply present. The difference between Heidegger and the ancients concerning practice can be seen when we recall that the nature or being of what is of paramount human concern—justice—is not, in the ancient understanding, something that all just things share equally. Indeed, there is no single Being of what is useful that allows all useful things to be equally usable, let alone to *be* in the same manner as the detrimental. Heidegger's ontological analysis of the ready-to-hand does not, as such, issue in ranked distinctions, and this will become even more apparent when we turn to his analysis of the possibilities for the sake of which *Dasein* is.

To point out this result of Heidegger's ontology of the ready-to-hand is not to attack it but to clarify its import. Indeed, Heidegger's discussion of Being in general is not simply a *counter* to Kant or Descartes or Aristotle, and the difference between Being as making possible and causality is not intended to be a difference at the same level. Rather, a discussion such as the discussion of readiness-to-hand indicates the manner in which Heidegger attempts to uncover a "Being" that is prior to and other than what is uncovered in traditional analysis. But here arises the basic question of my book: Does the Being described by Heidegger—here readiness-to-hand—force a new conception of the possibilities for practical activity that are explored in traditional analysis? Are some or all impossible to grasp as occuring within what Heidegger describes as Being? Or is his analysis simply neutral? In particular, if the traditional discussion of what is useful or good depends on an ultimately improper understanding of the possibilities of human Being, in what manner, if any, can the concrete results of this discussion be assessed?

I will begin to explore this question by considering the results of treating political entities as if their Being were readiness-to-hand in Heidegger's sense. Now, Heidegger's analysis of readiness-to-hand concentrates on equipment, on tools, on ways and means, and these are freed as entities whose Being is to be destined or involved. That is, they are freed as entities that show themselves in their concrete characteristics only by showing themselves in their connection and dependence on other entities, only by showing themselves in their lack of self-sufficiency. It is conceivable that tools are not the only entities that show themselves this way, but it is not conceivable that the things that are for their own sake can show themselves this way in those characteristics that are most their own. In traditional terms, what is useful may show itself as ready-to-hand, and what is both useful and beneficial or noble may show itself as ready-to-hand, but the noble as noble and the beneficial as beneficial could not show themselves as ready-to-hand. This means, in turn, that the independent attractiveness of entities that attract cannot be conceived properly as freed by their readiness-to-hand. Now, political institutions, laws, and judgments deal with ways and means or are ways and means. But they also claim to embody justice, to distribute goods and offices with proper equality or inequality on the basis of relevant equality or inequality in merit or in rights. Such justice never presents itself as being exclusively for the sake of something else and may well present itself as being for its own sake. But, then, such justice is not ready-to-hand. Insofar as politics deals with matters akin to the noble or beautiful, matters connected with proper distribution or formation for its own sake, political affairs cannot be exclusively, or primarily, freed as ready-to-hand entities. Indeed, this is also true to the degree that politics concerns power for its own sake. For, although power and its instances and effects may be conceived solely as a means to an end, power for its own sake and the distributive effects of the exercise of power for its own sake cannot present themselves simply as ready-to-hand. Whether the pure exercise of power and the suffering of its results falls under the rubric of justice as its debilitating extreme, or whether "justice" is an excessively illusory exercise of power and securing of its results, neither of these elements of politics is properly freed as ready-to-hand. In general, therefore, we must say that what presents itself as choiceworthy, or merely as chosen, for its own sake, and what presents itself as the effect of attraction or the effect of exercise or expression, does not present itself as ready-to-hand. This also requires that what presents itself as deficiently just cannot present itself with the imperfections of the imperfectly ready-to-hand. And this means that the possibility of political questioning and debate cannot be captured sufficiently under the rubric of deliberation about ways and means. Rather, such debate would center upon the limits of the things that are for their own sake as they present themselves to human concern.

If such possibilities do not present themselves exclusively as ready-to-hand, how may we understand their mode of Being, in Heidegger's terms? They may be present-at-hand, they may belong to *Dasein,* or they may belong to some other mode of Being. That all human affairs are misconceived as present-at-hand is central to Heidegger's analysis, and this means that political affairs could not be conceived properly as present-at-hand. Now, that Heidegger believes his discussion in *Being and Time* is insufficient for understanding the beautiful becomes clear in his work in the 1930s, and there statesmanship is mentioned in conjunction with the art work. But in *Being and Time,* beauty is mentioned under the rubric of readiness-to-hand, a painting is treated as a whole not clearly differentiated from present-at-hand wholes, and poetry is mentioned in conjunction with *Dasein*'s discursive expression of the possibilities of his moods. Moreover, Heidegger does not draw a connection between the beautiful and the noble. Thus, even if the political is indeed connected to the noble or beautiful, this does not, in *Being and Time,* connect it to a mode of Being other than presence-at-hand, readiness-to-hand, or *Dasein.* To the extent, then, that one argues that readiness-to-hand is the meaning of the central entities dealt with by political life, one is wrong, for such a meaning does not cover these entities sufficiently; but these entities are not present-at-hand either.

This is not to say that readiness-to-hand is the chief, or only, way to attempt to consider the political in Heidegger's terms. For it is not the discussion of readiness-to-hand but rather the discussion of *Dasein*'s possibilities that offers the most fruitful ground, in Heidegger, for exploring both what presents itself as Being for its own sake and political things insofar as they present themselves in this way. It is when discussing man's possibilities, for example, that Heidegger discusses morality and public law. Moreover, the status of *Dasein*'s possibilities is decisive for understanding the implications of Heidegger's analysis for the problem of ranking and choosing ways of life, a problem at the heart of political philosophy, as we saw when considering Heidegger's justification for his own enterprise. But even on the basis of what Heidegger has said up to now we might, in advance, question the adequacy of understanding as a possibility of *Dasein* everything that presents itself as being for its own sake. For although, say, justice may indeed present itself as a possibility that *Dasein* chooses for his own sake, does not justice as such present itself neither as standing in need of Being decided upon nor as requiring what is ready-to-hand in order to be what it is? Or is this no longer the justice that is politically relevant?

Although understanding politics on the basis of readiness-to-hand is insufficient, we must still explore the implications of readiness-to-hand for that material of politics that *does* come to light as useful and serviceable. As we have seen, if the Being of the useful is readiness-to-hand, then understanding the Being of the useful does not itself furnish a criterion for measuring or judging but merely frees entities so that they show themselves in their possible utility. Whether or not such an understanding distorts the manner in which the possibly useful presents itself depends on the status of the ends, the "for the sakes of" for which the useful is useful. Does an entity present itself in its ready involvment because it is properly ordered to an end or ends, or does it present itself as ready-to-hand because its Being is disclosed when man exists in a possibility that presents itself existentially? If the former is correct, then even the improper use of means is intelligible, meaningful, in relation to proper use. The food that presents itself to the glutton presents itself as eatable only because moderate use is first of all conceivable. Heidegger's analysis presumably is intended to allow such a possibility, which would be one of those possible understandings of economic things toward which his analysis is designed to be neutral. But if such an understanding, which we may identify with that of ancient political philosophy, can be worked out concretely, what function would remain to be performed by Heidegger's readiness-to-hand? Indeed, if it is correct, would not Heidegger's analysis distort it? For although Heidegger's Being is not causal, it is intended to allow the possibility of causal explanation among entities and, indeed, is intended to begin to clarify the manner in which discussion of causes' intelligibility informs us about entities in their Being. But Heidegger's discussion of significance appears to usurp the function of meaningful accounts in terms of nonhuman ends and forms, and usurp it in such a way that discussion in terms of *the* ends and *the* proper means could not be correct.

Does this, then, suggest that Heidegger's readiness-to-hand frees utilities in a manner more compatible with the place of economic things in modern political philosophy? For here things are presented as means for satisfaction with no natural limits deriving from the movement toward satisfaction or from the means themselves. Moreover, political matters in general, the political institutions, political activities within these institutions, and the founding social contract present themselves as a particular kind of means, namely, means that are produced artificially but still produced in accordance with natural necessities (natural laws). In this sense the presentation of political things in their nobility or in their status as distributive framework is obscured; and the chance or fortune traditionally connected with the clash of noble things presents itself as an effect to be overcome, not as chance truly. The status of the producing act itself, and, consequently, the status of its relation to the original movement toward satisfaction, then becomes the decisive question. But here we think of the Hobbesian analysis of death and the fear of it that enables one to see that desire itself is a motion without an end and potentially roots all producing in a new kind of openness. One might think as well of a Machiavellian understanding of glory as the production of the standards, traditions, and institutions by which one is judged oneself, and judged well.

Heidegger's analysis of the ready-to-hand does not preclude such understanding of useful entities—at the level of entities—in any obvious way, for it does not usurp any function performed by a purely utilitarian analysis among entities. Nonetheless, Heidegger's distinction between readiness-to-hand and presence-at-hand suggests the impropriety of reducing entities, in their meaning for human possibilities, to entities whose activities can be comprehended in terms of natural laws derived from understanding such entities in their pure presence. Now, the technological production of means to ends on the basis of physical laws may appear to be the overarching and fully developed example of utilitarian activity of the modern sort whose roots we identify with Hobbes or Locke; but, in truth, such production obfuscates the Being of the useful as useful, namely, its involvement as discovered within human concern. For, abstracting useful objects from their presenting themselves as destined or involved will treat as self-sufficient what always presents itself as dependent. Moreover, Heidegger's understanding of *Dasein*'s possibilities, although it will emphasize death, anxiety, and authenticity, is not compatible with conceiving man as subject to natural movements and natural laws, nor with conceiving him as, so to speak, his own tool, for his own self-production.

That the Being of the useful is obfuscated belongs to the implicit dominance of Being understood as presence-at-hand and to the continual failure to grasp properly the Being of man. What occurs among the modern political philosophers, from the perspective of *Being and Time,* is that human life is considered as a business enterprise, ultimately rooted in self-acquisition and self-promotion, but the readiness-to-hand of utilities is not grasped properly, enabling the results of natural technology to come to appear paradigmatic for all efforts; and the human possibilities themselves are then grasped within the horizon of what can be technologically produced and are not even mistaken for tools properly understood. But whether locating the useful in readiness-to-hand, and therefore more properly understanding the Being of technology, would lead to a new science of, say, economics, or a new economic practice in general, is another matter. For this would depend, first, on the connection of what is discovered on the basis of theoretical understanding of present-at-hand entities to what is discovered practically, second, on the status of sciences of practice, and third, on the concrete analysis of the status of man's possibilities; and we will return to these issues. For now, and despite these arguments, it is unclear how specifically the explicit understanding of useful entities as ready-to-hand would alter the current concrete analysis of useful entities.

We turn now to a more explicit discussion of the political implications of Heidegger's analyses of worldhood and the "they-self." Our discussion includes, but does not restate, the analysis just presented of readiness-to-hand, and, like that, cannot be complete until we study Heidegger's discussion of the temporality of worldhood and concern.

Heidegger explicitly contrasts his understanding of world with that in which world means Nature, or all the natural entities. In the *Essence of Reasons,* written shortly after *Being and Time,* he also distinguishes world from the ordered cosmos, a distinction already implicit in *Being and Time.*[10] But world might still appear to mean all nonhuman entities, natural or practical, or those nonhuman entities, natural and practical, that are connected to one's concrete concerns at any instant. Indeed, it is this sense on which Heidegger implicitly relies when he tells us that one reason the analysis of man can be a fundamental ontology relevant for all beings is that we are in the world. But we also free other humans, in their Being, from out of the world. World is not a totality of entities or an ordering of all entities in light of a highest entity, but that wherein *Dasein* is and that from out of

---

[10]For a discussion of *The Essence of Reasons* (*Vom Wesen des Grundes*) and of *Being and Time* in general, consider William J. Richardson, S. J., *Heidegger* (The Hague: Martinus Nijhoff, 1967).

which entities can be discovered. This suggests that world and its worldhood must not be confused with the political community and the nature of politics, a confusion tempting to the student of politics. For worldhood, the Being of world, is an existential structure of *Dasein*, and *Dasein* as such is neither practical nor theoretical: the disclosing of world frees both practical and theoretical entities. Moreover, the closest world is the domestic environment and not the political forum. Consequently, the public entities said to be freed within the world, public transportation for example, are not those things that *constitute* the world, any more than those natural entities that are freed as material that does not need to be produced constitute the significance of world, as they might were world equated with political community. Indeed, a world is neither itself an entity that is the supreme entity to which others are ordered nor the most general characteristic shared by entities at any time. A world is not an instance of, say, the form of justice that is found only imperfectly in a concrete community. Rather, world has the Being of *Dasein:* any world's concrete "particularity" is therefore found and lived *as* the possibility that gives significance, and the possibility that gives significance is itself always found in a concrete occurrence. It is in the light of world, which is *Dasein*'s existentially, that entities are discovered, and this happens without a world's normally being lit up as such, not to speak of the obscurity of its Being.

But does not the analysis of the "they-self," and the decisive importance of publicness, indicate the dominance of politics? After all, the possibilities guiding our disclosure of the world are the average possibilities of the public, and it is these possibilities that prescribe what can be ventured and what will be successful. We are always with others in such a way that we subject ourselves to them, and to ourselves as one of them. Is this not the dominance of the "common," the "public," the "political," from which I can never fully free myself as my own? Surely it seems that Heidegger is arguing that world is the political world of modern democracy with its "representability" of each of us by another, its reduction of all to the average, and its turning of all possibilities into tasks to be calculated economically by men who are what they do.

I must suggest, in reply, that the publicness of possibilities is an ontological structure. As such, Heidegger believes it to define the manner of Being of possibilities, and of ourselves as having possibilities, whatever the concrete ontic political status of the world. Thus, the analysis does not by itself point to the political community as *the* world. Moreover, the analysis does not by itself consider the *ordering* of various concrete possibilities or their origin: averageness is a manner in which possibilities are disclosed, not a statement concerning their worth. World for Heidegger need not require a ruler or regime from which the possibilities are commanded or a concrete natural source of these commands; the publicness of Being-with as the "they" is neither democratic nor aristocratic but that which makes common decision possible; the publicness of possibilities and of the world significance attached to them indicates the manner in which they are and can be disclosed. Possibilities are *present* to us in this public way and, everyday, each of us is this "one" to whom possibilities are made present. Similarly, the modes of solicitude do not themselves answer the question of the proper rules and occasions for such solicitude.

The political issues presented by Heidegger's analysis of the publicness of the everyday world are, therefore, not properly questions seeking to develop the argument that the political community is the chief or only entity that Heidegger believes could be a Heideggerian world. Rather, they must be the following questions, which are clearly connected to the issues we have begun to address in analysing readiness-to-hand. To what extent does Heidegger's analysis of the *Being* of the world of public possibilities permit the possibilities of political life, and the questions of political life? Here, for example, we will consider whether the distinction between theoretical knowledge and practical deliberation, and the averageness of the everyday, could allow the decisive political questions—such as the question concerning the nature of justice—to arise at all. Here as well we will consider whether and how Heidegger's analysis can permit the fundamental dilemmas of statesmanship to retain their meaning. Does, or can, Heidegger's analysis point in any specific direction for a "best" politics or humanity? For here arises the problem of whether the Being of worlds indiscriminately makes possible all worlds. Does what Heidegger says about significance and the ready-to-hand allow a sufficient ground for the distinction between the shoemaker who makes the shoes and the thief who steals them? Indeed, as I will argue in discussing history and tradition, the problem of the multiplicity and interconnections of those entities that can be as worlds is relevant in questioning not only the implications of Heidegger's analysis for the possible Being of the most significant political entities but also the adequacy of Heidegger's ontology in general.

3. *Human Possibilities and Human Being*

At this point in our discussion, it is necessary to clarify Heidegger's analysis of human possibilities. Let us begin by turning to Heidegger's exposition of the final element of man's Being-in-the-world, namely, "Being-in." In general, "Being-in" means that man is the opening or clearing within which other entities can become accessible. To use Heidegger's terms, man is always his own "disclosedness" and, in every case, his "there." Heidegger's first task in discussing "Being-in" is to spell out its three existential constituents: states of mind, understanding, and discourse.

[1]

States of Mind: Exposition

(§29–30) We begin with states of mind. States of mind (*Befindlichkeit*) are the ontological ground of what is familiar to each of us as our moods: they are moods understood in their possibility of disclosing man in his Being. A state of mind is, therefore, not to be interpreted as psychical, as an epiphenomenon of something material, or in any manner that fails to grasp it as an existential. Rather, states of mind disclose, and they disclose in three ways. First, moods reveal us to ourselves as always Being *this* disclosedness; the mood discloses to us that we *are* always as a fact. In each mood a man is opened to himself in the pure "that" in which he is and has to be: mood shows man to himself as the entity to which his Being has been "delivered over." To put this in other words, man always finds *himself* in the mood in which he is: moods disclose man to himself in his "thrownness" into his openness. Now, because moods belong to our Being, we always have them. Thus, even if we "can, should, and must through knowledge and will" become their master, moods remain ontologically prior to any willing or knowing, and we can control moods only when accompanied by counter moods.[1]

The second characteristic of states of mind is that they always disclose the current Being-in-the-world as a whole. In a bad mood, for example, we can see that our devotion to the world is diminished and our entire concern within an environment is closed off. But this is possible only because moods disclose Being-in-the-world as a whole. Third, states of mind belong to the submission to the world from out of which we can encounter something that matters to us. A thing can affect us as, say, threatening, something can be discovered in its detrimentality, only because it can matter to us. And it can matter to us as threatening only because our state of mind, say fear, belongs to the prior disclosing of world.

Understanding: Exposition

(§31–32) Understanding is the second characteristic of "Being-in." Just as a state of mind is the existential meaning of a feeling, so understanding is the existential meaning of what is evident concretely as reasoned explanation or assertion. Understanding is man's distinctive potentiality for Being: while a tool *is* by being seviceable, man *is* by being understandable. But who understands man? Man himself: man *is* by understanding his own ability to understand. More broadly, man is by disclosing what his Being is capable of, seeing himself more or less "transparently" as belonging to himself, freeing himself in his possibilities more or less authentically, more or less as his own. Now, according to Heidegger, existential understanding takes the form of "projection": understanding is *Dasein*'s projection of himself upon his possibilities. It is for this reason that prior ontological inquiry—such as Kant's—searches for "conditions of

[1] *Sein und Zeit*, p. 136.

possibility" when it seeks the Being of objects, and it is for this reason that the ready-to-hand comes to sight as service*able* and us*able.*

Heidegger defers a more thorough explication of the general meaning of "possibility" until the second part of *Being and Time,* where he discusses authentic understanding. But it is clear that we cannot, here, understand "possibility" to be inferior to "actuality" or "necessity" as a mode of Being; nor can possibility mean here, as it often does, the not yet being actual of something present-at-hand.

Man's projecting himself upon possibilities has already come to light in Heidegger's discussion of worldhood, for man understands significance by holding himself in a possibility of his own Being. On this basis, he can first see entities within the world as the entities they are. Now, *Dasein*'s projection upon his possibilities is not a mere selection of free-floating "possibilities," because man has always been thrown into his "there": along with every understanding there is also a state of mind. Moreover, we should not view possibility, in this sense, as equivalent to concrete contingency, for example, the contingency of meeting ends or goals: that man "projects" himself upon his possibility means that he holds himself in one or another mode of disclosure. Therefore, most of what one might think of as choosing "possibilities" ontically, to run or stay put, for example, is itself possible only because *Dasein* has already assigned himself to the everyday world, thereby uncovering the possibilities of the ready-to-hand and of himself as absorbed in the world. Indeed, a man's projecting his abilities primarily in terms of things of the world may be contrasted with authentic understanding, which is not absorbed in the world or others but projects itself upon the possibilities of *Dasein*'s own Being. But both authentic and inauthentic understanding can be genuine or fail to be genuine, that is, both can be or fail to be worked out and developed appropriately.

When a man works out the possibilities on which he projects his understanding, he is said by Heidegger to have "interpreted" them. Interpretation is explicit understanding, and Heidegger analyzes it by discussing man's interpretative understanding of the world. When *Dasein* understands the world, he discloses significance and understands the involvement an entity *can* have in terms of this significance. In this example, interpretation, explicit understanding, is the circumspective discovery of something ready-to-hand; it happens when, for example, we deal with something *in* its in-order-to. Interpreting, indeed, is always to deal with something *as* something. When, for example, we deal with the door *as* a door we have explicitly understood it in its significance: we have explicitly laid out its involvement. The "as" constitutes the interpretation: it "makes up the structure of the explicitness of something that is understood."[2] This explicitness need not be in the form of a verbal assertion. In fact, circumspectively seeing entities *as*, or solicitously seeing others as, or transparently seeing oneself as, is primary; merely seeing without seeing *as* is derivative and indicates failure to understand. But interpretatively to see something *as* does not mean that we see what is present-at-hand as a door, as having this "value." Rather, by understanding the world we have already discovered an involvement: interpretation makes this involvement explicit.

We have just seen that interpreting ready-to-hand things is a way of Being toward involvements that we have already understood as significant. Similarly, every interpretation is grounded in something had in advance, the "fore having." Moreover, all interpretation is based on fore sight, on something seen in advance: it is with regard to this that the understanding becomes explicit. Furthermore, every interpretation has decided in advance how to *conceive* the entities it interprets: this is the fore conception. The "fore" structure of understanding, and the "as" structure of something interpreted, can themselves be interpreted further by seeing their connection to the concept of "meaning." Understanding discloses entities in their possibility, and the possibility corresponds to the entity's kind of Being. Entities within the world are projected upon the world, upon "a whole of significance." When these entities have been understood, we say they have meaning. Strictly, meaning is that

---

[2] *Sein und Zeit*, p. 149.

wherein the intelligibility of something maintains itself; meaning is that which can be interpreted in the disclosure by which we understand. Therefore, we understand an entity, or Being, by projecting it upon its meaning. (Consequently, it is, strictly, incorrect to say that we understand the meaning itself.) "Meaning is the upon which of a projection in terms of which something becomes understandable as something: it is structured through a fore having, a fore sight, a fore conception."[3] "Meaning" is thus an existential of *Dasein:* it is the existential framework of the disclosedness of understanding. Meaning is therefore not a property of entities, and only man can be meaningful or meaningless: a man is meaningful when his understanding appropriates his own Being and the entities disclosed with it; *Dasein* is "meaningless" when he understands these inappropriately. Finally, the discussion of meaning helps clarify Heidegger's intention in asking about the meaning of Being. This question "asks about [Being] itself insofar as Being enters into the intelligibility of Dasein."[4] Consequently, the meaning does not stand behind Being, nor can it be contrasted with entities, nor can it be contrasted with Being as the ground of entites, for such a ground "becomes accessible only as meaning, even if it is itself the abyss of meaninglessness."[5] But we must note here the ambiguity of the first quoted passage. Does the entrance "into the intelligibility of *Dasein*" simply mean Being as it can be understood by *Dasein* on the basis of his Being, or Being-as-such as that which allows intelligibility, meaning, to belong to *Dasein*?

Discourse: Exposition

(§34) Heidegger develops his discussion of understanding by examining "discourse." Understood ontologically, discourse is the articulation of "intelligibility"; it goes beyond interpretation because interpretation merely makes something explicit in the meaning that discourse has already articulated. Heidegger calls the worldhood of worlds "significance" because we have always

[3] *Sein und Zeit,* p. 151. My translation.
[4] *Sein und Zeit,* p. 152.
[5] *Sein und Zeit,* p. 152.

discursively articulated a whole of significations from that which *can* intelligibly be articulated.

Discourse in this sense is the existential basis of language. Indeed, discursive articulation is expressed in language. But discourse as such is not identical to some totality of words, and language can itself be misinterpreted as a ready-to-hand tool or even as a present-at-hand collection of things.

Now in all discourse we find something said, and it is through this that discourse communicates: discourse takes hold of and articulates the co-understanding and co-state of mind in which a man is already manifest with others. To say that discourse expresses is to say that discourse makes known how one stands outside himself, that is, how one's mood places one in the world: discourse indicates this through intonation, modulation, and tempo.

The elements of discourse can be found in hearing and keeping silent as well as in talking. In hearing, as in all discourse, *Dasein*'s dwelling alongside ready-to-hand entities is prior to his relation to the present-at-hand: what we hear is a storm, or "the column on the march," and never a complex of sounds or pure noise. What we hear is always primary, for when we "hear" we are already alongside the entity and have some understanding of it beforehand. Similarly, keeping silent may develop a better understanding of what a discourse is about than the uttering of many words.

The Everyday Possibilities of Discourse and Understanding: Exposition

Because discourse, interpretation, and understanding are existentials, *how* they are is always an issue. But they are usually in an everyday manner, and Heidegger now turns to discussing the possibilities of discourse, understanding, sight, and interpretation that belong to the publicness of the "they." These everyday possibilities must not be misconceived as concrete ontic possibilities. Rather, they refer to the way in which all concrete possibilities are disclosed as possibilities in the everyday. (In this sense, whether man's disclosing is itself to be everyday or authentic is open to existent*iell* decision.) Consequently, Heidegger claims his discussion of these characteristics to be "far removed from any moralizing critique of everyday *Dasein*," much as it may sound like one.[6]

(§35-37) Everyday discourse is "idle discourse" or idle talk (*Gerede*). In discursive expression, there lies hidden a way in which *Dasein*'s understanding has already been interpreted. This is the interpretedness to which man is usually "delivered over," and it is this interpretedness that controls and distributes the possibilities of average understanding. An understanding of "Being-with" and of one's own Being-in has already been deposited in the way things have been expressed in the totality of significations. Now, in idle discourse, as in all discourse, there is communication. But usually communication attends to the dictum rather than to the entity the talk is about; and what is said in the talk is itself understood only in an average or common way. Consequently, everyday discourse loses its ability to let the entity it is about be appropriated genuinely. Things are only what they are said to be in gossip, in passing the word along, and in hearsay. These, together, make up idle talk. In this sense we can see that idle talk closes Being-in-the-world and covers up the entities within it, not by attempting to deceive intentionally but because we understand what is said as if it did indeed uncover something. Rather than keeping articulated understanding open, therefore, idle talk is "the possibility of understanding all without previously making the matter one's own."[7] *Dasein* is usually uprooted from what he is, and any genuine understanding and appropriating are carried out in, from, and against the public interpretation.

One counterpart of idle talk is curiosity. Curiosity is Heidegger's term for the characteristic form of sight that belongs to everyday understanding. For Heidegger, all *Dasein*'s understanding is accomplished as a "seeing" that frees entities: circumspection, for example, discovers the ready-to-hand, and transparency sees *Dasein* himself. Everyday seeing is curiosity. Curiosity is the mere looking at things just in order to see. In curiosity, circumspection is free from concern with the ready-

[6] *Sein und Zeit*, p. 167.
[7] *Sein und Zeit*, p. 169. My translation.

to-hand and brings the most alien things close. But, as opposed to theory, curiosity does not seek to understand the present-at-hand as such: it does not wonder at entities but looks by jumping from one thing to another, seeking novelty rather than leisure; in its being forever distracted, curiosity is a peculiar kind of abandonment to the world by never dwelling anywhere. Curiosity in this sense discloses man's possibilities by closing everything in apparently closing nothing: it belongs together with the idle discourse that "understands" all possibilities and decides in advance what we must all restlessly read and see.

Ambiguity is the third element of everyday disclosure. It refers to the impossibility of deciding what belongs to genuine understanding and what does not. Like idle talk and curiosity, it presents man's possibilities in such a way that they lose their power. Everyone "understands" what lies before us and what must be done, everyone is in on it, but the level of ambiguous public interpretation is betrayed by the inability to carry something out, face up to what has actually been carried out, or even genuinely to break down in the attempt. This ambiguous Being, however, is not to be regarded as deliberate, any more than the covering up by idle talk is deliberate. Rather, the "they" belongs to *Dasein's* Being, but what "one" genuinely is is hidden from each of us by the very structures of public disclosing we are discussing here.

Falling: Exposition

(§38) Heidegger concludes his examination of Being-in by discussing "falling." Falling is the most comprehensive characterization of everyday Being: it signifies that man is usually lost in the publicness of the "they," that he has fallen into the world and "fallen away from [himself] as an authentic potentiality for Being [himself]."[8] This fallen absorption in things and others is guided by idle talk, curiosity, and ambiguity, and it defines everyday *Dasein's* inauthenticity. As a mode of man's Being, fallenness *is* no less than authentic Being: Being fascinated by the world is a positive possibility of absorption in the world. More-

---

[8] *Sein und Zeit,* p. 175.

over, we must not confuse fallenness, as a mode of Being, with an ontic report of man's fall from a purer or higher status. Rather, fallenness is the movement inherent in man's Being itself. Consequently, no stage of "human culture" could possibly eliminate it: as long as a man is, he is thrown into a turbulence, plunging from his authentic possibilities into the they's inau-·thenticity and sham authenticity. This movement is a fact, revealed to man by his moods.

Falling is composed of the temptation exerted by things as groundlessly understood in idle talk, of the tranquility engendered by a public interpretation that claims to understand everything genuinely, and of an alienation from one's own potentiality for Being while one curiously busies oneself with everything. Together, these characteristics of falling make up our everyday Being. But precisely because it is an essential structure of man and man is not a static thing, fallen everydayness can be modified to the authentic seizing of everydayness itself.

Anxiety and Care: Exposition

(§39-44) Heidegger's discussion of falling completes his examination of the separate elements of Being-in-the-world. But Being-in-the-world is a whole: what is the Being of this wholeness and what concrete possibility can reveal this Being to us? The phenomenon that presents itself for the task is anxiety (*angst*).

Anxiety is a mood that discloses something different from other states of mind. In particular, it must be distinguished from fear, which had been Heidegger's example of a mood in his discussion of moods. Fear is always in the face of an *entity* that comes from a definite region within the world. We discover such entities in their detrimentality for our Being-in-the-world at a given time, and it is about this Being that we fear. But anxiety is not anxious in the face of any definite entity within the world, and in its oppressiveness it appears to come from nowhere in particular. Indeed, in anxiety all entities within the world *lose* their significance. But, in the insignificance of entities within the world, the world in its worldhood obtrudes itself; we are oppressed by the very possibility of the ready-to-hand rather than

79

by some definite ready-to-hand entity. Anxiety therefore discloses the world *as* world, and because worldhood belongs to man's Being, we may say that when we are anxious we are anxious in the face of our Being-in-the-world as such. This disclosure is prephilosophical: everyday man does not *thematically* interpret what he discloses in anxiety. Indeed, man does not hold himself in what anxiety discloses but flees from it: this flight is precisely that turning away from oneself that constitutes our falling into the entities within the world. Now, although we have established that we are anxious in the face of our Being-in-the-world, we have not yet established about what we are anxious. We cannot be anxious about any *definite* possibility nor can we understand our anxiety in terms of the public interpretation of entities, because anxiety is precisely what strips these entities of their significance. Rather, we are anxious about our very Being-in-the-world: in anxiety, what we are anxious about and what we are anxious in the face of is the same. Anxiety throws *Dasein* upon his authentic potentiality for Being in the world; it makes manifest man's own, individualized "Being free for the freedom of choosing and grasping [himself]."[9] Anxiety reveals man's authenticity as a potentiality that he always is: it discloses to man his Being delivered over to Being free for the possibility of authenticity and inauthenticity.

Because anxiety reveals Being-in-the-world as a whole, Heidegger's analysis of it enables him ontologically to grasp the whole of man's Being. The name for this Being is "care" (*Sorge*), and for this reason our Being toward entities within the world is "concern" and our Being toward others is "solicitude." Heidegger formally defines care as follows: "The Being of *Dasein* says: ahead-of-itself Being already in [the world] as Being-alongside (entities encountered within the world)."[10] "Ahead of itself" refers to *Dasein*'s understanding: man is by disclosing, by Being toward, his own potentiality for disclosing Being, and he is for the sake of this potentiality. This means that man is in each case already "ahead" of himself, beyond himself, not by transcending

[9] *Sein und Zeit,* p. 188. My translation (italics omitted).
[10] *Sein und Zeit,* p. 192. My translation.

to other entities but by Being toward his own potentiality for Being.

Dasein, however, is not a worldless subject. On the contrary, he has in each case already been thrown into a world: he has always been delivered over or abandoned to himself: he always is as this fact. Understanding is "factical": the "for the sake of" is always tied up with a series of assignments. But *Dasein* is not merely a general thrown potentiality for Being-in-the-world, for he is always "absorbed" in the world of his concern, always falling "alongside" entities. Indeed, in each of the elements of care the other two exist also.

We should not confuse care as an ontological structure with concrete worries and trials, although there are English expressions, like "I don't care anymore," that begin to reveal the range of care. Moreover, Heidegger argues, we must distinguish care from the concrete, ontic phenomena that appear closest to it and that lead us to misconceive it. Just as we must not confuse existential understanding with asserting and explaining, and just as we must not confuse states of mind with the content of any specific feeling, so we must not confuse care with will, wish, urge, or addiction.

Heidegger does not discuss the ontic limits and causes of these four phenomena; rather, he treats them as kinds of disclosure. His purpose is to show that, as kinds of disclosure, they are all grounded existentially in care but are not equivalent to it. In willing, something is seized upon as an entity with which one may concern oneself, or as someone toward whom one may be solicitous. But this is possible only because what is willed has already been projected on its possibility. Willing can seize only because *Dasein* has already disclosed the world. Now, because any man has fallen into the world, he takes his possibilities from the world in accordance with the "they's" interpretation. But this interpretation has limited possible choice to what is fitting and proper, attainable and respectable: man's possibilities have been leveled to what is at one's everyday disposal. This leveling so flattens the possible that the everyday self in fact busies himself with what is actual, willing no new possibilities but merely altering things to give a semblance of something happening. This tranquilized willing shows itself most fully as wishing. In wishing, man projects himself upon possibilities he has not taken over in concern and whose fulfillment he does not expect: he does not understand the concrete possibilities. In "addiction," one puts all one's possibilities in the service of the entities one is already alongside; Being ahead of oneself is completely absorbed in the entities one is pulled toward. And when one urges oneself toward something, one crowds out other possibilities and fails to let one's own care become free. Any urge—say, the urge to survive—is rooted in our being thrown into possibilities such that this thrownness always precedes our concrete understanding of choices.

Each of these four is thus made possible by, and is a modification of, care, but none can be equated with it.

Care: Analysis

I will begin my analysis by considering care and then turn to its constituents. Care is distinguished from what is similar to it: will, wish, addiction, and urge. This suggests that it takes the place of the classical *eros*, the early modern desire to acquire security or glory, and the late modern will as the fundamental constituent of human Being. Heidegger's "care" is meant to be ontological in the special sense of naming man as the discloser of Being; it is therefore intended to be on a wholly different plane from these others. Nonetheless, we may see that it newly interprets the fundamental openness of man, always central in the tradition, an openness that, like care, was never fully equated with the theoretical quest. As care, man is open to the possibilities of his Being, and in Being for the sake of these possibilities he discovers entities in their Being. He *is* for the sake of Being, he is open to Being, and he is this openness *as* his moods and understanding. But, for Heidegger, this openness does not direct us to a correct understanding of Being, which would be the fulfillment of reason and the passions. Man is not open by lacking something that completes him in its being striven for properly. One outstanding difference between Heidegger's analysis and the earlier analyses is, thus, that Heidegger's "care" is not oriented to any concrete understanding of the fulfilling end. Heidegger therefore cannot and does not argue that the proper analysis of man's Being can, as such, teach the proper way of life—say, a life devoted to fundamental ontology or philosophy itself. Moreover, although man's openness is ultimately destined to that for the sake of which he is, what he is for the sake of has his mode of Being: he is for the sake of his own potentiality. But this means that he is for the sake of his own possibilities of disclosure, of openness. Man is open for the sake of his own openness; he is not open "because" of anything but this openness. We will explore later whether and how this openness can further be understood as belonging to Being and not merely to man's Being. But whatever the outcome of that discussion, neither Being nor his own Being causes man by attracting him, and neither is disclosed because of this attraction. Even the difference between everyday inauthenticity and "authenticity," still to be thematically discussed, revolves around the different possibilities of deciding upon one's own Being as the entity who discloses Being. Authenticity is not perfect human *Dasein* and *is* no more than inauthenticity.

Our analysis distinguishes Heidegger's account of care as man's Being from erotic openness, but it may seem to equate his understanding with one that finds man's Being in a self-positing will—say, the will to power. Heidegger takes pains to differentiate care from will for precisely this reason. Man's Being is not arbitrary activity or the willful choosing of concrete goals, but the disclosing that first frees those entities, including goals, which can then be chosen. This freeing is accomplished as care. Man is always already ahead of himself in such a way that he can release the concrete possibilities toward which he directs himself. It is true to say that he is free to flee from himself as this entity who discloses Being—and, indeed, he almost always does so—but he neither creates his Being nor willfully determines what other entities are in their Being.

With these considerations we have introduced the theme of Heidegger's understanding of human openness; we have not closed it. The questions of the status of man's possibilities and abilities, of his "will" and resolve, and of the measures that guide him will be discussed once more in ensuing chapters. But now we will turn to a preliminary discussion of man's closedness, his "particularity," his spirited self-assertion.[11] The heart of Heidegger's description here is his analysis of moods, culminating in the uniquely individuating mood of anxiety. Indeed, the peculiar Heideggerian connction between self-assertion and the openness of the self is visible in the observation that individuating anxiety is the mood that most radically discloses care as a whole: care is simply and only as mine.

Moods disclose thrownness, facticity. That is, they disclose me to myself as *this* entity who is *Dasein*. A mood discloses the "general" fact that man is as this unique entity, and discloses this fact to me in my particularity. Here we are tempted to say that mood discloses my *Dasein* in its here and now, or discloses me as a soul with *this* body. But for Heidegger this traditional manner of grasping the peculiarity of each man mistakes human beings for present-at-hand entities. For the authentic temporality that he will show to be the meaning of man's Being is, at root, other than the now of ordinary time, and the "here" of man is his discovery of place and direction in the world, not his assignment to a point on an abstract spatial grid. Indeed, the mood that most radically discloses my inevitability as *Dasein,* and my responsibility for significance as *Dasein,* is anxiety, and anxiety is said to strip from man all here and now, all significant entities on which he can rely in order to understand himself. This means that the closedness or uniqueness of *Dasein* must be understood ontologically. It is what separates man as the entity who discloses Being from the other entities: thrownness belongs to the entity who is necessary for the Being of other entities, necessary because there is no discovery without the world and there are no horizons of significance without *Dasein*. Consequently, moods cannot be understood properly as disclosing our contingency, if a contingent fact means one that is nonessential, unnecessary, or meaningless. For man's thrownness is essential, he is necessarily as this fact, and the proximate source of meaning is his facticity. Even this, however, fails to emphasize that moods *are* by disclosing our *Being* as

[11]Consider Leo Strauss, *The Argument and Action of Plato's Laws* (Chicago: The University of Chicago Press, 1975), pp. 7-10.

fact: thrownness belongs to us insofar as we are the clearing in which entities, including ourselves, can be uncovered in their Being, and in which Being can be disclosed; it does not refer to our immediate factual content as an ontic affair any more than our caring understanding of possibilities refers as such to our ontic determination by qualities we hold with others in general. I must repeat that, for Heidegger, our openness and our individuation disclose a Being that is itself no entity, not even the highest and most general, and that is the condition for the discoverability of entities but not any ontic cause of them. Thus, the averageness of possibilities is the everyday mode in which we are toward ourselves as disclosing Being; and the thrownness, the individuality, that moods disclose is the condition for the possibility of a world within which entities are. We are "what" we are (our understood possibilities) by Being "that" which we are (the factical world we find ourselves in), and we are that which we are by Being what we are. Again, however, even these terms fail to secure rigorously the expression of man's existence in his characteristic as Being the clearing of Being. A full determining of the special connection that emerges in Heidegger between our closedness and our openness, as well as its political implications, awaits his forthcoming discussion of the negativity, in guilt, of our "thatness," the finitude, through death, of our possibilities (our "whatness"), and the ecstatic (open) and horizonal (closed) temporality on the basis of which we understand our Being.

The Elements of Human Being: Analysis

We must now fill in these general characterizations of existence by considering the omissions and commissions in Heidegger's particular analyses of understanding, facticity, and falling.

Let us, first, continue with our discussion of moods, that which discloses facticity. We may say that Heidegger's discussion attempts to clarify the ontological meaning and possibility of the passions that traditionally are considered to belong to the rational animal.

A mood's *Being* cannot be confused with what causally elicits it or with the physiological situation concomitant with it, for these do not tell us what the mood as a mood is. Moods *are* by disclosing thrownness. But if this is so, then the virtuous mastery of moods does not belong to their Being. Clearly, what moods *are* must enable us to see how a variety in virtuous control is possible—how, for example, fear can be met courageously or in a cowardly manner—and what they *are* must enable us to see this whether or not they allow the grounding of the superiority of courage to cowardice. But the mood as a mood *is* without dependence on virtue. Heidegger does not claim, for example, that fear *is* properly only when it is met courageously, any more than circumspective deliberation *is* properly only as prudence and not as cleverness. The ontological discussion does not yield the principles that govern activity. Moreover, no mood in particular is the essence of human passion, neither fear of violent death nor a "sweet" sentiment of existence. This is true even of anxiety, which illuminates man's Being, the source of significance, and which, when properly followed in what it discloses, is central to a man's grasping his ownmost Being. For the proper Being revealed in anxiety *is* no more than the self-forgetting turn to entities within the world that belongs to other moods. And "authenticity" is neither an ontic mastery of moods nor a calculable form of fulfillment. Anxiety is said to be different from other moods because it is in the face of Being-in-the-world and is about Being-in-the-world itself. Other moods are in the face of definite entities and are about my possibilities as I understand them in terms of these entities. The *fact* that I am, the disclosure of myself as *this* granter of worldhood, is, therefore, revealed more fundamentally in anxiety than in other moods. But this raises two questions. First, is anxiety the only mood that can disclose Being-in-the-world as such? Second, can the disclosure of thrownness be shown to be the Being of all moods, or are some impossible if this is their Being? We cannot fully discuss these questions until we consider Heidegger's exposition of the possibility of authenticity and the temporality of care. Here, however, we may prepare for this discussion by addressing a related question. If all moods *are* as the disclosing of thrownness, how can differences be accounted for ontologically? Or are these differences merely ontic?

Let us begin by analyzing Heidegger's differentiating of fear, terror, alarm, and dread. The differences among these, and between these and anxiety, indicate that the difference in moods has its ontological possibility in modifications of mood's structural elements. In particular, fear is in the face of present-at-hand, ready-to-hand, or human entities encountered within the world. When the involvement of an entity is detrimentality, when it affects a definite and well-known range, when it draws closer and closer to our neighborhood but is not inevitable, it is fearsome. This ability to come close to us belongs to the possibilities of entities within the world: it belongs to their spatiality insofar as this is significant nearness and farness, not simply measurable distance. But this possibility can be modified, and the possibilities of modification belong to entities as they are freed in their *Being*. For entities can come close in several ways, and their advent can be variously encountered. What is threatening, but still familiar, can break in suddenly: fear becomes alarm. What is threatening can be unfamiliar but not close by: fear becomes dread. And what is threatening can be unfamiliar and encountered suddenly: fear becomes terror. Timidity, shyness, and the like are other moods whose possibilities are modifications of fear: none is an ontic disposition.

I have already remarked that Heidegger's analysis of the Being of moods implies that virtuous control of moods does not belong to man's ontological disclosing. Similarly, Heidegger's discussion of the Being of what is fearful does not result in a listing or evaluating of the fearful as such. Entities are detrimental only within a world, and their very detrimentality does not announce any inherent evil or ugliness in them but, rather, only the manner in which they are defined in their Being involved. The fearsome must first be disclosed in its Being, and is always so disclosed before we can then consider and evaluate the "future evil" that traditionally is said to elicit fear.

Fear is neither defined nor modified solely by what fear is in the face of. For fear is *about Dasein;* only because man is existentially spatial can the fearsome be discovered in its detrimental closeness. In particular, in fearing about himself, man discloses himself in his abandonment to himself. But he does so in light of his possibilities as he understands these in terms of the entities with which he is concerned: he falls into concern with himself as providing shelter, food, and the like. The modifications possible here presumably belong to the various ways in which the characteristics of the public interpretation of possibilities, idle talk, curiosity, and ambiguity, can be modified, although Heidegger does not develop this now. But if Heidegger does not discuss the modifications possible in the manner in which a mood is *about Dasein,* we nevertheless can project the difference between anxiety and fear in these terms. Anxiety is about *Dasein* when *Dasein* loses those significant entities in terms of whose possibilities he can project himself. The difference between anxiety and fear is enabled by the different manner in which one's own *Dasein* is freed, for *Dasein* can be freed in his own Being as abandoned to the world, or his abandonment can be freed in flight to those entities with which he is concerned. Anxiety *is* by disclosing *Dasein* in his pure thrownness, a disclosure made possible by the fact of this thrownness and the possibility of projecting oneself upon this thrownness.

Let us conclude our discussion of moods by considering the power of Heidegger's analysis of anxiety. Whether or not moods other than anxiety can disclose Being-in-the-world as such, it may seem that the phenomenon of anxiety cannot be captured at all by the traditional analysis of fear and courage, and that a discussion such as Heidegger's is indispensable. Indeed, it may seem that the existential projection of anxiety is basic evidence for his entire analysis of man's Being as care. But it is, in fact, possible to capture the peculiar generality and lack of focus of anxiety in the following way. What is called "anxiety" is the phenomenon that reveals the radical imperfection of *any* concrete human endeavor or striving, and the falseness, the sham, the sophistry that belongs to any such endeavor. Any concrete enterprise falls short of its hoped for perfection because of the contingent and accidental; this can be seen in the way in which practical activities both take for granted and fail to live up to the validity or justice of their ends; and it can be seen in the pretentiousness of even the most divine contemplation. What is called anxiety amalgamates a kind of shame and a kind of fear in the face of the lie that pervades any activity, a shame and a fear that reveal one's own ignorance, mortality, and baseness. It is in this way a peculiarly unsettling experiencing of the possibility or, indeed, necessity, of one's own imperfection. At the extreme, such shame and fear almost obliterate any spirited self-assertion. But even at the extreme, the fearful shudder reveals the "self" capable of such imperfection. I leave open here the question whether such an experience is possible without experiencing the attendant perfection, and the question whether the possible generality of such "anxiety" can be experienced identically despite concrete differences in the activities connected with it. Moreover, we can hardly fail to recognize that even were such an analysis developed, it would appear to employ the concepts of the present-at-hand rational animal Heidegger seeks to understand more originally. But I do mean to suggest that the phenomenon itself can at first glance be captured adequately *without* reference to the kind of root uncanniness, insignificance, and projection of Being discussed by Heidegger, and that, therefore, Heidegger's analysis does not obtain special confirmation because of the being of such a phenomenon. We will return to this problem when we consider Heidegger's ontological exegesis of guilt and death.

To complete this discussion adequately, we would also need to discuss the phenomenon of laughter. Heidegger does not discuss laughter, as he need not if such a discussion is unnecessary for his ontological enterprise. He does, however, briefly discuss joy later in the work. It is not analyzed in detail, but it appears to be the "positive" mood analogous to anxiety in its range: we have joy in the possibility of our individualized ability to be and are freed from the everyday events our curiosity presents to us. Such joy is not obviously connected to laughter, although it is clearly connected to a powerful and overflowing amusement. Nonetheless, we may raise the question whether there is a traditionally understood possibility with the range and lack of specificity of such joy; and our attention is drawn to the ridiculous. Whatever the concrete cause and object of laughter, laughter seems directed at the foreign and strange—that is, the ridiculously uncommon—or at the too familiar, the pretentious and sophistic—that is, the inadequate imitation. Laughter at the ridiculous reveals the imperfection in which its "object" is clothed. Clearly, much laughter is improperly immoderate if rooted in a common that is not genuinely common and a "perfect" that is not genuinely perfect. But is there not a sudden sense of the pervasively ridiculous that is a twin of the fear we have just discussed, and a twin that more clearly announces the rootedness in the perfect, however inadequate that root, that makes possible the approach of the sham? Obviously, in developing such an analysis we would need to be aware of the same caveats just mentioned. But here we believe that the burden is on Heidegger's existential analysis: it is unlikely that either the joy in the individual ability to be, or the possibilities of understanding laughter by way of characteristics of the "they," could properly account for the generality of the ridiculous.[12]

The manner in which modifying existential structures makes different characteristics ontologically possible, which we have just considered in the context of moods, can also be understood by recalling the differences among will, wish, urge, and addiction. For Heidegger analyzes these according to their different ways of projecting possibilities, of disclosing them in their average characteristics, and of discovering the entities within the world with which we are concerned. He does not differentiate them according to a listing of human faculties that are ontically expressed and fulfilled in different degrees in relation to concretely different entities.

As existent, each of these possibilities belongs to the fallenness of care. Fallenness is one mode of the ontological interpretation of what would be understood traditionally as the dependence, neediness, or finitude of man. By arguing that it belongs to *Dasein*'s ontological structure, Heidegger is suggesting that dependence on things of the world is essential to man and not accidental. Consequently, man's Being could not be grasped by understanding him on the basis of ontic characteristics that

[12]Consider Plato, *Laches,* on courage, fear, and the ludicrous.

"transcend" concern, as if submissive Being alongside what is within the world could then somehow be grasped in light of these "transcendent" characteristics. This does not mean that factual needs and the meeting of them *cause* theoretical reason or so-called "pure" morality, only that such possibilities must be understood for the entity to whom fallenness belongs essentially. Similarly, fallenness must be understood as belonging to the entity for whom both understanding of Being and anxiety are possible. Consequently, Heidegger's understanding of the ontological meaning of our needy dependence on the things within the world is rooted in his broader characterization of the openness and closedness of existence. He will progressively consider existence itself in its temporal "finitude," but this finitude is not to be confused with an ontic report about our concrete dependence on other entities and other men. Fallenness is merely the characteristic of man's Being by which he projects his potentiality upon the possibilities of entities within the world: it is the most comprehensive characteristic of everyday Being, it is how the entity who discloses Being "has" these other entities, and it indicates as well the primary manner in which man discloses his own Being to himself. Both everyday moods and everyday understanding belong to "fallen" *Dasein:* he *is* his possibilities in temptation, tranquilization, and alienation. That is, we are toward the average possibilities interpreted by the "they" *as* tempted, tranquilized, and alienated.

Understanding: Analysis

We turn now to understanding. Understanding takes the place of reason in the traditional view of man as the rational animal. As one of man's existential structures, understanding belongs to that which makes possible all his actions, but, more specifically, it makes possible assertion, explanation, and practical deliberation. To comprehend Heidegger's "understanding" we must see that existential understanding is of Being, and of entities as determined by Being; it is not of entities in their concrete ontic characteristics, even the highest entity and the most general property. To "understand" an entity is to free it in its Being, its possibilities; and to interpret this entity is to develop the understanding explicitly. Now, man's *self*-comprehension is central in existentially understanding *any* entity because of the connection between man's understanding and the forming of worlds. Man's self-understanding is *Dasein's* projecting of possibilities *as* belonging to *Dasein*. If, for example, a man is for the sake of justice, this "end" can form a world because it is a possibility released to *Dasein* as possible for a man; and in freeing this possibility *Dasein* both releases himself as *this* self through the mood that exists along with every choice and frees himself as submitted to the entities that are significantly involved in his choice. Heidegger's argument suggests, therefore, that whatever the status of justice, of righteousness, as an entity beyond human possibility—indeed, whatever its status as a "biological" preference or changeable and fleeting historical inclination—it is only this end as freed for *Dasein* that forms a world within which nonhuman entities, preferences, or inclinations can be understood. Whatever the nonhuman entities' causal relationship to ends as *Dasein's*, they cannot effect the world-releasing function of these ends as man's.

But what of this status? Does Heidegger's argument further suggest that the questions we have asked concerning the status of the attractiveness of what can be chosen—the questions of the independence of the goals that inspire and form human virtues—are irrelevant because to understand these possibilities as man's in fact exhausts their Being? Does it mean that these questions remain relevant but secondary because the entities that are for their own sake and cause their own distributive effects are *within* the world and, therefore, ontologically subordinate to *Dasein's* ends? Or, do such entities indicate that Heidegger's analysis of the transcendence of significance and world can indeed be located in *entities*, and man's openness to them, rather than in Heidegger's Being and *Dasein*? I will now develop a critical analysis of Heidegger's concept of human possibilities by exploring these issues.

Just as the Being of the most politically and morally significant entities cannot be equated with readiness-to-hand, so too, I will argue, the Being of entities such as justice, courage, and moderation is not exhausted by understanding them as *Dasein's* possibilities. For justice and the like would be relevant to entities other than those whose Being is existence—namely, men—if such entities were actual. If there are immortal thinking beings, the very justice that forms men would be expected to form them. Indeed, human justice and human power are fully intelligible, fully meaningful, only in conjunction with a possible purity and possible omnipotence beyond human attainment. But, Heidegger might reply, this view belongs to our ordinary misconception of ourselves and our possibilities as present-at-hand. Even if this is true, however, Heidegger does not believe that his grasping of man's possibilities solely from *Dasein*'s Being speaks against, or for, the possible ontic existence of a god. But, then, insofar as man's possibilities—indeed, the most comprehensive of man's political goals—are possibly relevant to what is not *Dasein,* and insofar as the meaning of these possibilities for man is never fully severed from these possibilities as they might belong to immortal entities, the Being of these possibilities is not explored sufficiently if we consider them only as possibilities for *Dasein.* Indeed, the possibilities of *Dasein* that may also be possibilities for other entities can further be conceived to be wholly on their own, that is, to be entities that can be without Being freed as the possibilities of man—or of a god. Here we are referring to the Platonic understanding of "ideas," in which, say, political justice or courage—even the justice or courage in the philosopher's soul—is impossible without justice and courage themselves; but justice and courage *are* in themselves whether or not they actually attract man's theoretical or practical activity.

If the Being of such entities is not exhausted by their presenting themselves as *Dasein*'s possibilities, what is their Being? I have already suggested that such entities are not ready-to-hand and that they could not be those present-at-hand entities Heidegger has been discussing—namely, those discovered primarily in theoretical science. We have provisionally called them the "noble" entities, or those entities that can present themselves as being for their own sake. One might reply that, in Heidegger's view, they *are* in some sense present-at-hand because they can ultimately be freed for pure theoretical observation even where they first present themselves in practical pursuits. But if this is so, then it is unclear how they present themselves from themselves in their independent *choiceworthiness,* because Heidegger has not mentioned characteristics such as attractiveness and comprehensiveness in his discussion of presence-at-hand. Consequently, Heidegger's criticism of both the ordinary and ancient philosophic "misinterpretation" of man's possibilities as present-at-hand is *not* directly relevant here because we are arguing that these possibilities are not sufficiently accounted for by *any* of the modes of Being discussed by Heidegger.

Assuming we are correct that, say, freedom, justice, and courage are not comprehended properly as ready-to-hand, not developed or comprehended properly as present-at-hand, and not simply comprehensible as *Dasein*'s possibilities, one might still suggest that the status of these ends as man's is primary. Are not the "noble" entities still inner-worldly entities released only by *Dasein*'s understanding of his possibilities, released only by man's understanding of possibilities such as Being just, but *as Dasein*'s, as world-forming?

Let me begin our discussion of this issue by remarking that even if it is true that such ends are entities within the world, we would still face the problem of understanding the connection between *Dasein*'s ends as they present themselves to man's existent*iell* choice and these ends as they present themselves in themselves, regardless of whether a man chooses them practically or chooses to explore them theoretically. I have suggested that several of *Dasein*'s ends, and those most significant politically, present themselves to man's choice as entities that do not completely, or even partially, require his choice in order to *be* and are not in principle limited to man. Indeed, their choice worthiness and meaning for man requires that they be beyond man. But, *ontically,* we would then be forced to account for man by means of entities whose Being is not his, forced to ground man on what is not human. To attempt such an account, within Heidegger's framework, would be to face a problem similar to that of connecting present-at-hand and ready-to-hand entities, given their difference in Being. The problems would not be identical because the human and nonhuman possibilities under discussion are freed in similar discursive terms, unlike the ready-to-hand and the mathematical-physical entities. Still, the Being of *Dasein*'s possibilities does not exhaust the Being of those entities that can present themselves as *Dasein*'s possibilities—what presents itself as, say, good-as-such would not present itself simply as good-for-man—and, thus, the ontic relation of the entities freed on the basis of such presentations remains unclear.

Now, in opposition to Heidegger, I may begin to clarify this problem by attempting to explain even existent*iell* choice in terms ultimately derived from, and congruent with, the status of ends that present themselves as Being for their own sake. Here one might suggest that the necessity of existent*iell* choice derives from an imperfection that comes to light only in our striving for the ends that perfect us; similarly, our mistaken judgments concerning the worth of these goals and the apparently contradictory status of these goals—say, liberty or just distribution—derive from such ends as they present themselves to us. For these ends fully to govern us, they must indeed be chosen, but choice is intelligible only in light of these ends as they *are* without being chosen. An imperfect entity is what it strives to be, and its imperfection or finitude is not conceivable fully in itself precisely because the choiceworthiness of what presents itself as a human goal belongs to what is beyond finitude.

One could suggest, as a possible Heideggerian reply, that the status of man's finitude, of death as death, of moods as moods, of the human body as body (dependent submission) does not appear to be grasped fully by such a discussion. We could not simply deny this suggestion. Nonetheless, existent*iell* choice is surprisingly explicable in other than existent*iell* ways. We are open to a variety of ends and a variety of means or modes of production to satisfy these ends because we must be free in order to be what we are; what we are is the practical attempt to be those unchanging things we imitate, to achieve immortal glory or to order our affairs with perfect righteousness; such practice, however, attempts to include our very imperfection in the perfection it imitates by failing to relinquish our own body, our own name. Ultimately, therefore, we must be free existen-

tielly in order to be what we are, and what we are is the attempt to be what we understand through reflection—that is, to be a microcosm. But if, despite this, Heidegger's analysis does more accurately depict man's possibilities *as* man's, we may remind ourselves that it fails to bring out the peculiar status of these ends as not his. Consequently, we face the problems of existen-*tiell* interrelation that we have been discussing.

Our analysis faces a graver Heideggerian objection. For if the ends that guide *Dasein* are, or are connected to, "noble" entities released within the world, and if the world is constituted by *Dasein's* projecting his possibilities, is not the Being of "noble" entities subordinate to the Being of *Dasein* which, according to Heidegger, is a priori to the possibility of dealing with, or being attracted to, these entities in any concrete way? If Heidegger is correct, then possibilities as belonging to *Dasein* constitute world and release entities such that possibilities *as Dasein's* function in a manner beyond and irreducible to what is for the sake of itself or what conceivably guides entities other than men.

As I have stressed throughout, it is necessary to understand Heidegger's description of man and his possibilities as ontological descriptions in his distinctive sense. But this view does not eliminate the problems that we have been considering. Nor does it guarantee that there is Being, and human transcendence to Being, in Heidegger's sense, or even guarantee that what Heidegger ascribes to Being and man's transcendence to Being may not properly be discussed in other ways. Here we will explore the possibility that what Heidegger ascribes to *Dasein's* projection of his possibilities is thinkable as connected to the dependence of man's possibilities on the nonhuman status of ends. That is, we will explore the possibility that world, signifi-cance, and the freeing of entities within the world belongs to man, but to man only insofar as he is *not* thought primarily from the existential being of his own possibilities. The function of transcending to and constituting the world belongs to man, but in his subordination, and therefore ultimately can be grounded in what is not simply his own. If this possibility is established, the status of what Heidegger calls Being-as-such then becomes simi-larly questionable.

In discussing anxiety and the ridiculous, we considered the possibility that the phenomena that appear to reveal *Dasein*'s possible freedom from ontological submission to innerworldly entities can be explained by means of the disproportion between the entities with which man deals and these entities as they truly are. Man's homelessness is experienced as such on the basis of the true community and true goods for which he strives. In discussing readiness-to-hand, we considered the possibility that the useful has its meaning, its intelligibility, in terms of the genuinely useful, what this is useful for—namely, human character or virtue expressed most fully politically—and what virtue reflects. In the present discussion, we have explored further the connection between those ends that are self-sufficient and human striving for them. Does this relationship not indicate that the meaning, or intelligibility, of entities—their Being, in Heidegger's sense—is sufficiently explained in light of the truest entities, or that intelligibility belongs to entities that *are* in the emphatic sense? Those entities that come to light in their connection to man's particularity—to his moods, to his ontic submission, to his tradition—intelligibly come to light because they are rooted in what is beyond their particularity, come to light because they are released from openness to the entities that are for their own sake insofar as these can be human ends. Now, this also suggests that only insofar as *man* is for the sake of such possibilities can *certain* entities be revealed at all. Consider concrete political institutions and imagine them to be ordered by a particular understanding of justice. Insofar as these institutions form particular material and govern particular ways and means, they are revealed as such only for man in his particularity. For the justice-as-such that renders the whole order significant does not require these institutions, ways, and means; and *these* institutions, ways, and means achieve their result only imperfectly. In this sense, that certain entities come to be freed in a certain intelligibility does depend upon man's freeing of his possibilities, and even if there is an order of fully noble things, it is not identical with all intelligible or significant things. But, nonetheless, the intelligibility of what is freed by man's projection of possibilities is dependent upon these noble things themselves as they make possible the various ways in which entities become meaningful in particular activities, for particular human orders.

We are left with the problem of how the noble entities could be intelligible as such. If the root possibilities—to be just, to be in the truth, to be an immortal and unique recipient of worship and glory—have a being beyond their presentation as that for the sake of which man is, if the human transcendence to world is ultimately a transcendence to these, how can they be understood as such? That is, how can we know them except as they are for human practical or theoretical activity? Here we have suggested that they are for this activity in a manner that reveals their elusiveness—that is, for example, that justice is for us, attracts us, precisely in a manner that reveals it not to be merely or primarily for us. Indeed, is this not the genuine source of the peculiar elusiveness of what *is* that Heidegger, in *Being and Time,* locates in the coveredness of Being as it enters the fallenness of man?

I do not pretend that my discussion of human ends is fully conclusive. At the least, I have not explored the understanding of *Dasein*'s possibilities that comes to light in Heidegger's analysis of authenticity and history, or begun to explain how an account other than Heidegger's could ground the possibility of natural science in the mathematical-physical sense. Nonetheless, I believe that I have sketched a legitimate alternative to his analysis up to this point.

Let us return now to the attempt to clarify what Heidegger means by existential understanding, and, in particular, to the broader conception of existential understanding as our understanding of the possibilities of all entities, not only men. Such understanding cannot be true or false in any ordinary manner, because its truth and falsity cannot primarily be understood as a property of entities; it is a property of neither the subject making, say, an assertion, nor of the entity about which he asserts. The truth of disclosing must be interpreted differently; we will consider this presently. But existential understanding must make possible truth and falsity in dealing with entities, as well as the manner in which such truth and falsity are discovered—mere seeing, calculating, deducing, and, in general, the giving of causes, reasons and grounds. Much of Heidegger's discussion of these issues was to have belonged to the unpublished portion of *Being and Time,* where Heidegger intended to use the Temporal meaning of Being as the basis for interpreting both the classical *logos* and phenomenology. And in the *Essence of Reasons,* Heidegger attempts to show how concern with grounding arises from *Dasein's* existential submission to the understood world. Here, we will consider Heidegger's analysis of assertion and its derivation from entities as we interpret them practically. This discussion will help clarify what it means to understand entities in their possibilities and will further prepare the ground for Heidegger's later thematic exploration of the ontological genesis of theory from practice.

Assertion: Exposition

(§33) We usually consider making statements like "this hammer is heavy" to be the chief manner in which men uncover entities. We interpret such assertions as asserting a predicate (heaviness) of a subject (hammer). But this interpretation depends on first letting the heavy hammer be seen from itself. This is assertion in the more fundamental sense that, in our example, discovers the entity in its readiness-to-hand by saying, "this hammer is *too* heavy." The mere subject of which a predicate is asserted is, therefore, a narrowing of what is originally discovered. The pointing accomplished in the subject-predicate assertion, thus, depends on the "fore having" of what is originally discovered, which the assertion then points out by giving it a definite character. It further depends on the "fore sight" of that with regard to which we are considering the entity and defining it, namely, the "predicate" that we loosen from the entity and make stand for it. Finally, insofar as assertion communicates, it works with significations that have been articulated in accord with a particular way of conceiving. Thus, assertion also depends on the "fore conception" by which the discovered entities have been articulated: it is this that enables us to say the hammer is heavy, or the hammer has the "property" of heaviness.

This entire discussion lets us see that the primary interpretation of the entity is found in the "too heavy," and that the theoretical assertion whereby heaviness is a "property" of the thing has leveled the entity: the ready-to-hand entity with which we do something, the entity we have in advance, becomes an entity about which assertions are made. It becomes so insofar as our fore sight is no longer the interpretation found in circumspection but merely looks *at* the present-at-hand in the ready-to-hand.

Indeed, assertion ultimately levels entities to a uniform plane on which we exhibit things by just looking at them. In between such merely theoretical assertion and full circumspective interpretation are a variety of intermediate possibilities: accounts of the ready-to-hand, assertions about environmental happenings, narrations of events, descriptions and reports of situations and states of affairs. But in all these, as in theoretical understanding, the root is circumspective interpretation. In sum, the ancient understanding that, according to Heidegger, considered the *logos,* the assertion, itself to be something present-at-hand, and that considered the entities discovered by *logos* to mean presence-at-hand, mistakenly understood Being-as-such as presence-at-hand. In fact, assertion is possible only as existential understanding and interpretation, and the entities that assertion discovers are first discovered and, presumably, always held in advance, in their readiness-to-hand.

This discussion helps to clarify the meaning of understanding and interpretation, just as it helps to clarify Heidegger's understanding of the priority of readiness-to-hand (and of *Dasein*) and their irreducibility to presence-at-hand. The discussion itself, however, raises the following problems, which I will mention here and elaborate in Chapter 5. First, how precisely can we understand the change from the fore having, fore sight, and fore conception of what is ready-to-hand to the interpretation of the present-at-hand: how is this understood in light of Being itself and man's understanding of Being, and can these ontological possibilities ground the concrete ontic causes of such change? Second, does Heidegger's discussion make understandable, or even permit, the interconnection between the properties of present-at-hand things and the characteristics of *Dasein* and the ready-to-hand things? We wonder on what grounds, say, technological entities constructed on the basis of theoretical knowledge can then become entities within a practical environment. Indeed, it is unclear to what extent we can discuss meaningfully why particular characteristics, say, too *heavy,* belong to interpretation of the meaning, the Being, of the ready-to-hand: is there limit and order here that is explicable ontologically, or, at least, capable of Being understood ontologically?[13] Third, to what extent does Heidegger's analysis of the derivative nature of assertions about entities obtain for his discussion of Being-as-such? For one might argue that his discussions are necessarily a leveling of the Being first revealed in an existential disclosure that lies a priori even in explicit fundamental ontology. Indeed, Heidegger's discussion of *logos* suggests that the traditional priority of assertion, and the coordinate priority of Being as presence-at-hand, explains why Being itself is so often seen as a kind of present-at-hand entity. But if this is so, we wonder how Heidegger can prevent his discussion from becoming a series of assertions that level Being.

[2]

Reality and Truth: Exposition

I shall elaborate these questions and further consider the connection of truth and understanding by summarizing the next section of *Being and Time.* Here, Heidegger attempts to orient the results of Part 1 to the problem of Being-as-such, and here, as well, he explicates the connection between Being and truth.

(§43-44) Because we are normally "falling," we understand ourselves as entities within the world, and this is so even for previous philosophers. Their clue for ontology is things conceived as simply present, and they understand Being primarily as "reality." Indeed, they see man himself as a real entity. Consequently, we must briefly examine the question of "reality" in order to advance the discussion of man and Being.

The problem of Reality traditionally has been seen as the

---

[13]Consider Kant, *Grundlegung zur Metaphysik der Sitten* (1795), section 3.

problem of how men can know the external world. But, Heidegger argues, knowing entities, knowing the so-called external world, depends upon Being-in-the-world. That is: Being-in-the-world lies a priori to any dealing with entities within the world, including knowing them. Therefore, the question of the reality of the external world is a nonquestion because the entity who asks it is already in the world. It is precisely the Being of the man who demands proof of the external world that has been insufficiently clarified. Moreover, the priority of *Dasein* also shows that the question of Being-as-such cannot be guided by the question of the Being, the Reality, of the real entities, because these entities can be discovered only within the world, and the Being of the world is "*Daseinal.*" Further, the clue to man's Being cannot be the isolated present-at-hand ego, the subject, because the conceiving of such a subject also takes for granted the a priori structure of man as he who uncovers entities that we can then deal with or behave toward. It is, consequently, this a priori structure that must be our chief guide in uncovering man's Being and the Being of the real.

This discussion of Reality demonstrates the inappropriateness of conceiving man as something real, because all modes of Reality "are founded ontologically upon the worldhood of the world" and, therefore, upon man's Being, care.[14] Indeed, we may understand "Reality" to designate the Being of all entities within the world so that both readiness-to-hand and presence-at-hand are modes of Reality. If, however, we restrict Reality so that it means the presence-at-hand of things—and this is its traditional signification—we then see that such Reality lacks ontological priority even among the modes of Being of entities within the world. Such entities include not only the ready-to-hand but also nature when we understand by this the nature that surrounds us and not the present-at-hand things of nature. But precisely because even the surrounding nature is itself within the world, its mode of Being is also ontologically grounded in the Being of Dasein.

Yet, Heidegger continues, the ontological priority of *Dasein*'s

[14]*Sein und Zeit,* p. 211.

Being surely does not mean that only as long as *Dasein* exists can the real entities be what they are in themselves. It does mean that only as long as an understanding of Being is ontically possible— that is, only as long as *Dasein* is—is there Being. For without *Dasein*'s existence, "independence" and "in-itselfness"—say, the independence of the real—are not, and they can neither be understood nor not understood. Indeed, without *Dasein* and, consequently, without Being, entities within the world cannot be hidden, cannot be said to be or not to be. But now, as long as there is an understanding of Being and therefore of presence-at-hand, one can say that entities will continue to be. Being is dependent upon the understanding of Being and, thus, Reality, a mode of Being, is dependent upon care. Only "if the understanding of Being *is* do entities as entities become accessible."[15] But this does not mean that entities in general, or the real entities in particular, are dependent upon care.

Heidegger develops this discussion of Being in his analysis of truth. Although truth has long been understood to be a property of statements and to lie in their correspondence with entities, the fact that statements or assertions are themselves derivative modes of Being-in-the-world indicates that assertion is not the primary locus of truth. The assertion's lack of priority cannot mean merely that the entity is primary and the statement secondary, because this still locates truth within the realm of assertions about entities already uncovered in their Being. The heart of truth is the uncovering of entities rather than correct statements about entities already uncovered: the truth of entities is their uncoveredness.[16] Now, uncovering entities belongs to *Dasein* as Being-in-the-world. Being-in-the-world as an uncovering of entities is grounded in *Dasein*'s disclosing, and this, in turn, is grounded in man's disclosedness of himself to himself. Such disclosedness, therefore, brings us to the basic phenomenon of truth.

This argument requires that truth be an existential of *Dasein;* and because truth belongs to *Dasein*'s Being, man is always in the

---

[15] *Sein und Zeit,* p. 212.
[16] "Discover" and "uncover" have been used equivalently to translate *entdecken.*

truth because he is as disclosing. This does not mean, however, that he has interpreted all entities at any time or that he correctly understands all the ontic characteristics of what he uncovers. Moreover, because man ordinarily flees from his own Being and understands himself in light of the "they" and the entities within the world, Being untrue, covering up, hiding, is existentially equiprimordial with Being true. Furthermore, because truth is an existential, it is not to be confused with the willfulness of the subject, as if truth were left to the subject's discretion; for man's most proper uncovering, his ownmost uncovering, brings him face to face with the entities themselves and takes asserting away from subjective discretion.

Heidegger supplements his discussion of truth with an argument similar to his argument showing the priority of care to Reality. There is truth only as long as and insofar as *Dasein* is, and entities are uncovered only when and as long as *Dasein* is. Because there cannot be disclosing when *Dasein* is no more, and because there could not have been disclosing before *Dasein* was, there was no truth when *Dasein* was not and there will be no truth when *Dasein* is no longer. This is so for all truths, including, to use Heidegger's example, Newton's laws and the principle of contradiction. It is not that such laws were *false,* or will become false when ontic discoveredness is no longer possible. Before Newton his laws were neither true nor false, but the entities that become accessible after Newton's discoveries show themselves as entities that already were. "Truth" is thus this primary uncovering. Whether or not there are eternal truths depends on whether or not *Dasein* has been or will be for all eternity (and, to say the least, proof of eternity is still pending); but, to repeat, lack of eternity does not make truth relative to the discretion of *Dasein* as if any entity is as he claims. On the contrary, *Dasein*'s uncovering entities and setting them free brings us to the entities themselves. Indeed, only because *Dasein* can uncover entities can there be universally valid truths. For "entities in themselves can be binding for every possible assertion,"[17] only if they have first been uncovered and set free. Fi-

---

[17] *Sein und Zeit,* p. 227. My translation.

nally, if truth has the ontological structure just displayed, it is clearly not a "value" outside or above us toward which we comport ourselves. Rather it belongs to the Being that frees entities such that we can comport ourselves to them.[18]

Reality and Truth: Analysis

We must remember that Heidegger's remarks on Being and truth are provisional, for he has not yet elucidated the connection of Being to its meaning, to Time. But one can see precisely from this discussion why Being and Time must be elaborated, because so many of the issues in these passages depend on the question of Time. With this in mind, what are the issues raised by these passages?

Whatever Heidegger's protestations to the contrary, his analysis seems to make truth and Being relative to man. In order to consider this issue fairly, two points must be kept in mind. First, Heidegger's Being is not to be confused with the highest and most general entity. Consequently, several of the peculiarities of his analysis that stand out if Being is understood as the highest and most general entity lose their peculiarity in the context of Heidegger's understanding; and different, but related, issues emerge. Second, Heidegger makes clear that man is not eternal, or, at the least, that he cannot be understood properly with the categories applied to ever-present entities, and he makes clear that truths such as the principle of contradiction are not true if *Dasein* is not. But he argues strenuously against understanding truth and Being as subject to man's will, and he does not make this argument simply on the unsatisfactory grounds that because man is not a "subject" nothing can be "subject" to him. Consequently, we must genuinely ask whether the specter of relativism, which Heidegger's discussion suggests, can be exorcised only with reference to what is eternally unchanging.

There is no Being without *Dasein* because Being is "there" only in *Dasein*'s disclosure.[19] One might say: this need not make

---

[18]Heidegger's understanding of truth is discussed in the monographs already cited, and is especially central in Richardson's work. To these, add Lazlo Versenyi, *Heidegger, Being and Truth* (New Haven: Yale University Press, 1965).
[19]*Sein und Zeit*, p. 230.

Being simply subject to man any more than Newton's laws become what we want them to be even though they could not be discovered without *Dasein*. For entities such as these laws, the question forced by Heidegger's analysis is: what "are" they before they are discovered, before they are either hidden or not hidden? We will return to this. Being, however, is not an entity. Whatever its connection to entities, it *is* only as Being, and Being and its modes *are* only in *Dasein*'s disclosure. Does this mean that Being is subject to man even if the entities discovered on its basis are not? But man does not create Being. He understands it. His understanding is not an assertion about an object already there but a projection of Being upon its possibilities: Being "is" "at the same time" that man is. But if Being is understood in light of its possibilities, it is not at our subjective disposal even though it is not an "object." That is, its comprehensibility cannot be equated with its Being understood. Yet, is not the direction of the projection at man's disposal? For however we may discuss the manner in which, say, Newton's laws are effective prior to any disclosure, Being *is* only in disclosure. It is the a priori condition upon which entities are discovered, but it is this only in conjunction with the variable direction of human understanding. Is it not true, then, that Being *is* only as far as we understand it, and that although we do not create it, our understanding is not subject to it? That is to say, is it not true that there is no correct or incorrect understanding of Heidegger's Being but that Being is only as it is projected, even if this projection does not create Being to our specifications? But what, more precisely, is our understanding of Being? Our understanding belongs to the entire structure of care that lies a priori in any discovery of entities. We have our own Being as an issue, but our Being implicates itself whenever we are: we can fail to be ourselves only as ourselves. This, however, does not mean that care is eternal, or is before concrete humans. Rather, care is only a priori "at the same time" as ontic *Dasein*. Is Being, therefore, a priori to ontic *Dasein* in this sense as well, "there" when men are, and only when men are, but nonetheless a priori? If so, how does Being-as-such differ from care? Is Being a priori to care or are Being and care equi-primordial? Whatever the outcome, it seems that the most one could say in support of the argument that Being-as-such is at man's disposal is that it is at the disposal of man in the same way that man's own Being is at his disposal, and even "less" so if Being-as-such lies a priori in care.

But in what way is man's Being at his own disposal? *Dasein* is necessarily in the truth, but truth is a possibility for the sake of which he is. When he projects his ability to be upon his possibilities, he must do so *as* disclosure, *as* care. But he normally projects himself as fallen. In what way is man's understanding of Being-as-such affected by the manner in which he projects himself upon his own possibilities? Presumably, whether or not he is disclosed to himself properly, authentically, as his own, he always understands Being and "cares" for it. Now, given Heidegger's argument, we cannot equate true disclosure with correct ontic statement, and, given his argument, we cannot grasp *Dasein* properly as a thing or tool, with the properties of things or tools, governed by the standards applicable to things and tools. Thus, we could not equate the distinction between authentic and inauthentic *Dasein* with correct and incorrect understanding of Being. Truth is neither a "value" arbitrarily posited nor an end properly fulfilled by the proper activity of human faculties, but, rather, a potentiality of *Dasein*. Presumably, however, when *Dasein* is authentically, his Being is disclosed to him properly, and Being-as-such belongs together with this proper *Dasein*. We must wonder, therefore, whether this distinction between authentic and inauthentic does harbor some standards of proper and improper understanding of Being, and whether Being in any way determines the propriety of its own disclosure.

We cannot consider these questions further until we have analyzed authenticity and care's meaning as temporality. Consideration must also be deferred for the related question of how (or whether) Being and man's understanding of Being comprehend all the possibilities of Being that could be, as Heidegger seems to suggest. But we must now consider two further points and then discuss the issues raised by the connection between Being and entities suggested in Heidegger's summary passage on Being and truth.

Our previous discussion had assumed that Heidegger connects Being's "Being there" with *Dasein*'s factical ontic existence. But one might suggest that Heidegger merely says that Being "is there" only when an understanding of Being is ontically *possible*. But this ontic *possibility* is none other than *Dasein*'s Being. Consequently, one might argue, Heidegger merely suggests that Being-as-such is understood only when it has care as one of its modes and that Being's "dependence" on care is merely Being's dependence on itself. Therefore, several of the problems we have discussed are not genuine. But we remember that *Dasein* is possible only as "actual." That is, he is his Being only as *this* concrete "factical " *Dasein*, and only as factical *Dasein* is his Being possible. Consequently, we cannot separate his Being possible from his factic existence as if man's Being existed separately from particular men. Therefore, although Heidegger's claim that Being and truth are "there" only as long as man is there does refer to man in his Being, to *Dasein*, man in his *Being* is not simply separable from man ontically, and the problem of the understanding of Being cannot be separated simply from the factic understanding of Being. Nonetheless, Heidegger is indeed not suggesting that this or that man in his concretely definite characteristics has mastery over Being. That he is not can be seen further in the following manner. Being is in no sense an entity, but is beyond ontic characteristics. Just as it is not itself the highest cause, it cannot be caused. Consequently, any attempt to make it causally dependent on man's objective or subjective ontic characteristics must be incorrect, if Being is as Heidegger attempts to show. This must also be true for the understanding of Being. If man's projection of Being is the area within which Being can be revealed, he lets Being be only in relation to a Being that is no entity. Man's freeing of Being and of entities in their Being, his letting Being be, is what it is as a "relation" to what is no entity. Therefore, it cannot itself be reduced to an entity or a nexus of entities. Just as one may claim traditionally that reasoning *as* reasoning cannot be reduced to physiology, so Heidegger's argument may formally defend itself against any reduction of Being and its understanding to ontic casuality. Consequently, neither the understanding of Being nor Being itself is *caused*, and, if we are to clarify the Being that Heidegger investigates, the problems we have opened concerning the precise relation between Being and the factical understanding of it can be pursued properly only as ontological problems. But this guarantees neither that Heidegger himself separates Being from ontic causality with complete success nor that there is "Being" as Heidegger seeks it.

The question of the connection between Being and entities is also involved in attempting to understand Heidegger's remarks concerning the truth and Being of entities such as Newton's laws. That they are neither true nor false until discovered is not difficult to comprehend. Moreover, it is clear that real entities in general cannot be *said* to be independent or in-themselves unless *Dasein* is, because when there is no *Dasein* there is no Being. Presumably, characteristics such as "independence" belong to an entity in its Being, although Heidegger gives no exhaustive presentation of the ontological attributes of the present-at-hand. Moreover, it is possible to see that once *Dasein* is, entities can be discovered to have been before *Dasein* is. But in what way are they when Being is not there? Does this mean that they can retain purely ontic characteristics without Being, that entities can be without Being? This seemingly impossible suggestion may seem more possible if we keep in mind that Being is not causality. But then four questions arise. In what way do beings need Being if some beings—most clearly, present-at-hand beings—can be without Being? Is Being more or less complete and significant than beings; and, if it is less complete, with what right does Heidegger usurp the title Being for what he is discussing? If beings can be when man and his Being are not, need not man and his Being be understood as aspects of them? Or are all these questions misguided because they are asked and askable only on the basis of the Being and human Being that is here now?

If it is true that Being and human Being cannot be explained by means of the present-at-hand, then Being and human Being need not be grasped in subordination to entities that are when man and Being are not. Even if there are eternal entities, but man is not eternal, such entities cannot be understood as the efficient or final causes of man and Being. The a priori need not be eternal nor even universal, if a universal truth is one that applies only to present-at-hand entities or if it is "universal" only for entities discovered on the basis of *Dasein*'s noneternal disclosure of Being. Moreover, insofar as it is a question of the act of explaining and understanding, the entities that are when *Dasein* is not enter the field of discussion only when they are freed in their Being. To be grasped in their causal characteristics, they must first be freed within the world. If Heidegger has properly uncovered Being, Being lies a priori in them precisely when we would attempt to discuss them as "causing" Being or human Being, a priori precisely when we would attempt to see them as the structure within which Being emerges. Indeed, the prior disclosing of Being runs ahead of any discovery of entities. This suggests that Being is more full and more complete than the totality of entities, let alone those that are before Being, even if this completion and fullness is difficult to specify without thinking of causal laws, or Platonic *eide,* or the end of history. Thus, although we leave open the question whether Heidegger's Being *can* free such entities, particularly those causal ends relevant to the direction of human action, Heidegger's remarks about the entities that are when Being is not do not necessarily detract from Being's fullness or make Being dependent on them. Nonetheless, the precise manner is unclear in which such entities are before and after Being is "there"; and the need to discuss the problem of Time and Being becomes all the more apparent.[20]

[20]It might be suggested that Heidegger's Being in some sense *is* even when *Dasein* is not—that Being's Being "there" speaks to the "discoveredness" of Being but not to Being simply. Heidegger's very distinction between the dependence of Being on ontic understanding and the "independence" of entities from ontic understanding, however, speaks against this, and Heidegger's discussion of Being is always of Being as it "is there." But if Being "is" before it can be "there," the connection between such Being and the prehuman entities, and the connection of these to Being as "there," would need to be discussed in ways similar to those I have just elaborated. In any event, the argument that Being's dependence on *Dasein* does not make Being subject to man does not depend on distinguishing Being from Being's Being "there."

4. *Death, Authenticity, and Political Possibilities*

Heidegger cannot yet discuss how time is the meaning of human Being because his analysis of human Being is incomplete. First, he reminds us that he has neither sufficiently demonstrated the ontological possibility of authenticity nor sufficiently clarified it as a possibility for concrete existent*iell* choice. Second, he suggests that his discussion of *Dasein* to this point has brought to light neither man's Being as a whole (his Being from beginning to end) nor the ontological condition of this wholeness. The discussion has stayed within everydayness, that which is between beginning and end. Third, Heidegger claims that only after his analysis of authenticity and wholeness will he be able to uncover a phenomenon that can support the articulated structural whole of man's Being—namely, the resolute understanding of death. This will point to temporality as its meaning; and we will then be able to understand how, and that, temporality is the meaning of man's Being in general. These analyses, in turn, will enable us to understand temporality both as the meaning of *Dasein*'s being historical and as the meaning of man's everyday understanding of time. In this way, Heidegger sets the program for the remaining six chapters of *Being and Time*.[1]

[1]Heidegger explicitly puts his discussion in the context of the structures of interpretation he outlined earlier. Indeed, Heidegger's account of how his own activity is possible if man's Being is what he claims can, in general, be found in his attempts to elucidate the deficiencies of any stage in the analysis, and the path for remedying the defects, by means of the very existential structures he is bringing to light.

[1]

Dying: Exposition

(§46-53) The first theme discussed by Heidegger is man's possibility for Being whole, a possibility that depends on man's end,
without which there cannot be a whole. Man's end is death, but
death, for *Dasein,* is only in an existent*iell* Being toward dying:
as man's, it cannot properly be conceived to belong to a present-
at-hand or ready-to-hand thing. Heidegger's task, therefore,
is to comprehend death through existential concepts.

One possible procedure is to seek to understand the death of
others. But it is wrong to suppose that my experience of the
death of another can substitute for my experience of my own
death. For no one can take another's dying from him: death is in
each man's case his own, something each *Dasein* must take upon
himself. Indeed, Heidegger claims it is precisely the characteristic "mineness" of death that distinguishes it from the possibilities
of Being-with one another. In everyday affairs, another can represent me within the environment with which I am closely concerned, contributing what I would have contributed. This extends from the "more refined modes of publicly Being with one
another" through possibilities restricted by occupation, status,
and age.[2] Precisely because everyday *Dasein* understands himself
by means of that with which he is concerned, such representa-
tion is "constitutive for our being with one another. *Here* one
Dasein can and must, within certain limits, '*be*' another."[3] Dying,
however, is that which concerns no thing; it can only be as mine.
Man, therefore, cannot be represented in his dying. But what is
dying? It is the coming to its end of an entity to whose Being
belongs a "not yet," something constantly outstanding. To
understand this statement in a manner appropriate to human
existence, we must clarify the meaning of this "outstanding" or
"not yet." Here the first point is that we must in fact distinguish
man's not-yet from something outstanding, however similar they
seem. What is outstanding already belongs to an entity but is

[2] *Sein und Zeit,* p. 239.
[3] *Sein und Zeit,* pp. 239-40 (italics omitted).

missing from it; it is not at one's disposal. Heidegger's example is a debt not yet paid off. When it is paid off, what is outstanding is filled in and pieced together with the rest; the joining of what was missing does not modify the Being of what is already there. The entities for which something is outstanding in this sense are ready-to-hand, and their togetherness is that of a sum. Consequently, "sum" and being outstanding cannot signify man's whole and not-yet because man's togetherness is not constituted by adding on already handy entities, and, rather than being together when his not-yet is filled up, this is precisely when man is no longer.

The remaining alternative is that man's not-yet belongs to *Dasein* in the sense that "Dasein must as [himself] *become*—that is to say, *be*—what [he] is not yet."[4] We can see this more clearly by considering other entities, such as the ripening fruit, "to whose type of Being becoming belongs."[5] The ripeness a fruit goes toward is a characteristic of its Being. Nothing one adds to a fruit could eliminate unripeness if it did not bring itself to ripeness of its own accord. In this sense, the fruit is its unripeness as it ripens, unlike the ready-to-hand entity whose sum is indifferent to what is missing. Similarly, *Dasein* is already his not-yet: his constant ahead of himself makes up his lack of wholeness in such a way that *Dasein* is his not-yet or is not *Dasein* at all.

But does this mean that man's wholeness is equivalent to the wholeness of a fruit or animal? We can see the difference if we consider the Being of the end itself, for ripeness as an end and death as an end do not coincide. Ripeness as an end is "fulfillment" (*vollenden*), the exhausting of the thing's specific possibilities. But in death, *Dasein*'s possibilities are taken from him: death usually comes after a man's ripeness; indeed, for the most part man "ends in unfulfillment." We may wonder why Heidegger has not, then, compared death with the rotting of the fruit. The reason is that death is not properly understood existentially as something like the disintegration of the fruit or as the stopping of something present-at-hand, any more than it is properly

[4] *Sein und Zeit*, p. 243.
[5] *Sein und Zeit*, p. 243. My translation.

understood as fulfillment. In general, things can end by no longer Being present-at-hand, like the rain that stops or by Being present-at-hand when the end comes, like the road that stops. Things that stop can either be unfinished, like the road that stops in the middle, or finished. And what is fulfilled is a mode of such finishing, for what is fulfilled must reach the finishedness possible for it: but not everything finished must be fulfilled. All these modes of ending must be distinguished from *Dasein*'s because they belong to present-at-hand or ready-to-hand things. Therefore, although man is already his not-yet, like the fruit, his ending must be of a different kind. In particular, *Dasein* is already and constantly his end. For his end is in no sense a thing or point: *Dasein* has his end by Being *toward* his end rather than by Being at his end; death is a way to be that *Dasein* takes over as soon as he is.

In order further to grasp death existentially, one must first see that although man in a sense perishes like anything living, life is a privative kind of Being in relation to *Dasein*. Strictly, man does not perish but demises, and even demising, man's "animal" death, is an ending without authentically "dying," the term Heidegger now uses to stand for the way in which man is toward his end: Man's dying is not the experiencing of demise but concerns Being toward his end, the end that we still seek to clarify. Second, we must not confuse the existential interpretation of death with an existent*iell* decision about whether a higher or lower Being, or immortality, is possible for man after death, or with a series of "norms and rules" for comporting oneself to death. Rather, the ontological analysis interprets death as a possibility of human *Being:* only on the basis of this interpretation could one meaningfully ask what may be after death and even decide whether this could be a theoretical issue. Finally, all questions about the meaning of death as an evil among entities are also dependent upon ontologically clarifying death, entities as a whole, and "evil and negativity in general."[6] Death has always been projected ontologically before any ontic discussion of it,

[6]*Sein und Zeit*, p. 248.

and although the psychological and physical facts of death and sickness can be understood fully only after the existential interpretation has been secured, the ontological analysis is itself peculiarly formal and empty when considered in ontic terms. Because *Dasein*'s end belongs to *Dasein*, existential analysis of this end can proceed by considering how the structures of care reveal themselves in death. *Dasein* exists: he is always disclosed to himself as something ahead of himself. Now, death stands before us as something impending, but death is different from other impending possibilities because it is the uttermost not-yet, the possibility that is not to be outstripped. It is the uttermost not-yet because it is disclosed as the possibility of the impossibility of *Dasein*, the possibility of no longer Being able to be there. Moreover, because no one can represent me in dying, when *Dasein* discloses the possibility of death—that is, when he lets death impend—he stands before his own potentiality for Being, a potentiality in which relations to others are undone. "As the ownmost, non relational, unoutstrippable possibility," death is the "primordial concretion" of the ahead of itself.[7] Now, because death belongs to care, it is also a possibility that we can disclose as something into which we have been thrown. That *Dasein* is delivered over to death is disclosed in anxiety, not in theoretical contemplation. Anxiety reveals that *Dasein* "exists as thrown Being towards its end," for one is anxious about, and in the face of, the potentiality for Being that is one's own, nonrelational and unoutstrippable.

Precisely because dying *is* by Being disclosed as a possibility by *Dasein* to *Dasein*, I can existent*ielly* maintain myself in it in different ways. Consequently, we must understand death ordinarily to be by way of falling: "at first and for the most part" man covers up his own Being toward death by fleeing in the face of it, by being absorbed in the entities with which he is concerned. We find this flight in the public interpretation expressed in idle talk.

Death is talked about as an indefinite thing not yet present-at-hand for oneself that belongs to everyone and therefore not

[7] *Sein und Zeit*, p. 250. My translation.

to me in particular: "one dies also sometime, in the end, but proximally one stays unaffected."[8] Its character as *my* possibility is ambiguously leveled by passing it off as an actual case constantly occurring. This evasive concealing is joined by the constant tranquilizing in which we console ourselves and others about death by immersing ourselves in the world of things. And it is completed by the "they's" tacit regulation of the mood, and the comportment to the mood, by which death is disclosed. For "they" do not allow the courage for anxiety in the face of death: such anxiety is understood as mere cowardly fear. Anxiety in the face of one's ownmost potentiality is alienated into an ambiguous fear in the face of an oncoming event, and this fear itself is considered to be weakness: the fitting response to death is thought to be indifferent tranquility. Alienation, tranquilization, and temptation, we recall, make up falling: everyday *Dasein* flees in the face of death.

The next clue in comprehending death, Heidegger argues, is to see how evasive *Dasein* grasps the truth of his end. When everyday man concedes that death comes sometime but not right away, he concedes that death is certain. But his certainity is not a certainty appropriate to death's distinctive possibility. To be certain is to hold something for true *as* something true, where truth has the existential sense Heidegger discussed earlier; we may then say that the entity so held is certain. When our certainty is grounded in the uncovered entity itself, and when the appropriateness to the entity of our disclosure is transparent to us, we hold ourselves in the truth properly. Now, everyday "certainty" of death must be inappropriate. Specifically, because we ordinarily encounter death as an event pertaining to every man, we understand its certainty as the certainty of demise; and when we then think about this demise, we see its certainty to be "only" empirical and not theoretically apodictic. But the true peculiarity of death's certainty is that it is possible at any moment: this is precisely what anxiety discloses.

Heidegger next attempts to clarify what it means to comprehend death as a *possibility*, in order that we may then see how,

[8] *Sein und Zeit*, p. 253. My translation.

existentially, we can understand death's possibility *authentically*. First, Being toward a possibility may signify "Being out for" something "possible" in the sense of trying to actualize it: this is the characteristic "possibility" of ready-to-hand and present-at-hand things that we use. But *Dasein* is not a thing: we should not see the possibility of death as man's actualizing his demise. Moreover, even the ready-to-hand *is* essentially in its possibilities, not its actuality, for its Being is its involvement, its "in order to," its possibility for doing something. Second, we should not interpret understanding death's possibility as expecting this possibility, because to expect death is to understand it with regard to whether and how it will actually be present-at-hand: one leaps from the possible into the actual and considers it in light of the actual. Third, Being toward death's possibility cannot mean brooding over it, because in brooding about it we are considering when and how it may be actualized so we may have it at our disposal.

To understand death as a possibility, therefore, is not to understand it in any way that subordinates possibility to actuality, but, rather, to disclose it as and cultivate it as a possibility. Heidegger's expression for such understanding is anticipating death's possibility. Anticipation (*volaufen*) is not concerned with making death actually available; for genuine death, the possible impossibility of all possibilities of existence, gives *Dasein* nothing to be actualized. The closer my understanding comes to death, the greater and more measureless is the possible impossibility of every way of comporting myself: there is simply no actuality to picture and calculate. Anticipating death is what first makes possible this "possibility" and "sets it free as such."

We will deal soon with the problem of the "positive" meaning of possibility. Here Heidegger's task is to reveal the connection between anticipating death and the ontology of authenticity. In anticipating death, man discloses his uttermost possibility: he understands in terms of, projects himself on, his ownmost and uttermost potentiality for Being. But this is to say that in anticipating he is existing authentically, existing as his own; anticipation is the possibility of authentic existence. Authenticity can therefore be clarified by making visible the structures of anticipation that "must belong to [an anticipatory disclosure] so that it should be able to become the pure understanding of the ownmost, nonrelational, unoutstrippable, certain and as such undetermined possibility."[9] Anticipation discloses man's ownmost potentiality to himself: it reveals that *Dasein* can wrench himself from the "they" but is usually lost within it. Moreover, anticipation discloses my Being as radically individualized, as nonrelational: my uttermost potentiality for Being cannot be taken over by any other men or things. This does not mean that authentic *Dasein* lacks concern and solicitude, because these belong to his Being, but, rather, that authentic *Dasein* cannot find himself by fleeing to the things of concern: in authenticity his Being alongside things and Being with others is projected on his "ownmost potentiality for Being but not on the possibility of the they self."[10] Furthermore, anticipation frees me for death as the possibility that is unoutstrippable. It liberates me from the accidental possibilities of the "they" by shattering my grip on the existence I have already reached, and it enables me authentically to understand and choose the concrete possibilities lying "ahead" of the end. Anticipation frees me for my own possibilities, which are now all understood as finite because they are now all determined by an end, an "uttermost," that consists of "giving oneself up." And because anticipating my possible impossibility discloses all the possibilities that lie ahead of this uttermost end, it therefore also includes the possibility of existenti*elly* taking over my *whole* potentiality for Being.

It is also only in anticipating that we can be certain of our ownmost Being, because only in anticipating death can we disclose *Dasein* as he is and hold ourselves in this disclosedness. But such certainty must be distinguished from our certainty of the present-at-hand. When we uncover something present-at-hand, we let it be encountered most purely in itself by just looking at it; it is in this way that we are certain of it, and it is for such uncovering that there can be graded orders of evidence. But the certainty in which we hold ourselves is different, and more orig-

---

[9] *Sein und Zeit,* p. 263. My translation.
[10] *Sein und Zeit,* p. 263. My translation.

inal, first, because it relates to Being-in-the-world as a whole, not merely to entities within it, and second, because we can hold ourselves certainly only in the full authenticity of existence, not in any particular kind of behavior. This also indicates that the certainty of ourselves in death is more basic than the evidence of any experiences of the "I" or of consciousness; such experiences "necessarily remain behind the certainty which anticipation includes" because such experiences fail to be certain of that of which they claim to be certain, namely, *Dasein* himself, which "I" myself *am*.[11] But I can be my ownmost only in anticipating, and the "self" disclosed in secondary experiences therefore cannot be the decisive clue in understanding man's Being. Finally, anticipation discloses the proper indefiniteness (indeterminateness) of death, and holds itself in this constant threat: it can do so existentially because anticipation co-discloses with anxiety. In summary, then, authentic existence is *ontologically* possible as anticipation, which frees us for, makes possible, and lets us be as, dying.——

Dying: Analysis

We may begin our consideration of Heidegger's analysis of death by elaborating the conditions that compel him to take this approach.

If man is neither ready-to-hand nor present-at-hand, his end cannot be the kind of end appropriate to the ready-to-hand and present-at-hand, and his wholeness cannot be their wholeness. But whatever substantive differences exist concerning man's proper end, all interpretations of this end have treated the end and the whole it constitutes as ready-to- or present-at-hand. Consequently, any understanding of man that takes its light from man's end understood as the fundamental human purpose cannot be true, because this purpose has been conceived inappropriately ontologically. In particular, the kind of "whole" constituted by fulfilling an end is normally conceived ontologically in a manner that grasps man as, in principle, a plant or animal, however unique. We may say, for example, that, in Heidegger's

[11] *Sein und Zeit*, p. 265. My translation.

terms, the Aristotelian analysis of the mature man's moral virtue, or the self-sufficient man's intellectual virtue, projects in advance an ontologically inappropriate understanding of "faculties" and their proper use and fulfillment. But if man is not ready-to-hand or present-at-hand, is there any way in which he can be a whole and have an end? If he cannot be a whole, how can we be certain that the ontological interpretation considers all of man? The solution is to analyze death as rigorously conceived in its *existential* possibility. But why could not Heidegger have chosen another possibility—say, moral or intellectual virtue or happiness—as the end of man that constitutes his wholeness, as long as *it* was conceived existentially? Presumably, the end must be an end for man as he discloses Being. But Being-as-such is no entity, even if to disclose Being is always also to disclose entities that have this Being. What end could be understood to be the end of the whole man, when this end belongs to an entity, man, who discloses Being before discovering entities? Such an end cannot itself lie within the world or depend on what lies within the world, as would the satisfaction of desire or moral virtue; rather, it must be transcendent just as Being is transcendent. Consequently, although all happiness within the world depends upon the nonphilosophical disclosing of Being, this happiness does not, as such, lie beyond what is within the world. But death lies beyond what is within the world, and, in addition, clearly ends and completes man's existence in *some* way. Death and dying, which can never be conceived positively because they negate all the entities in which such conceptions are grounded, therefore appear to be the end men have that accords with our transcending entities to Being. Obviously, this negation of entities must not be equated with negation or destruction within the world, but must be conceived in terms of Being, which is not an entity.

Because death is *Dasein*'s end, it cannot be conceived as a possibility that is occasionally there for some men but not for others. Rather, death is always disclosed as *Dasein*'s end, and we are thrown into death in every world. But how death is disclosed is an issue. That is, we must understand death to *be* in the same manner and with the same permanence and necessity as the

structures of care, however this permanence is itself to be understood. As long as *Dasein* is, he discloses himself to himself in his
end. More than this, both his end and the wholeness that it
constitutes have *Dasein*'s kind of Being, and man's true end is
not to orient himself by other entities he is not but to orient
himself by himself as disclosing what is not any entity. In traditional understanding—say, that of Socrates in the *Republic*—
man can become whole and reach his end by knowing what is not
human, but superior to the human. Although Heidegger would
argue here that Socrates has not differentiated the *Being* of man
from the Being of the eternally present ideas, the ancient intention is to understand man's openness, completion, and end in
light of beings he is not. But Heidegger's analysis of the end of
the being who discloses Being interprets this end as having no
orientation to any entity other than *Dasein,* and to *Dasein* only
insofar as he is ontological. Consequently, the end discussed by
Heidegger cannot as such guide our actions in any manner re-
served for the ends of man understood as proper fulfillment of
powers or satisfaction of desire. It is not clear, indeed, that it can
guide us at all. Similarly, the whole that we are always "not yet" is
not wholeness in the sense of completion or fulfillment and is
not as such better or worse than incompleteness.

But must we not say, as we pursue the question whether existential "death" can furnish man's guiding end, that Heidegger's
purpose in discussing this question is to uncover authenticity,
and that authenticity is a way of life that guides us? Authenticity,
however, merely means that man discloses himself in his ownmost Being, grasps his end as the end belonging to man in his
Being, and, as we will see, grasps as his own the significance that
constitutes the world within which entities are. To be authentic is
to understand oneself as the discloser of Being. But just as care
and death themselves can give no ontic guidance in any ordinary
or philosophical sense because they do not have the Being of
goals, powers, or standards, authentically Being my Being and
Being at my end cannot give such guidance. Authenticity is a
way we are as disclosers of Being, and as disclosers of Being we
transcend the kinds of standards, ends, and wholeness that can
be suited to us only as entities already disclosed. When Heideg-

ger claims that the averageness and alienation of the "they" are not moral categories, we must take him at face value; and this must then be true for authenticity as well. Indeed, understanding how such structures are not moral categories is the chief manner in which those immersed in the tradition of political philosophy can begin to understand Heidegger's intention.

Nonetheless, we may raise about authenticity the question we have raised about care in general. Can authentic Being make possible the genuine standards of political action? If not, does this mean that these standards are not fully, or that Heideggerian authenticity is not? Indeed, it seems as if authenticity could hardly free any entities, insofar as we let these entities be only when fallen into the world. But the Being freed by authenticity is the Being of beings. Consequently, we must discuss more fully both authentic thrownness and the authentic analogue to fallenness if we are to see whether purpose, wholes, and standards can be freed only by the "they" (if indeed they can be so freed), and if we are to see whether there is a general guiding attraction to what is freed by authenticity, whatever the variations in concrete authentic choice.

We begin by considering briefly Heidegger's remarks on the neutrality, or ontic emptiness, of his ontological analysis of death. We know that the ontological analysis as such does not provide norms and rules for dying; neither does it provide an answer to the question of immortality after death nor to the question of the meaning of death as an evil in the aggregate (*All*) of entities. But can the ontological analysis allow these questions as questions, authentically or inauthentically, or allow the conditions in which such questions could be answered correctly? Strictly speaking, dying as an ontological characteristic is beyond all these questions because it is not a characteristic of entities. It is neither mortal nor immortal, but is a characteristic of Being. As such, it is man's finitude, his Being at an end or limit, but such finitude is not itself mortality or sickness. Presumably, nothing Heidegger says about dying would be changed in principle if men became, or came to think of themselves as, ontically immortal, because dying refers to our finite Being as disclosing Being and not to an ontic regularity. Therefore, dying as an ontological characteristic cannot be an affliction in the aggregate of entities, and for man as dying—for man in his Being—the question of immortality does not arise.

Similarly, whatever we might say about the possible grounds for choosing authenticity or inauthenticity, these grounds cannot be comprehended as norms governing entities. In Heidegger's own understanding, the finitude of *Dasein*, and what will prove to be the history and Temporality of Being, could not by itself make him a relativist or an historicist because such characteristics of Being do not prejudge the issues concerning entities. But our question is whether an entity can be freed by *Dasein*, authentically or inauthentically, to whom such issues of demise genuinely apply, in a manner that could uncover norms for death or justifications for evil among entities. Presumably, the "they" deals with *Dasein* as he falls into conceiving himself as an entity to whom such things as norms apply; but fallenness itself is not wrong insofar as it is a mode of Being. Can there, then, be permanent norms for the "they," at least for those possibilities such as "demising" that have, as their counterpart, possibilities inherent in man's Being itself? Or can there simply not be such norms? The latter could be the case for the following reasons. First, whatever I discover inauthentically I may also discover authentically in a manner that conflicts with inauthentic directives and therefore is not necessarily subject to "they." Second, "they" may simply never discover permanent possibilities, leaving their norms and the possibilities to which they relate in flux. Third, the relationship between what is discovered theoretically and what is discovered practically, as Heidegger develops it, leaves unclear the relationship between theoretically permanent entities and the possibly permanent practical.

Fourth, certain possibilities that are meaningful for the "they" may be simply meaningless, or even undiscoverable, authentically: authentically dealing with entities, and with ourselves as entities, may make the "they's" "permanent" rules and standards "impossible" in the sense that when we fall back into the "they" we cannot fall fully into those authentically meaningless entities with which rules and standards deal. What *now* appears to be uncanny is the uncanniness of the everyday. Indeed, Heidegger's discussion of authenticity's being wrested from inauthenticity (a discussion he soon develops) raised the problem of the *Dasein,* or even the people, caught in this process.

Some of these problems may be illustrated briefly by Heidegger's remarks concerning the courage for anxiety. Everyday *Dasein* discloses death in the fear that flees from death and in the understanding of man that his public interpretation articulates. For such *Dasein,* anxiety comes to light as cowardly fear, and the fitting response is not to follow up what this fear discloses but to disperse himself into the things of the world. The courage for anxiety, what Heidegger will soon call resoluteness, is, therefore, a vice in the everyday. This is apparently not simply a random interpretation that may or may not belong to some specific everydayness, but is essential to everydayness as such, because fully genuine fear in the face of death can, ultimately, only be anxiety in the face of *Dasein's* impossibility, his nothingness. But everydayness is constituted precisely by the tranquility, alienation and averageness that cover up the possibility revealed in anxiety. What, then, of that which the everyday finds to be appropriate courage? Whatever specifically is found to be courageous, the courage for anxiety could not be found to be courageous. The courage for anxiety, for following up the phenomenon that, when connected to the anticipation of death, grounds authenticity, could not be an everyday virtue and would always be an everyday vice.

But, nonetheless, would it not be incorrect therefore to say that "man" should not pursue this courage? For man as such is not merely everyday *Dasein.* His ownmost self, his "proper" self, is the self who is authentic. These, indeed, are not terms of virtue or excellence precisely because moral terms have meaning only inside a disclosure. But *how Dasein* will be his disclosing is the ontological issue for man; this is a choice or decision, a resolve or failure to resolve, of a different sort from any choice within the world, and therefore it cannot be guided by standards within the world. But what then of the everyday measures of the fitting? Although both anxiety and the call of conscience, which reveal us in our proper Being, cannot be willed, we can flee or not flee, follow up or not follow up, what is disclosed in these phenomena. (We will consider the call of conscience in the next section.) Even if the everyday standards *are* permanently appropriate, or appropriate in some manner as long as man is, fundamental phenomena of authenticity are truthfully pursued only inappropriately by these standards. But could it be wrong simply to follow one's ownmost possibilities? Does the possibility of authenticity, then, take precedence, and do the paths and directions revealed in authenticity take precedence over the everyday? This problem is especially difficult if there is conflict between what is most genuine in the everyday, or what essentially characterizes the everyday, and what is revealed in authenticity. For even if authenticity could not disclose us as simply obedient to the rules that govern the present-at-hand, it does reveal its own possibilities for taking action in what Heidegger will call the "situation."

One might argue, however, that whatever is revealed in an authentic situation does not conflict with whatever is genuinely revealed in the everyday. Thus, although courage for anxiety is craven fear by everyday standards, and must be so because the fully pursued courage for anxiety is the overturning of the everyday mode of Being, nothing revealed about who and what we are alongside authentically is different from what is genuine in the everyday. In this sense as well, the call of conscience may not lead to concrete discovery of "right" and "wrong" different from what is revealed by what is genuine in the traditional conscience and morality whose mode of Being has inappropriately projected the everyday. Or, if something different is discovered, it is not in conflict with what is genuine in the everyday but merely develops it. But we doubt the likelihood of these possibilities. For we face the difficulty of concretely ascertaining what is genuine in the specific everyday and its specific authentic counterpart, a difficulty compounded by Heidegger's upcoming discussion of the historical quality of the possibilities that we disclose. It is further compounded by the apparent contradiction we see today among a variety of standards and goals that once were genuine. And, in any event, there remains the impossibility of grounding the choice of authentic Being, the problem we have just discussed in our analysis of the courage for anxiety.

This discussion has been the first step in considering the implications of authenticity for the problem of the guidance that is offered by the possibilities freed by *Dasein* and for the problem of the permanence of that guidance. Because Heidegger's analysis of authenticity and its temporal meaning is incomplete, we will return to the critical analysis of these issues in the following sections and chapters. We must now consider the fact that Heidegger's analysis of death does not uncover man's possibilities in their possible nonhuman status. For the present topic this means that man's wholeness, and dying as his "end," needs to be reconsidered in the light of what we called the "noble" entities. Here we would refer back to the analyses Heidegger implicitly rejects which find man's wholeness in his being ordered to the attractive entities which transcend him. For it is in fact incorrect to equate such classical discussions with mistaking man for a present-at-hand or ready-to-hand thing. Rather, in these analyses man's wholeness and not-yet are his orientation to what he cannot fully possess; his wholeness is not viewed as his coming to a fully acquirable ripeness. For this reason, to argue that man is whole through such orientation, rather than through projecting his possibilities upon dying, is *not* to argue in a simple teleological manner as we would with the fruit. Nor is it to argue that we are potentially whole and currently "not yet" as a sum; for it is true that we do not become whole by adding on a unit identical to that which we already possess. Furthermore, it is not to argue that we become complete by stopping, whether we are fulfilled or unfulfilled, because we cannot "stop" as a whole when our wholeness is constituted by what cannot be our own. Indeed, Heidegger's admittedly provisional description of the modes of Being a whole does not consider the wholeness that I am now describing, nor does his analysis attempt to discuss the possibility of entities that are whole in that they both lack nothing and cannot be conceived to stop or start or be in any way not-yet. Indeed, he uses a painting as one example of what comes to an end by stopping, but this ignores the ordinary status of what is whole by being beautiful—that is, of what is whole because every part fits, however these parts developed into their fittingness.

But how is man whole if he can never possess what completes

him? Are we not in fact arguing that man cannot be grasped as a whole? Here we must distinguish between arguing that any man is a whole, or can be his end self-sufficiently, and arguing that a man can be grasped in his wholeness. For to understand a human being in his wholeness is only to grasp him in his attempt to be whole, in his reflection of what is whole. What makes us whole is that we can be like what is whole, not that we are fully completed. All our possibilities more or less fit together in the attempt practically or theoretically to be justly ordered or gloriously ruling, to be a ruler or an order which is self-sufficient, and in which, or in whom, nothing is superfluous. But because we are not our possibilities simply and sufficiently, we are not fully whole: to understand a human being in his wholeness is also to understand him as he is not whole.

Now, such an argument may again seem to mistake Heidegger's ontological analysis of death's Being an end for an ontic characterization. But I have argued that the transcendent ontological characteristics ascribed by Heidegger to *Dasein*'s freeing of possibilities can be accounted for as man's yearning for, but not fully capturing, possibilities that are not exclusively his own. Similarly, the end that allows the freeing of man's possibilities as a whole is the very attempt to be the whole of things, or to be each possibility as it belongs to this whole. Indeed, it is not my individualizing death that is the source of the possibility of my wholeness but, rather, that very striving to be, or to be the source of, what is common. Death's intelligibility as the possible impossibility of possibilities is itself dependent on the full intelligibility of our possibilities. But if our possibilities are fully intelligible only in terms of characteristics that transcend our attaining them, dying, or impossibility, is not intelligible solely in Heidegger's "Daseinal" terms. Rather it must be understood analogously to the manner in which our other finite characteristics are intelligible. In this sense our finitude, and the experiences that reveal this finitude, is indeed pervasive, but it does not constitute our wholeness.

This suggested analysis would also allow us to understand how a man's possibilities can present themselves to him in concretely disordered or contradictory ways without forcing us to say that man is in no way whole. For the very imperfection of man's striving prevents his grasping his ends in their full possibilities of independence and interconnection, and his ends present themselves to him with an immediacy and urgency not necessarily equivalent to their importance. Indeed, this may be the most humbling experience of the prudent statesman, the lover of truth, or the decent man. But the striving, the humility, and the order are intelligible in light of these ends as they present themselves beyond man's possession. It is not clear, however, that Heidegger's analysis of death as our end can render this disorder possible, because death in its pervasiveness equally includes all possibilities. One might say that the disorder among our possibilities is always an ontic matter and is therefore irrelevant to the ontological question. But if, as Heidegger says, the manner in which an entity's possibilities can be whole belongs to its ontological characterization, then the possible disorder that belongs to it must also belong to it ontologically. As we will see in the next section, Heidegger will attempt to conceive what we cannot be, or can never be, as fundamentally identical to our Being a whole. But he does not consider the questions raised by the apparently contradictory or disordered presentation of our possibilities.

We will also return to these problems of properly understanding human disorder when we critically analyze Heidegger's description of the relation between theory and practice and the phenomenon of history. Here, I will point to an analogous issue. Heidegger's general analysis allows every entity fully to possess its mode of completion because its characteristic wholeness belongs to its Being, and each entity fully is. Thus, a debt that is paid off or a road that stops can serve as sufficient examples of types of wholes. But the debt or road is obviously dependent ontically because these are not self-sufficient entities, and even in Heidegger's analysis a useful entity *is* by Being involved. But does this not suggest that useful entities or groups of entities must always present themselves in a wholeness that reveals their insufficiency, that they are only imperfectly whole because considering them as wholes requires an artificial practical or analytical limit? The road that stops can never present itself as genuinely ended because the road's meaning is dependent on what is done with it, and it is never necessary that this purpose be served by exactly this road built in exactly this way. Here too, therefore, we may wonder if Heidegger's analysis of the wholeness belonging to entities properly describes the instability of such entities precisely as they appear to come to their ends.

Let us conclude our analysis of Heidegger's discussion of death, here, by considering how this discussion helps to clarify his intention concerning the meaning of the "possibilities" that *Dasein* understands. Any possibility that is merely an entity, that is merely an actuality, or that has the mode of possibility of a real entity cannot be the uttermost and certain possibility that we understand in "dying." Rather, we must understand possibility as an ontological characteristic, and we must understand *Dasein*'s possibilities to specify *Dasein*'s Being. For any concrete "end" or goal to be a possibility we are for the sake of simply means that a goal forms a world as that goal is disclosed in its Being and as man discloses his Being to himself by Being for this possibility. Only as *Dasein*'s, even if this is fallen care, can a goal be a possibility that forms a world-structure within which entities are freed. To understand man's final end, death, properly, in its ownmost, as a possibility is to understand it simply as belonging to our Being and to let this uttermost element of our Being become the basis of the variety of significances, of worlds, that become a whole in it. They become an authentic whole in *Dasein* precisely insofar as they are *all* released from an authentic disclosing of the possible impossibility of *all* my possibilities; as the uttermost not-yet, possible at any moment, death can authentically release the other goals that lie before it in their finite participation in the whole constituted by our end.

This, too, we can develop further only after we discuss resoluteness and history; Heidegger could hardly yet give the full positive meaning of possibilities because he has discussed neither Being-as-such nor Temporality. Consequently, Heidegger primarily seeks here to distinguish anticipating from all understanding of possibilities that conceives them either as entities or as elements of a mode of Being that does not belong to *Dasein*. There is a sense, however, in which Heidegger's own discussion of the characteristics of death partially obscures *their* status as ontological characteristics. For he plays with the certainty of death as it is ordinarily understood, and with the unpredictability of death as it is ordinarily understood, when these characteristics refer to death as man's ontic demising. And although he shows how authentic certainty and unpredictability project death in its ontological possibility and hold it open there, he does not bring out the positive meaning of possible impossibility, of indefiniteness, and of what is nonrelational. In fact, they too become more intelligible only when Heidegger discusses resoluteness in his next chapter.[12]

[2]

Conscience: Exposition

Heidegger's analysis of death attempted to prove that authentic existence is ontologically possible, possible in terms of the structures of existence. But he has not shown that there is an *ontic*, an existent*iell*, potentiality into which man throws himself and which demands such authentic Being toward death. Indeed, in what way could there be ontic authenticity given the existen-t*iell* inauthenticity of our everyday existence?

(§54–60) Heidegger begins this inquiry in the second chapter of the second division, where he examines the phenomenon of conscience. For, he argues, it is in conscience that a man testifies to the existent*iell* possibility of, and demand for, authentically Being himself.

Because we are to interpret conscience as a phenomenon belonging to *Dasein*, questions about whether, factually, there is such a thing must be questions about the facticity of *Dasein*, not of something ready-to-hand, and any discussion of experiences of conscience, any biological explanation of conscience, and any

---

[12]For a discussion of death, consider, among others, Karl Lowith, "The Nature of Man and the World of Nature for Heidegger's 80th Birthday," in Edward G. Ballard and Charles E. Scott, eds., *Martin Heidegger in Europe and America* (The Hague: Martinus Nijhoff, 1973); and James M. Demske, *Being, Man and Death* (Lexington: University of Kentucky Press, 1970).

theological exegesis of conscience must follow upon the existential analysis. As a phenomenon belonging to *Dasein,* conscience can be seen to call us from our listening to the idle talk in which the "they" presents the possibilities into which we are thrown. It calls us from this to itself, thereby enabling us to hear ourselves and project possibilities as our own. We can explicate this once we grasp that the call of conscience, like the idle talk in which we listen to others and let them present possibilities, is, existentially, a mode of discourse. This means, first, that discourse, as a call, appeals to something; in this case the call appeals to *Dasein* himself as the they-self who is concerned with things and with others in the average everyday manner. But to whom does conscience call everyday man? To *Dasein's* own self: man as he is understood in worldly concerns, man as what he counts for and can do, is passed over; the they-self and the public interpretation I fall into as "they" is pushed into insignificance and the self who I am myself is brought to listen. But what is said in this discourse, what is said in this call? Strictly, nothing: no information is offered about any events in the world. Rather, we are summoned to our ownmost possibilities, in a silent utterance. This silence forces us "into the reticence" of ourselves, in such a manner that what is called does not expect to be communicated. Precisely in its silence the call unequivocally discloses that it is I myself who am called; how I hear this call, how I understand the possibilities of the self that has been called, depends on whether my understanding is authentic or has been perverted by the they-self.

The analysis must still tell us who does the calling. We experience the call of conscience as coming from something beyond us, against or without our will. Moreover, we experience it as coming from something that holds itself aloof. This leads us to believe that what calls is something other than *Dasein*—say, God. But we can also understand these characteristics to belong to a kind of Being in which *Dasein* himself is the caller. For it is the man authentically revealed in anxiety, the man who finds himself in uncanniness, who calls; the caller lacks that very definition by anything in the world, and possesses the bare fact that he is in the nothing of world, that is disclosed in anxiety. Indeed, once we understand conscience' connection to anxiety, we can see how conscience is ontologically possible on the basis of care: "the caller is the *Dasein* that, in [his] thrownness (already Being in . . .) is anxious about [his] potentiality for Being. The appealed to is this very *Dasein*, summoned to [his] ownmost potentiality for Being (ahead of [himself] . . .). And *Dasein* is summoned through the appeal from fallenness into the "they" (already Being alongside the world of [his] concern)."[13]

Heidegger's discussion is incomplete in two ways. First, it appears to make unimaginable the everyday experience of conscience as something that warns and reproves about specific matters. Second, it has not yet clarified how conscience gives exist*entiell* testimony to authenticity. We can deal with these issues only after we clarify *what* is heard in this silent call of *Dasein* to *Dasein*.

All interpretations of conscience agree that what we hear in the call is, "Guilty!" How can such guilt be understood ontologically, and how is it connected with the foregoing interpretation of conscience? The leading concept in Heidegger's interpretation is, once more, that the phenomenon under discussion lies in *Dasein*'s Being: so far as any man exists, he is also guilty.

Guilt ordinarily signifies owing something, and being guilty ordinarily signifies having debts: it is related to matters of concern. It also signifies being responsible for something. Neither of these two necessarily implies the other, but they can come together when one makes oneself responsible. Making oneself responsible is found in lawbreaking in which one is responsible for, and punishable for, a debt owed others, but it goes beyond this to include my responsibility for endangering or ruining another's existence even if I have not broken public law. It is in this sense that moral requirements are breached. Formally, then, Being guilty means Being the ground for a lack of something in another, in such a way that this grounding determines *itself* as lacking in relation to that which it grounds; it is a failure to satisfy a requirement of one's existence with others.

Guilt so understood remains within the domain of concern, and we interpret the lack that it is as something missing because

---

[13] *Sein und Zeit*, p. 277. My translation.

it is not present-at-hand but ought to be. Consequently, we must conceive Being guilty as it authentically belongs to man in a way that goes beyond legal and moral guilt. In particular, we must understand the "not" at the ground of our Being in light of *Dasein*'s Being, and this means that we cannot conceive our Being guilty, our nullity, in relation to some thing that is missing. On the contrary: concrete indebtedness becomes possible only "on the basis" of a primordial Being guilty. We can clarify this guilt, Heidegger argues, by grasping the not that is at the ground of existence itself. As an entity, *Dasein* has been brought into his disclosure, but *not* of his own accord: as long as he is, *Dasein* is constantly this fact, this entity to whom he has been delivered over. *Dasein*, therefore, does not lay his own ground, and never gets behind his thrownness in order to release his "thisness" from his Being itself. Now, in his existing, *Dasein* is the basis of his potentiality for Being as *this* entity. This means that man *is* his thrown ground by projecting upon possibilities, is a self who must lay the basis for himself (make himself possible), but that he projects himself upon possibilities into which he has been thrown: man is his own ground in a manner that never has "power over one's ownmost Being from the ground up."[14] *Dasein*, therefore, is the disclosedness and disclosing, the Being, of his ground, but he is not the ground of his Being because his ground does not first arise from his projection; rather, *Dasein* is released to himself from this ground and "constantly remains behind his possibilities."[15]

The nullity at the heart of man's Being is also evident in projection itself. For man understands himself in light of possibilities, but in doing so he always stands in one possibility and is existent*ielly* not the others: this nullity belongs to our very Being free for existent*iell* possibilities. In general, indeed, *Dasein*'s Being means Being the ground of a nullity where the grounding is itself null. Because this is equivalent to the formal definition of guilt, Heidegger says that *Dasein* as such is guilty. This guilt does

[14]*Sein und Zeit*, p. 284. "Ground" and "basis" are used synonymously in this chapter.
[15]*Sein und Zeit*, p. 284. My translation.

not mean that man is ontically worthless, that he falls short of some ideal, or that he is evil or valueless, for the nullity in question belongs to *Dasein* and is in no sense the privation of something present-at-hand. But all concepts of good and ideas of value originate in the ontology of the present-at-hand. Anything *Dasein* concretely projects and attains is, according to Heidegger, null in advance, because the Being that makes achievement possible is itself null in advance of these achievements. This primordial guilt is the ontological condition for "moral" good and evil, and "for the possible factical forms" of morality overall. Morality thus always presupposes such guilt; guilt cannot be defined by it.

Such Being guilty is what the call of conscience gives us to understand: the relation between guilt and conscience is, simply, that "Guilty!" is what conscience calls. Hearing the call therefore means to project oneself upon one's potentiality for becoming guilty. But such "hearing" means *letting* myself be called forth to myself, freeing myself for my ability to be called forth and called back to my own Being as my own. Heidegger calls such understanding choosing oneself, or "wanting to have a conscience": this means that I free myself for, disclose myself in and for, my unavoidable Being guilty. Any existent*iell* possibility of being good or of coming to owe something depends on existen*tielly* projecting my own possibilities upon this inevitable nullity in my own Being, and, therefore, in my Being with others.

Thus, the call of conscience attests an authentic potentiality for Being, that is, a potentiality for disclosing Being for the sake of my own Being. The ordinary interpretation of conscience covers up this authenticity because the "they's" "common sense" (*Verstandigkeit*) knows only success or failure in satisfying manipulable rules and public norms: in the everyday we interpret ourselves as one more object of ready-to-hand concern to be managed and reckoned up. Consequently, ordinary interpretation and the theories based on it cannot be adequate. Still, ordinary experience must "somehow" reach the genuine phenomenon of conscience. For example, conscience is in a sense grasped genuinely in the ordinary experience of its critical character, for this experience indicates that conscience does not give practical directions for action. But because man interprets himself as a household or business procedure that can be regulated, he understands conscience' critical character within the same horizon: the call of conscience recommends nothing positive and therefore disappoints us in our expectation of being told something useful about available, calculable, and assured possibilities for action. The authentic meaning of the critical character of conscience is that it calls man to his possibility of Being himself. Consequently, it cannot disclose anything with which we can practically concern ourselves. The expectation of a series of unequivocal maxims, indeed, denies the possibility that an existing entity could act at all. But such an expectation also underlies all demands for material ethics of value as opposed to merely formal ones. In fact, Heidegger argues, even the theoretical understanding of conscience and morality that we find in Kant is inadequate because it is based on the understanding of Being as presence-at-hand. Conscience is encountered as the arbiter who stands over a sequence of experiences, but the Being of such a sequence, of such physical processes, is left undetermined. Consequently, although Kant's conception of conscience as a court of justice, and the idea of a moral law in general, is "far removed from utilitarianism," the concept of Being on which it is based is unclarified. All theory of value is based on an ontology of *Dasein,* of existence, on a "metaphysic of morals," whether or not this is recognized. But *Dasein* is always misconceived as an entity with whom one concerns oneself, and this is so both when we see such concern as actualizing "values" and when we understand it as satisfying "norms."

Resoluteness: Exposition

(§60) The elements of the authenticity to which conscience attests can now be gathered together. When *Dasein* is authentically disclosed, he *wants* to have a conscience: he projects himself upon his *own* possibility of having his potentiality for Being-in-the-world. Corresponding to this projection is the uncanniness of individualization that *Dasein* discloses and understands in anxiety. And corresponding to this readiness for anxiety is the reticence in which I hold my own guilt unconcealed through a silence that comes from uncanniness and summons me from idle talk to my own stillness. Together, Heidegger calls this authentic disclosedness "resoluteness" (*Entschlossenheit*): resoluteness is "the reticent, ready for anxiety, self-projection upon one's ownmost Being guilty."[16]

Now, the discussion of conscience and its culmination in the definition of resoluteness seem to suggest that authentic man is fully his own in a kind of free-floating detachment from the world. But if resoluteness is the authentic disclosedness of *Dasein,* it discloses Being-in-the-world in general and therefore discovers the entities possible within the world. We recall that *Dasein* frees the current wholeness of involvements by understanding significance: in disclosing significance a man has submitted himself to what he encounters as ready-to-hand. A man's understanding of significance, in turn, is based on the possibilities for the sake of which he is, and his understanding of these possibilities is inauthentically guided by the "they." But when disclosedness is authentic, the things within the world and the others within it are discovered and disclosed in a modified way: in *Dasein*'s resoluteness for himself, he is authentically freed for his current Being alongside the ready-to-hand, and solicitously liberates others, letting them be with him in their authenticity. Resoluteness, therefore, is not free-floating detachment. Nonetheless, because resoluteness is the disclosive projection of the Being of what is possible at some time, it is not a seizing of previously proposed possibilities. Nor can one say in advance what any resolve resolves upon. Resoluteness, "by its ontological essence," is always the resolution of "some factical current *Dasein*" and becomes definite only in a current resolution.

Such resolute disclosedness is authentic truth insofar as truth (as we remember from Chapter 3 above) ultimately means disclosedness.

Heidegger's name for the disclosedness opened in resolution is the "situation" (*Situation*). A situation is not a present-at-hand framework of circumstances and accidents within which we find

[16] *Sein und Zeit,* pp. 296–97. My translation (italics omitted).

ourselves, but *is* only through resolute disclosure. Accidents befall us from within a context of involvements, and this context is "there" only insofar as a man has resolved upon this "there" as that which he must be in his existence. The resolute man is called forth to the situation and what is disclosed in it, thus making his existence possible for himself, unlike the "they's" losing of itself in the generality of opportunities and accidents. Such root resoluteness is the authentic action that grounds any later authentic behavior, whether this is distinguished as practical or theoretical. Resoluteness is not itself a way of behavior, but the authenticity of care.

Heidegger's uncovering of resoluteness does not yet complete his discussion of authenticity, because he must now return to the phenomenon of dying in order to explore the possibility of authentically Being a whole. The question that remained there concerned the possibility of authentic existent*iell* Being toward death. He has now shown resoluteness to be the phenomenon in which authenticity is existent*ielly* possible. Can the anticipation of death now be connected to it in a way that is adequate to the phenomena themselves? It can if Heidegger can show that anticipatory resoluteness is an existent*iell* modification of authentic resoluteness demanded by resoluteness itself. But this is indeed the case, because *Dasein* can fully project himself upon his ownmost nullity only when he understands his utter and whole nullity, the possible impossibility of all care. And he can fully resolve upon his possibilities of guilt only when his nullity is understood to belong to a possibility that cannot be outstripped and in which *Dasein* is related to no other. Moreover, only in anticipating death can resoluteness hold itself in its disclosedness, hold itself in its certainty, because only in anticipating can it hold itself free for itself constantly, over the whole of *Dasein*'s Being. Any resolve must hold itself free for its current possibility and it can do so only by resolving to repeat itself, only by holding itself free for taking the resolve back. But this lack of rigidity is fully possible only when resoluteness can hold itself free for *Dasein*'s whole potentiality. Similarly, the indefiniteness of *Dasein*'s Being disclosed by resoluteness is fully disclosed authentically only when wholly revealed in anticipating the indefiniteness of the moment of death. In all these ways, then, resoluteness "is authentically and wholly what it can be only in anticipatory resoluteness."[17]

Conscience and Resoluteness: Analysis

The discussion of conscience and anticipatory resoluteness develops several issues that we have analyzed. First, it makes particularly clear the connections and differences between Heidegger's understanding of the openness at the basis of man's Being and the traditional understanding of that openness. To hear the call of conscience is to understand what anxiety discloses. This understanding is not be be confused with Heidegger's philosophic uncovering of the wholeness of care by interpreting anxiety. It refers to a possibility that is prior to thematic ontology: to be resolute does not require one to have mastered fundamental ontology. Moreover, man is guilty in the ground of his Being and carries this guilt ahead of and behind all his existence whether or not he authentically understands himself in its light. His guilt is his essential connection to the "not" of his *Being;* it is different from any "not" among entities, such as concrete debts or lacks. The "not" at the ground of our Being corresponds to the proper way in which man is by Being what he is not-yet. The repeating of resolve is the holding of my not-yet, my becoming, in the uttermost not, death, which makes me whole. Consequently, by Being toward his uttermost not-yet, man discloses himself in the "not" that is behind his Being and can disclose his present situation as it exists by Being on the basis of this "not."

The "not" can be seen in the three dimensions of care because care is by Being this "not." But just as care cannot be equated with any willing of entities, so too authentic care—anticipatory resoluteness—cannot be so equated. In falling, we fall into entities we are not, but we do so as a necessity of our Being. In understanding, we disclose these possibilities and not the others, but without such disclosure they are not. In thrownness we are

[17] *Sein und Zeit*, p. 309.

this entity and not any other. In Heidegger's analysis, therefore, openness cannot be reduced to preexisting dependence on entities, even on the eternal: authentic care is not any ontic need or lack. Nor can openness be equated with a yearning for Being-as-such, which Being our concrete existence imitates only palely, and which yearning it appears to hinder in its purity. Similarly, our "factical" existence, our "closedness," cannot be equated with a brute particularity that is alien to Being. Nor can our "thisness" be treated as if it masters our transcendence to Being by making it impossible or extraordinarily difficult. Rather, our Being is thrown existence, resolute anticipation. For political philosophy, Heidegger's claim that our authentic Being is resolute anticipation may be likened to the claim that the nature of political communities is not without convention and that convention is not, as convention, without nature. But Heidegger's claim is made from a standpoint beyond the traditional understanding of Being as nature (whatness) and convention as nonbeing (thatness). For, in Heidegger's understanding of human Being and the "not" at its basis, we are our Being and, therefore, are not merely as entities. But we are our Being only as *this* entity. Our "Being" is not simply our root "possibilities"—for example, our most general characteristics as they are without Being "attached" to us in particular—and our specific world and what is within it is not simply arbitrary but is, rather, the basis of our Being. Our thrownness into this world characterizes our Being; consequently, our thrownness, our thisness, is not an accident having nothing to do with our Being or "essence," but is ours as a characteristic of Being. And our "possibilities," our essential possibilities, including our most authentic disclosing of Being and our own Being, are only as based on thrownness. We do not cause our Being as entities—that is, we *are* not as results of ontic historic occurrences—but neither does our Being cause our concrete thrownness, nor can it be apart from thrownness. In this sense, we are only as what we are not, because we are only as this thrown entity, not the others; we are for the sake of these possibilities, not the others. But although we can never get behind this thrownness to, say, create it, we are it only insofar as we are disclosing Being and our own Being. I am the "ground" for the lack in my Being insofar as *Dasein* is the disclosing of, the possibility of, his ground.

Guilt, Morality, and Law: Critique

Heidegger claims that the guilt in our Being is the condition for the responsibility and debt characteristic of public law and morality. He does not show, however, that guilt is the basis of morality in a manner any more specific than the sense in which guilt and care are the basis of all our Being. Nor does he demonstrate that "care" can in fact free the true claims of morality, if there are any true claims. Furthermore, he does not specify the grounds on which he separates morality from public law such that morality has wider scope.

If the claims of morality are wider than the claims of public law, *Dasein* apparently can free others from a horizon that goes beyond his particular public, just as he can free natural entities that are more common than the laws and public goods of a particular country. Still, moral requirements can be released only from the "they" into which we are thrown, however transformed the "they" must become if the moral obligations are to be held in their truth by authentic *Dasein*. Moreover, such requirements must be finite if they can be released authentically by finite *Dasein*. This finitude, however, need not mean that moral obligations are any less permanent than other entities released by *Dasein*, some of which are whether or not *Dasein*, or Being, is. Nonetheless, Heidegger treats moral requirements as if they are solely for *Dasein*, as if, indeed, they are only with *Dasein*'s Being; for the call of conscience that reveals the "not" that can free *Dasein*'s more specific lacks is a call from my *Dasein* to my *Dasein*. Consequently, moral requirements exist *only* when *Dasein* exists, morality is in principle finite, and its authentic ground is precisely the disclosing of our finitude. It is only everyday falling into the world that causes us to misunderstand morality as a series of rules and regulations appropriate to a ready-to-hand entity, or to an unchangingly present one.

But does not this finitude rob morality of its obligatory nature? For although there can be morality only for the entity who can free an obligation for himself, and although such letting morality *be* is possible only for the entity guilty in his Being and finite in his Being, how can a moral obligation be binding for such an entity? Indeed, Heidegger suggests that "material" ethics of value is precisely an attempt to close the openness that belongs to *Dasein* as *Dasein*. Now, Heidegger has already wondered, in his discussion of truth, whether a truth is less true merely because it is not eternal. If it is not less true, and if what is true of *Dasein* must be a finite truth about his finitude, the moral requirements need be no less true because, authentically, they are finite. Indeed, we may say on Heidegger's behalf that, in principle, there may be obligations that will prove binding for a *Dasein* as long as he is; and there may certainly be obligations that are experienced as binding for every *Dasein* up to any now.

On the other hand, no *Dasein* could authentically reveal more that is binding for it as an entity than what is binding for it in its situation or for it from out of the "they." This may accord with what has been, but *such* binding could not properly be grasped or experienced as necessarily and immutably obligatory. Nor could it be experienced as binding for what may result from future projections, and insofar as the past is revealed as past in the light of future projections, what has been binding up to now may itself need to be freshly understood. Heidegger's analysis is powerful because it forces us to ask how obligations must be revealed by and for man if we are to grasp them in their possibility of not Being obeyed; but we must also explore them in their possibility of *guiding* us. Of course, if, contrary to our argument, what is obligatory *can* be revealed in its finitude, then Heidegger's finitude need not mean relativism, even though his existent*ial* analysis makes no explicit decision concerning what is existent*ielly* binding.

Our point, thus, is that the *full* obligatory presence of a moral requirement cannot be revealed to authentic *Dasein*, and, therefore, that misinterpreting *Dasein* as ready-to-hand or present-at-hand is not a mistake about the Being of moral requirements but is necessary for them to be freed in the usual sense. But if such misinterpreting is necessary, does this not suggest that there is no morality that can be freed for *Dasein* as he truly is?

The finitude explored by Heidegger speaks against morality strictly. Now, I have argued that man's finitude can be grasped in a manner that permits his orientation to possibilities that can be more fully than merely as human. But my argument would also speak against the possibility of universally or absolutely obligatory *rules,* because man is not an entity to whom what is absolutely obligatory can practically apply. This is because he can only imperfectly possess the ends for which he strives. He can imitate, but not be, a just or wise god or what is just in and of itself. Indeed, human finitude makes it unjust that those human actions clothed with mortality, insufficiency, and inevitable conflicts over scarce resources should be judged as if they could be absolutely other. A just political order cannot perfectly distribute goods because the goods it seeks to distribute are too few for those who deserve them. And this is most obvious among those goods whose very scarcity makes them attractive: honor, glory, reputation, luxuries. These goods are reflections in the human material granted to most of us of the possibilities of justice, eminence, and wisdom that we cannot fully attain. But, then, absolute moral rules, and political rules whose effect is identical to morally absolute rules—the demand for perfect equality or inequality in rights, for example—distort the achievement and expression of human possibilities. It might even be wondered if the injunction to the thinking man that he never at any moment allow a lie in his soul would not, if faithfully obeyed, perpetuate more error than is necessary. In general, therefore, Heidegger's analysis of authentic *Dasein*'s releasing of his finitude, his "Guilt" and his dying, suggests that absolute moral requirements could not genuinely be released authentically. But, I have just argued, it is also possible to understand this fact in the light of ends that are not finite.

The advantage of such an understanding, when compared with Heidegger's, is that it does not leave unexplored the status of these nonhuman possibilities, and, therefore, their relation to the possibilities presented to man. It thus enables us to investigate the status of the attractiveness, and therefore possible order, among these possibilities as we can strive for them, whereas

Heidegger's analysis has not so far dealt sufficiently with their independence and the questions of order among them. We are thus able to grasp more fully certain concrete issues of ambiguity, uncertainty, and contradiction in our possibilities, their order and attainment. Indeed, such an understanding would even enable us to explore the problem of defending the superiority of "authentic" possibilities, and what is discovered when pursuing them, to "inauthenticity," because the difference between acting and failing to act as the entity one is becomes a difference in degree of likeness to what is truly desirable.

For these points to be developed, we will need to consider Heidegger's forthcoming analyses of the connection between practical and theoretical activity and his discussion of tradition and history. There, the most striking questions are of the possible unity of possibilities and disjunctions among the entities discovered when these possibilities are pursued. Now, however, we can pursue our issues in the following ways. First, we must see that Heidegger has still left incompletely resolved the problem of the connection between what is discovered in the authentic situation and the inauthentic and average norms. Whatever the status of what we discover authentically, but especially because morally binding rules could not be freed authentically, the problems we considered in the first section of this chapter still remain in force.

Second, we must consider more systematically the status of conscience as testifying to the existent*iell* possibility of man's authentically Being a whole. For here the question arises whether there is a genuine phenomenon of conscience at all. Indeed, Heidegger's discussion of everyday conscience and the Kantian interpretation of conscience cannot as such speak to the problem of whether the phenomena "genuinely" understood as conscience phenomena are indeed conscience phenomena. Beyond the problems this raises for the proper interpretation of virtue, law, and "morality," the issue here is the authentic care that makes the hearing of the call of conscience possible. If there is never a call of conscience that cannot be understood properly in other ways—that is, if there is no conscience—does some other phenomenon reveal our ontological guilt and the possibility of projecting ourselves upon it? More radically: is there such ontological guilt at all?

The heart of the question is whether the guilt Heidegger uncovers is a genuine phenomenon that can then be grasped properly only by understanding man as Being in his sense. But here we wonder whether root guilt might not be treated analogously to our treatment of anxiety and the ridiculous. Cannot the "guilty" heard in the call of "conscience" be understood sufficiently as the experiencing of the fake and the imperfect as necessary correlates of every activity? Cannot heeding this experience be understood as the courageous and moderate attempt to act and to understand within these limits? In this sense, the "self" revealed in anxiety and guilt is a self only within the limits of, only *as*, the good character or properly ordered soul—the just man—and in this sense as well, courageously anticipating death belongs to the manner in which we are imperfect imitations of more self-sufficient possibilities and is intelligible in this way without death's losing its character as a misfortune.

But, one might reply, our argument once more appears to project man upon an inappropriate understanding of his Being, not to speak of its own formality. Still, if the fundamental phenomena leading one to conceive man as finite care can be interpreted sufficiently in light of the possibility of perfection, its limits and its lack, Heidegger's analysis loses its evidence. But what, then, of Heidegger's uncovering of the priority of meaning to the concrete characteristics of entities? Or have we not shown sufficiently the connection between the intelligibility of our possibilities (and the intelligibility of what we use) and the noble status of the possibilities that we seek to imitate?

If conscience is a questionable phenomenon, then the grounds on which Heidegger distinguishes between morality and public law also become questionable: does Heidegger intend this to be an essential distinction or only an occasional one? For what is the precise connection between the demands of morality and the standards and actions required in the everyday work world? Heidegger rejects the understanding of human ends as values and considers even "good" to belong to the ontology of the present-at-hand. He modifies his opinion about "good" in his discussion of history. Here we ask how the "they" frees both morality *and* the standards belonging to ourselves as business enterprises: can they be consistent or are they at root inconsistent?

We are tempted to say that, in Heidegger's analysis, moral rules seen as ready-to-hand regulations, the enforcing of everyday debts and lacks by public law, and the standards of everyday success form a unit; the moral demands of this unit are broader than, but consistent with, any political and economic demands within a public. Moreover, we would also say that there is nothing essentially necessary about any of these kinds of tools. But if this is so, why is morality not simply subservient to politics: why is conscience in any sense independent? Here we see that moral rules are an inauthentic fleeing from what the call of conscience authentically reveals, and in this sense even idle discourse about morality is grounded in the authentic issue at stake in conscience. The ordinary legal or political treatment of the issues of everyday concern belongs to our fallenness, and, therefore, also belongs to our covering of authentic *Dasein,* but, apparently, this treatment does not so immediately cover the root individualization and finitude set free in conscience. Therefore, morality is a clue to possible authenticity; in this way it is separate from the limits of public law and potentially is inconsistent with these limits. But if, as we have argued, the conscience on which morality is dependent is properly interpreted in other ways, then we must reopen the issue of the concrete scope of public rules and the phenomena that reveal horizons beyond this scope. And, consequently, we must also reopen the question whether one must resort to "*Dasein,*" authenticity, and Heideggerian Being to grasp these phenomena. In this sense, the discrepancy between the justice found in ordinary politics and law and the righteousness presumably revealed in morality may in fact be interpreted sufficiently as an indication of the discrepancy between all political justice, justice simply, and justice as it can be theoretically or poetically imitated. And the existent*iell* possibility of "anticipatory resoluteness" is then interpreted sufficiently as the experience of the fake and imperfect to which I have referred. Indeed this interpretation then enables us to clarify both the discrepancy between political life and possibilities drawn from horizons beyond it and the pervasiveness of political life. For if political practice is imperfect in its justice—in the courage, moderation, and wisdom it permits—it will inevitably be open to the possibility of a full virtue, because it cannot be what it is and be blind to what it attempts to embody. But the flowering of such openness prevents the full exercise of the pretense to perfect completion that is necessary for the political community to achieve the most exact justice by its own lights. Similarly, the possibilities that more closely imitate what political practice seeks—let us say, art and philosophy or science— inevitably are dependent on the production of goods and the protection afforded by the political community. Political concerns are therefore necessary even for those least obviously concerned with political ends.

Man's Wholeness: Critique

Even if Heidegger's analysis of the meaning of conscience is correct, the indeterminateness of his understanding of the relation between political entities such as laws and moral rules reminds us of the murky status of political possibilities in his analysis; and, as I have argued, it is precisely the attempt to clarify this status that leads us to question Heidegger's analysis in general. How must political entities *be* if we are properly to understand their ontic comprehensiveness, but also their lack of comprehensiveness?

One way to develop this issue is to consider further Heidegger's understanding of wholes and Being-a-whole. Heidegger's discussion of wholes belongs to ontology: he is not formulating generalizations about the types of wholes that can be abstracted from a variety of concrete conditions. Rather, the way in which an entity is freed as belonging to a whole belongs to the manner in which it is intelligible in its Being. Indeed, I would argue, the understanding of something as whole and "part" has always belonged to the comprehension of its being, however that being has traditionally been conceived. If, for example, justice is considered the being of political communities, it *is* this precisely by being that which makes an agglomeration of people, places, and things into a whole. But Heidegger does not understand Being as the highest entity, or as the most general property of entities, or as the totality of entities ordered by the highest entity. Therefore, if we say that whole and part are ontological characteristics for Heidegger, we mean that they belong to Being and the understanding of Being as that which releases entities as entities. A political community as an entity, therefore, is not simply analogous to whole and part as these belong to Being. Rather, it must be understood as a kind of entity freed by *Dasein* that is grounded in *Dasein*'s ontological wholeness. I repeat, therefore, that the relevant question concerning the political community as a whole is how Heidegger's analysis of Being allows the freeing of the political as a possibility of concern, and whether the ways in which political communities are wholes can *be* if man's Being is what Heidegger claims. And here I have argued that Heidegger's analysis either mistakes the decisive political things for ready-to-hand things, rather than seeing them as human possibilities, or sees all the human possibilities in a way that overlooks or misinterprets both the completeness and incompleteness, order and disorder, among the possibilities that men pursue. The concrete political implication is, as we have suggested, that the peculiar "ontic" status of the political community as a whole that is not fully whole is also misinterpreted.

But perhaps Heidegger's analysis of how *Dasein* is a whole contains further material for resolving these issues. It is true that Heidegger finds man's wholeness to belong to the individual *Dasein*. For Heidegger this does not mean that man either is or is not a political—or sexual—animal, because *Dasein*'s wholeness is man's wholeness as a characteristic of the being who understands Being. Just as dying does not mean perishing, just as *Dasein*'s end cannot be understood as the satisfaction of desire of the individual entity, so too the end and the whole it constitutes is not social or political. Rather, it belongs to man in his Being before he is concretely disclosed as the entity to be individually satisfied or politically fulfilled in this or that way. Nonetheless, it is true that the wholeness of man in his Being belongs to *Dasein* as he is radically individualized in death. But is there a way in

which such wholeness, especially when it is authentically revealed, is communal? If so, might not a discussion in Heideggerian terms at this level deal with the issues that seem obfuscated
in his analysis of individual authenticity? But if there is such a
communal wholeness, is this equiprimordial with, prior to, or
posterior to the wholeness constituted by dying? What would be
the connection between such communal wholeness and the political community? One answer might be that man's Being is essentially Being-with, and that Being a whole authentically or inauthentically discloses other men in their Being. Precisely as part of
his Being, man reveals his dependence on men and things, and,
consequently, can disclose others in authentic solicitude. But
which men and things? There is no ontological necessity in this
particularity any more than there is ontological necessity in the
content of the particular possibilities that I disclose in resolutely
anticipating death. But do "dying" and the resolute disclosing of
guilt reveal a "we" in which dying belongs? Does my own self
when resolutely seized newly reveal the "they" but in a manner
that clarifies how my possibilities, perhaps even death, belong to
this new "they"? If anticipatory resoluteness transforms the averageness of possibilities and wrests *Dasein* from the "they," can
this mean that these possibilities are freed from any attachment
to "us," or only that they are newly revealed in their attachment
to an authentically complete "us"? Is there a "we" to which we
authentically belong that is as different from other "we's" as I am
authentically from others, but that must no more be ontically or
bodily conceived than is my dying?

Although I will develop these problems · fully only after
explicating Heidegger's analysis of history, I may say here that
the "political" analogue to the authentically whole *Dasein* is indeed *this* people and generation in its destiny. That is, the way in
which I am whole in anticipatory resoluteness does belong together with a communal whole of which we are part. This whole
is not as such the political community. But it is not altogether
clear how authenticity could exist in this whole, or what could
replace death as its "end," or guilt as its "before." For presumably, if not necessarily, a people is not yet whole and not yet at its
end in a manner similar to each *Dasein*. If so, the "people" would

need to be conceived historically in a manner analogous to the terms of individual history—death, thrown facticity, Being what one is becoming—in which a *Dasein* is conceived, but precisely when these terms do not refer to the concrete material of perishing and thrown facticity. But this indicates that the problems we see in understanding individual authenticity will be repeated at this communal level, that Heidegger's interpretation of the wholeness of the people will fail to resolve the problems of comprehensiveness and interrelation among possibilities, and that the difficulties that emerge in treating political entities as ready-to-hand or as human possibilities, in Heidegger's terms, will recur.

5. *Temporality, Theory, and Practice*

The analysis of death and guilt completes Heidegger's discussion of human Being. He turns now to showing that the *meaning* of *"Dasein"* is temporality. I will once more summarize Heidegger's arguments, analyze them, and attempt to clarify their significance for the moral and political issues we are discussing.

[1]

The Temporality of Man's Being: Exposition

(§61–66) Heidegger begins by repeating and developing his analysis of meaning. To understand something is to project it upon its possibilities; any entity that we subsequently examine we have first implicitly discovered in its possibility. The condition that makes the projected entity possible is, therefore, identical with that on which it is projected, and this is what meaning signifies: the meaning of entities is their Being. To clarify this meaning is to study the projection so that the entity projected is clearly grasped with reference to what makes it possible. The task now is to clarify the meaning of man's Being.

Because man's existence *is* to understand Being, the meaning of his existence is no more apart from man than is his Being itself. What, then, is this meaning? Heidegger seeks to demonstrate that temporality (*Zeitlichkeit*) is the ontological meaning of care. Man's Being has just been existentially interpreted. One might therefore expect Heidegger to ask: upon what did he thematically project this structural whole so that it was understood? But he does not, because he needs to uncover the meaning of man's Being as it is understood in any authentic or inauthentic existence. Consequently, he first seeks to show that temporality is the meaning of care by interpreting the meaning of the three elements of care that make up authenticity. In anticipating, *Dasein* lets himself come toward himself in his ownmost possibility as a possibility. That is to say, *Dasein* is "futural": only because he can come toward himself as futural and is always coming toward himself as futural, can man *be* toward his death authentically or inauthentically. In resoluteness, man takes over his thrownness into nullity. But this means that *Dasein* is authentically as he already was, that he always is as "having been." This authentic coming back to my own having-been arises from the authentically futural anticipation of the uttermost possibility of dying. Such anticipatory resoluteness is itself not isolated, for it discloses the current situation in which we are circumspectively concerned with the ready-to-hand. But we can "take action" authentically, letting ourselves be encountered and seized by what has presence environmentally, only by making entities present. Resoluteness, therefore, can be what it is only as the present, in the sense of "making present." This authentic making-present is itself released from the future that is by having been: it is this unitary phenomenon of the having-been–making-present–future that Heidegger calls temporality.

To say that temporality is the meaning of authenticity is not yet to show that it is the meaning of care in general. Heidegger begins this task by demonstrating that temporality is the meaning of care's unity. Care was formally defined as ahead of itself—already Being-in (a world)—as Being alongside (entities encountered within the world). The existential "ahead of itself" is grounded in the future, which makes it possible for man to make himself intelligible in light of the "for the sake of" himself. The "ahead" is based on the kind of future that can make an issue of man's potentiality for Being. Already being *this* thrown entity is grounded in the having-been: man does not have the past of a real entity, some of which is no longer present, but can *be* his past only as long as he finds himself as the thrown fact that he is and already was; he finds himself this way in his state of mind. Finally, making-present is the meaning of our falling into the present-at-hand and ready-to-hand things with which we concern ourselves. But such making-present, even the "moment of vision" in which the authentic situation is disclosed, is included in the future and in having been. In general, temporality makes possible the unity of the elements of care, a unity that is not first pieced together from separate elements. Such temporality itself has not been pieced together: it is not an entity at all, but "temporalizes" possible ways of itself that make possible *Dasein's* authentic and inauthentic modes of Being.

Heidegger further explicates temporality by indicating its character of being outside itself. The future is a coming *toward* oneself. The having-been is a back *to*, the present is letting oneself be encountered *by*. This character of being outside of themselves, of being "ecstatic," leads Heidegger to call the three phenomena of temporality the ecstases of temporality. Temporality is outside of itself in and for itself. That is, it is not an entity before being outside itself that somehow emerges from itself, but its "essence is a process of temporalizing in the unity of the ecstases."[1]

Common sense misleadingly levels this ecstatic character of temporality, because ordinary time, like everything else in the everyday, is understood as something present-at-hand. In particular, we ordinarily conceive time as a series of nows—the present now; the past, which is now no longer; and the future, which is not yet now. But so to interpret authentic care's meaning results in just that understanding of death as the stopping of a present-at-hand thing, and of guilt as a reckoning of past debts, that Heidegger seeks to avoid. Indeed, man's temporality cannot mean that he is fundamentally an entity *in* time, because the kind of entities that are in time are not human beings.

The commonsense view of time also misleads concerning temporality's finitude: not only is authentic existence essentially finite, but so is the temporality that makes it possible. Temporality's finitude can be seen in the future: for this is my coming

[1] *Sein und Zeit*, p. 329 (italics omitted).

toward myself as the possibility of nullity. This coming toward myself closes off my potentiality for Being and is itself closed. As such, it makes possible resolute existent*iell* understanding of my nullity. The ordinary understanding does not grasp this finitude, and, indeed, believes time to be endless. Heidegger does not dispute that time goes on and that an unlimited number of things happen despite my no longer Being. But the meaning of endless time is unclear. In particular, Heidegger will show in the final chapter how inauthentic temporality arises from authentic temporality in such a way that it temporalizes infinite time. But that is to say that endless time is subordinate to authentic temporality's finitude.

Heidegger now seeks to confirm his analysis by grounding everyday Being in temporality: this discussion also serves to develop and clarify his original description of care.

(§67–68) Heidegger begins with understanding. *Dasein* "understands," when understanding is thought of existentially, by throwing himself into an existent*iell* possibility and by developing the possibilities of sight that belong to it. Now, in all comprehension, man lets himself come toward himself by projecting his possibilities upon that Being for the sake of which he is. When a man lets himself come toward himself in his *own* potentiality for Being, he understands authentically, and the condition for authenticity has proved to be the future. But the future grounds all understanding, all of which is ahead of itself. In what way, then, does it ground inauthentic understanding, in which man is for the sake of possibilities that are not his own? In everyday concern *Dasein* projects himself upon the things with which he is concerned. This means that *Dasein* comes toward himself in his potentiality for Being alongside the things with which he is concerned. He does not anticipate his ownmost and uttermost possibility, but "*awaits*" himself, himself as "they," in the context of his possible success or failure with regard to the things with which he is concerned: the inauthentic future, the inauthentic ecstasy that makes possible such inauthentic understanding, has the character of awaiting. Such awaiting, in turn, is a "mode of the future which temporalizes itself authentically as anticipation."[2]

Because temporality temporalizes the three ecstasies equi-primordially, the inauthentic future must be connected to the inauthentic present and past. Corresponding to the inauthentic future is the inauthentic way of Being alongside things: this is the present or the "making present." It is to be distinguished from the moment (of vision), the *Augenblick,* the authentic present in accordance with which one discloses a situation and the possibilities and matters of concern encountered in it; in this one is brought back from distraction in the matters of one's closest concern. The inauthentic present is the existential meaning of that falling into the world of one's concern from which authenticity brings us back.

Inauthentic understanding also temporalizes an inauthentic having-been. Authentic having-been is called "repetition": here I come back to my own self, come back to my thrown individualization "at the same time" that I come toward myself. Only this coming back makes possible resolutely taking over the entity I already am. But inauthentic projection is possible only if my own thrown Being has been forgotten. Such "forgetting," the inauthentic past, means backing away from what I already am in such a way that what is backed away from, and the backing away itself, is closed off. Having forgotten is thus "the temporal meaning of that type of Being in accordance with which I *am* at first and for the most part as having-been."[3] Consequently, *such* forgetting is a basis on which present-at-hand and ready-to-hand entities are retained when we awaitingly make present, and ordinary forgetting means a nonretaining on this level.[4]

Forgetting is the mode of temporality that makes possible in-authentic states of mind. A mood can concretely affect us as the mood it is only because it discloses the pure fact that I am the entity I am. But in what way can we see precisely that a mood's disclosing thrownness is possible only on the basis of having-been and, in particular, that forgetting is the condition of inauthentic

[2]*Sein und Zeit,* p. 337. My translation (italics omitted).
[3]*Sein und Zeit,* p. 339. My translation.
[4]Consider Leo Strauss, *The City and Man* (Chicago: Rand McNally, 1964).

thrownness? In inauthentic irresoluteness, we flee from the thrown individualization disclosed by the mood. That is, we flee in the face of the disclosure that we are authentically. But this is possible only if we come back to ourselves in the mode of forgetting ourselves. In fear, for example, entities are freed in their detrimentality for a possibility of *Dasein* when *Dasein* has assigned himself to a particular area of concern. Fear awaits these detrimental entities and makes them present in such awaiting. But I can discover such entities as fearsome only if I allow them to come back to the entity I am. Consequently, it is the way I am as having been, in this case my inauthentic temporalizing, that makes it possible that fear and feared entities have existent*iell* significance.

My inauthentic temporalizing can further be seen to be the basis of fear if we examine the bewilderment characteristic of it. Fear forces a man back to his thrownness, but he backs away from his resolute ability to be and closes it off, clinging to the possibilities of self-preservation and evasion that he has already disclosed. But we disclose these possibilities as present for fear, and seize them in fearful concern in a manner that leaps from one to another, only as they are encountered within an environment in which we no longer know our way. We thus make these possibilities present in a bewilderment based upon our having forgotten, and await them in a manner similarly modified by bewilderment.

Heidegger concludes his discussion of the temporality of moods by discussing anxiety, and he then completes his analysis of the temporality of everyday care by elucidating the temporality of falling. For us this analysis also clarifies the connection between various potentialities and concrete modifications in temporality itself.

The present is the ground of falling: the nature of such making-present has already largely been elucidated. The present is the ecstatical horizon within which we let something be encountered in the way it "looks" in general and within which entities can have bodily presence in particular. Heidegger develops the analysis by explicating the grounding in the present of curiosity, which is one of the elements of falling. Curiosity makes present-at-hand entities present, but not to tarry alongside and understand them, not to uncover them by projecting them upon their possibility. Rather, curiosity sees only in order to see. Curiosity's craving for the new is a way of Being toward what is not yet, but curiosity leaps away from any awaiting of definite possibilities and simply desires the possible as something actual. Consequently, it does not hold on to what it makes present but merely makes it present, immediately leaping away from what is made present. When this awaiting is such that *Dasein* no longer lets even inauthentic possibilities of concern come toward him, but lets come toward him only possibilities for a making-present that leaps in this way, it is the ground of distraction. Finally, we may make present simply for the sake of a making-present that is not held onto. Here *Dasein* is so entangled that he never dwells anywhere: we thus have the making-present that is at the "opposite extreme from the *moment of vision.*"[5] Making-present is more inauthentic the more it comes solely toward itself, fleeing in the face of any definite potentiality for Being: in this sense we can see the connection which Heidegger brought out in his discussion of fear between the degree of inauthentic making-present and the degree of forgetting of one's thrownness.

The Temporality of Man's Being: Analysis

Heidegger's discussion begins his elucidating of the temporal meaning of *Dasein*'s Being. We begin our analysis by noting that Heidegger's treatment here does not complete his discussion, because he has not yet taken up the connection between authentic repetition and history, between ecstatic and "horizonal" temporality, and between *Dasein*'s temporality and ordinary time. But, we may ask, what is the precise connection between the temporality (*Zeitlichkeit*) of *human* Being and the Temporality (*Temporalität*) of Being-as-such to which Heidegger referred in his introduction? Heidegger's discussion of the Temporality of Being was not completed in publishable form. But what could possibly be missing once the temporality of

[5] *Sein und Zeit*, p. 347.

human Being has been established along with the fact that "there is" Being only when there is *Dasein*? What is missing is a discussion of how *Dasein*'s understanding of *Being* and the Being projected in this understanding have their meaning in Temporality. The entire matter has not yet been conceived in a way that thematically projects Being upon Temporality; the temporal projection of *Dasein*'s Being does not suffice for this task. We may say that Heidegger has now discussed the temporal basis of the structures that make it possible for *Dasein* to experience entities in their possibility; but we must add that he has not discussed how the possibility itself, the Being itself, of these entities is first projected upon its meaning, and that he has not done this either for the modes of Being or for Being itself. If this is so, he could hardly yet display the Temporality of such Being or Being's precise meaning in Temporal terms. But this need not mean that the Temporality of Being is additional to the temporality that gives *Dasein* his meaning. For it may be, and, indeed, likely is, nothing but this temporality, understood as making Being-as-such possible.

We are nonetheless forced to ask the following questions even at this juncture. If to understand is to project something upon its meaning and then interpret it in that meaning, upon what does Heidegger project Temporality when he explicitly understands and interprets it? Why is not the uncovering of greater and greater circles of meaning continually necessary? Does this uncovering just happen to come to an end because we can see nothing beyond temporality, or must temporality be the final horizon? Now, *Dasein*'s temporal meaning is in his projection and is not other than his projection. Perhaps, then, this meaning need *not* be within a broader meaning even if *Dasein*'s Being as care is itself only within temporality. But even if this is so, how are we to conceive the possibility of temporality's explicitly coming to light? This question would only be exacerbated if we were to attempt to conceive it in reference to the Temporality of Being itself, acting as if temporality could be explicitly understood only within the horizon of Being-as-such and *its* Temporal meaning. If this is too abstract, we might ask concretely: precisely in terms of what does temporality reveal itself as *meaning*

and the ecstases reveal themselves as the elements of *meaning?*
Here we see that Heidegger hardly seems to think Temporality
for itself, from out of its own openness or truth, but rather to
think it exclusively as the meaning of Being, or more narrowly
here, as the meaning of man's Being. But perhaps the "meaning" of Temporality is nothing but its belonging together with
Being and with *Dasein* as that which lets Temporality "be" by
projecting Being upon it. In this sense it may well be that "there
is" Temporality only when and as there is Being. This would
then place Temporality in essential unity with man as the comprehender of Being, because there is Being only when *Dasein* is.
At the very least, Heidegger suggests this relationship when he
suggests that *Dasein's* meaning—temporality—is not something
floating free apart from, or above, *Dasein.*

Indeed, we may also in this way understand the *finitude* of
temporality. For one may also ask: even if *Dasein* is finite, and
projects himself authentically upon temporality only in anticipating death, why should this lead us to say that temporality
itself is finite? Surely, this seems to identify *Dasein* and temporality. In fact, we need *not* identify temporality's finitude with man's
finitude, an identification Heidegger does not wish to make.
But, temporality can come into its own, can "be" temporality
only when *Dasein* and his understanding of Being are "there."
Temporality, and Being, are finite insofar as they "are" only in
their making possible *Dasein's* understanding of Being, an understanding that is most its own when it anticipates its uttermost
impossibility, its finitude, in resolving upon guilt. This does not
mean, however, that temporality and its finitude are identical to
Dasein and his finitude in all respects. Here, however, we again
may wonder whether there must not be an authentic "infinity"
coordinate with man's finitude if he is to understand that finitude
as finitude. Moreover, we must also wonder how Heidegger's *explicit* disclosing of Being-as-such and of temporality are grounded
in care. This disclosing could not be successful unless sometimes
authentic; but the explicit attempt itself would also need to be
grounded in inauthenticity. Yet, it is unclear that the disclosing
can be grounded in either authenticity or inauthenticity, given

that the ordinary discovery of entities in their Being requires that we pass over phenomena such as equipmental wholeness and world. Can one successfully bring to light as it is what is by Being obscure?

To clarify the foregoing questions, I must emphasize that temporality is not an entity. Moreover, the Being of which it is the meaning is also not an entity. Temporality does not "cause" Being. Rather, it is the widest openness in which Being and entities are. But at the same time it is nearest to man because without the temporalizing of the ecstases he could not begin to come toward himself. The future, for example, enables *Dasein* to come toward his ownmost and his inauthentic possibilities *as* authentic or inauthentic possibility. This, in turn, enables him to interpret these possibilities and deal with them ontically. Making-present enables man to Be-alongside other entities and let them be encountered in their Being. Heidegger's remarks on *Dasein*'s temporality, therefore, are not intended to assert that man is in time and caused by time-bound contingencies. And they are not intended to assert that *Dasein*'s "Being" is subordinate to "becoming" when Being and becoming refer to general characterizations of entities. Rather, temporality is connected to Being and "becoming" only as we conceive these in light of the projective disclosing that first enables entities, and therefore their most general characteristics, to be uncovered. This still leaves unclear the precise difference between Being and Temporality as fields in which possibilities can be encountered. Yet, we may at least say that Temporality releases that which is no entity, while Being releases entities. This issue depends on the meaning of Temporality itself, and the sense in which Temporality, here, has been projected upon the understanding of Being.

The three dimensions of authentic temporality are the basic ecstases to which the usual past, present, and future correspond. One may wonder, however, why it is that authentic temporality conveniently has these three ecstases. Here we must see that in whatever manner authentic temporality yields ordinary time—a topic Heidegger discusses in his concluding chapter—the ordinary interpretation of time arises from man's *pre*thematic

understanding of Being's meaning, and, therefore, always remains an important clue in grasping temporality. It could be
suggested that the central difference between Heidegger's
analysis and ordinary analyses is the decisive importance of the
future, which, by grounding man's awaiting of possibilities,
holds sway even in inauthentic *Dasein* who conceives time as the
"now," that is, the present, and can be shown to do so because
awaiting has fallen into things within the world. But the heart of
Heidegger's analysis is not so much the priority of the future as
it is the wholeness of temporalizing, the truth that temporality
temporalizes all three ecstasies equally. When all three are
thought genuinely from this wholeness, they are being thought
from the ecstatic nature of temporality and can then be interpreted in their connection to *Dasein*'s authenticity. This is similar
to the sense in which the heart of man's Being as care is the
wholeness of its structures even though one structure, understanding, shows its priority. Indeed, the structures of care correspond to the ordinary articulation of man into reason, the
passions (the heart), and the body. Thinking through the meaning of these phenomena as ordinarily experienced is the chief
clue in working out existence, and thinking through the wholeness of these phenomena reveals their grounding in care. Anxiety is the decisive phenomenon because it reveals this wholeness
as a wholeness such that the three "parts" of man can be thought
in light of this wholeness and can then be disclosed authentically.
But this reveals the fourth, and superior, dimension of man—
namely, his possible understanding of Being—just as the wholeness of temporalizing reveals the "fourth" dimension of man's
comprehension of time—namely, its essential connection to the
understanding of Being.

We may continue to analyze Heidegger's discussion of temporality by attempting to uncover the level of specificity with
which temporality makes possible specific ontic possibilities. In
particular, we will consider Heidegger's discussion of moods,
keeping in mind his treatment of curiosity. Indeed, Heidegger's
temporal analysis of moods enables us further to clarify the
limits and scope of existential analysis. Existential analysis discusses a phenomenon by analyzing it in terms of the structures

which first make it possible, as these structures are grounded in time. The analysis clarifies a human phenomenon *as* a possibility by discussing the possibilities the phenomenon uncovers and, in particular, by discussing the possibilities of man's own disclosing that the phenomenon reveals. Whatever cannot be comprehended in this way does not belong to Heidegger's analysis. But it might seem that such ontological analysis would be empty and formal: whatever mood we discuss, for example, we analyze identically with the others in terms of the temporality of thrownness. This cannot be true, however, because Heidegger discusses fear differently from hope and anxiety. Moreover, the moods Heidegger discusses existentially retain many of their commonsense characteristics. The difference cannot be limited to the difference between disclosing what is authentic and what is inauthentic because fear and hope are both inauthentic. Rather, as I have already argued, the differences in the moods must be taken back into the different combinations of the structures of care. But this, then, also means that they must be taken back further into the different combinations of temporality's temporalizing. This requires that inauthentic moods be interpreted as different modes of forgetting, awaiting, and making-present. Yet, although Heidegger does discuss the moods as modes of the ecstasies, he does not do so systematically and it is therefore not always clear where specific temporal variations must be brought to the analysis and where it is sufficient to point to a possibility of mood as "based on" one of the ecstasies in particular.

This difficulty is partially overcome by the consideration that Heidegger does not set out to provide a complete ontological analysis of man. It is also partially overcome by the fact that any discussion of a phenomenon based primarily on one mode necessarily implicates the other modes. In fearing, for example, we encounter entities in their detrimentality. According to Heidegger's earlier analysis, when the detrimental entities are familiar and not approaching immediately, we fear. When they are familiar and encountered suddenly, we are alarmed. When they are not familiar and not encountered suddenly, we dread; when they are unfamiliar and encountered suddenly, we are terrified. The modes of fear appear to be different ways in which what is made present as detrimental is encountered in its ontological characteristics of familiarity and immediacy. But Heidegger does not clarify the precise relations of the temporality of awaiting, forgetting, and making-present that makes this possible. Moreover, he also does not explicitly clarify their connection to the bewilderment characteristic of fear.

Heidegger discusses the way in which bewilderment frees possibilities for Being encountered. The possibilities he discusses, however—the jumble of hovering possibilities, none of which we take hold of—appear to concern man's dealing with his fear for the sake of possibilities he fears about, rather than man's dealing with the fearsome entities themselves. Bewilderment modifies the manner in which I await my possibilities and the manner in which I see entities within the world. A bewildered man assigns himself to his world in such a way that the order of significance can free entities with only the most fleeting and inconstant possibilities of usefulness: one loses one's way around one's environment. Yet, the threatened entities themselves presumably have been disclosed in such a way that they are not made present in this bewildered manner. When I am bewildered, I fail to take hold of any definite possibility; but the threatening entities connected to bewilderment have themselves been more definitely disclosed. How can this be, assuming that we are in the same order of significance? The precise interconnections of the threatening possibilities and the jumble awaited and made present, and their precise relation to modifications in temporality is, thus, unclear. But the connections are like the similarities and differences in the temporality of curiosity and distraction; we might suggest that bewilderment is grounded in a greater degree of, a fuller closing of, oneself in forgetfulness similar to the fuller abandonment to awaitingly keeping present that distinguishes distraction from curiosity. Indeed, Heidegger mentions that there can be mixed modes of authenticity and inauthenticity, he speaks of greater and lesser authenticity in his upcoming discussion of historicality, and he indicates that there are degrees between the authentic moment and the inauthentic present. These differences may be connected to the variations in certainty, in holding an entity as true, which he has mentioned, and we could develop a detailed discussion of the temporal variations. But Heidegger himself does not do so.

[2]

Theory and Practice: Exposition

The discussion of the temporal ground of the structures constituting care is tantamount to a discussion of the temporal unity that makes it possible for *Dasein* to be cleared, to be open and bright for himself. But the concrete temporal discussion of Being-in-the-world still needs to be achieved. What is the temporal basis of the circumspective concern that frees ready-to-hand entities by letting them be involved? What is the temporal meaning of the way in which circumspective concern is modified to theoretical discovery of the present-at-hand? What is the temporal meaning of the transcendence of world itself? The following explication will focus on Heidegger's discussion of the arising of theory from circumspective concern.

(§69*a*) Concernful dealings discover ready-to-hand entities by letting them be encountered in the involvement in which we have previously understood them. We discover an item of equipment when we let it be involved in that "toward which" it is, namely, the work to be produced in order to meet our everyday needs. The basis of this "toward which" is our existential understanding of it; the temporal basis of such understanding is awaiting. Together with this awaiting, our concern comes back to that with which it is involved, and the unity of this awaiting retention makes possible our making present of equipment in specifically manipulative ways.

Temporality is also the basis of modes of circumspectively letting things be encountered such as conspicuousness, obtrusiveness, and obstinacy. Heidegger's general point once more is that we never encounter an entity as damaged, or missing, or unserviceable by merely representing the thing, but always encounter it within concernful dealings. Even those entities with which I cannot cope are revealed as insurmountable only when I encounter them circumspectively. Here, my concern resigns itself

and lets entities be revealed in their resistance to it: the temporal
ground of this possibility is a nonretaining that awaitingly makes
present, letting things be ready-to-hand, but unsuitable. In this
sense, *Dasein* can understand himself "in [his] abandonment to
a 'world' [of things] of which [he] never becomes master."[6] One
might say that even what is beyond man's control can be this way
only on the basis of *Dasein*'s temporally grounded understanding.

If this is the ontological ground of the ordinary, of practice,
what is the temporal ground of the theoretical discovery that
arises from such practice? We cannot answer this question by
reporting the concrete examples of such a transformation.
Rather, we seek to know how, given what man is, theory is possible and, in particular, how it is possible for it to arise from
practice. (Notice that, for Heidegger, this issue cannot be discussed in terms of natural faculties, tendencies, and ends because such a discussion would misinterpret *Dasein*'s ontological
status. One could not argue, for example, that the goals sought
by practice and the faculties that it develops require the results
of theory for their fulfillment, nor could one point to the
theoretical life itself as what most fully satisfies these ends and
develops these not yet developed faculties. For such "ends" and
"faculties" are being interpreted in light of what is outstanding
for, and what is not yet for, entities other than man. Heidegger's
ontological discussion of theory must, therefore, clarify theory's
possibility in terms of the temporal basis of existence.)

The change from practical use to theoretical observation,
from concern with the ready-to-hand to explanation of the
present-at-hand, may appear to consist of a disappearance of
practice in which we hold back from manipulation and just look
around. But such tarrying is itself a mode of circumspection, still
dealing with equipment by inspecting it, looking it over. Con-
versely, theoretical research has its own kind of practice: mea-
surements are read, instruments are prepared, books are written. These observations are trivial but they make clear that the
ontological boundary between the theoretical and atheoretical is

---

[6] *Sein und Zeit,* p. 356.

hardly obvious. The chief clue in uncovering this boundary is to consider the sight and seeing, in the broadest sense, that belong to understanding, because theoretical knowledge traditionally has been interpreted as something based upon, or directed toward, intellectual intuition. To understand how practical concern can change over to theoretical contemplation, therefore, we must consider the change from the seeing that is characteristic of practice to the seeing that is characteristic of theory. The seeing characteristic of practice is the "circumspection" that guides all concern. Circumspection operates in the involvements of a context of equipment, guided by a survey of the current wholeness of equipment and the public environment. The heart of this survey, and that from which concern begins, is understanding the context of involvements as this is structured by that for the sake of which *Dasein* is. Circumspection "surveys" by interpreting what is seen in this understanding. Its interpretation brings ready-to-hand entities and the environment close to *Dasein,* although this is not a physical nearness. The specific name for such circumspective interpretation is "deliberation" (*Überlegung*), which operates as an "if then": if this is to be produced, then these ways and means are needed. Deliberation never *affirms* that an entity has such and such properties or is present-at-hand, but concretely illuminates *Dasein*'s situation in the environment that concerns him. That is, deliberation concretely frees an entity in its readiness-to-hand.

The primary existential meaning of deliberation is making-present: deliberation brings closer the ready-to-hand that has been retained. That is, deliberating lets that in which something has an involvement be seen as this very thing. But such deliberative interpretation is possible only if what is ready-to-hand has already been discovered. Indeed, this prior discovery is what Heidegger means by suggesting that *Dasein* understandingly awaits possibilities, that deliberation follows the primary survey of involvements. This primary understanding, whereby something first *can* be seen as something, is the root of all concern. Moreover, for deliberation to bring the ready-to-hand things close, this primary awaiting must come *back* to those ready-to-hand things that are for the work the concern is about. For without such retaining of the ready-to-hand, there is nothing for deliberation to work out.

How, then, may we now clarify the ontological genesis of theory from practical deliberation? Theoretical talk, Heidegger argues, it not spoken within the horizon of a context of equipment. When the worker calls a hammer heavy or too heavy, he is using it and discussing it circumspectively. But when someone says that this hammer has a certain weight, has the property of heaviness, falls if what it presses on is taken away, he is talking of, letting the hammer be seen as, what is suitable for an entity with a mass, a bodily thing subject to gravity. This talk is not possible simply through abstaining from hammering with the hammer but requires that we look at the ready-to-hand entity as something present-at-hand. But this means that the understanding of Being that guides concernful dealings has changed. Such a change cannot mean that theory must understand the entities it discovers to possess a changed Being, for it is possible for a science such as economics to make the ready-to-hand its object and to understand its object to have the Being of equipment.

Heidegger continues his discussion by developing his earlier analysis of theory, in which his theme was the discovery of physically natural entities within the world. (He thus leaves aside both the question of theorizing about equipment and the theoretical activity of previous ontology.)

In physical science there is a change in the understanding of Being, one in which suitable tools encountered in their place are now objects of assertions about abstract properties and spatio-temporal positions, each indistinguishable from the other. In this way entities are released from environmental confinement and the aggregate of the present-at-hand becomes thematic. That is, the realm of the present-at-hand is marked off on the basis of an understanding of Being as presence-at-hand.

The ontological meaning of science can be seen most clearly in the rise of mathematical physics. The heart of mathematical physics is neither a high regard for facts nor an application of mathematics, but the way in which nature is mathematically projected. Matter is uncovered beforehand as something present-at-hand and the physicist is guided by looking at its quantitatively determinable constituents: motion, force, location, and time. Only on the basis of nature projected in this way can any fact be found and set up for experiments; there are no bare facts. Indeed, the reason that mathematical physics is paradigmatic for all sciences is not that it uses the mathematical as such or that it is binding for all of us, but that it discloses something a priori in its projection; it discovers entities in the only way they can be discovered, namely, through a priori projection of their Being.

This discussion enables us to grasp more clearly the temporal and existential meaning of science. The whole of the projecting that makes up science is "thematizing," and thematizing is a distinctive kind of making-present. In science, already encountered entities are projected in a way that allows their Being to be understood in a manner that manifests the possibility of the pure discovery of entities. The whole of this projecting, in which an understanding of Being is articulated, an area of subject matter is marked off, and ways of conceiving entities are sketched, is thematizing. Thematizing frees entities so that they can throw themselves against a pure discovering: it allows them to be objects, frees them so that they can be determined objectively. Such freeing makes them present in a distinctive way: the Being of thematizing is rooted in this making-present that awaits the pure discoveredness of the present-at-hand. But how can *Dasein*'s awaiting make present a pure discoveredness? Only because he can project himself upon his potentiality for Being in the truth—that is, only because he can resolve existent*ielly* upon that potentitality. But Heidegger does not clarify the precise way in which existen*tiell* resoluteness is the source of science. For such existent*iell* resoluteness can yield thematic science only because we are in the world. Consequently, he argues, it is necessary to explore the temporal meaning of transcending to the world if we are to understand further the meaning of both theoretical and circumspective discovery.

For man circumspectively or theoretically to discover entities, he must transcend the entities he objectifies or uses. And, for man's understanding of Being to be modified in thematizing, it must be possible for him to understand Being. Indeed, he must always understand Being even if his understanding is so neutral that he has not distinguished presence-at-hand from readiness-to-hand. The transcendence required for circumspection is transcendence to the world. How, then, does temporality make possible Being-in-the-world? The point of Heidegger's discussion is to show that the ecstatical unity of temporality has "something like a horizon." (In this sense his discussion is the rigorous heart of analyses that consider concepts such as context, horizon, and perspective to be central in understanding knowledge in general and political knowledge in particular.)

We remember that a world is constituted by significance, and that significance is the unity of relationships of "in order to," "toward this," and "for the sake of." In his existence, a man understands himself in the way in which his "for the sake of" is connected to the current "in order to"—that is, he understands himself inside of the world. But if care is grounded in temporality, then significance must be similarly grounded. This is accomplished, Heidegger argues, because temporality has something like a horizon. The three ecstasies do not merely carry one away but each carries one somewhere: these three "whithers" are the three "horizonal" schemata that, in their unity, determine that upon which entities are disclosed. That is, they determine worlds. In Being futurally toward himself, *Dasein* is for the sake of himself; in Being as having-been, *Dasein* is disclosed in terms of, is carried to, that in the face of which he has been thrown and to which he has been abandoned; in his making-present by concernfully Being alongside, *Dasein* is carried to his "in order to." Indeed, because this horizonal constitution belongs to temporality essentially and is not merely occasional to it, whenever *Dasin* temporalizes himself, a world is temporalized too. The world "is" neither present-at-hand nor ready-to-hand but is temporalized, is "there," with *Dasein*. If no *Dasein* exists, there is no world.

Because the world is grounded in this horizonal unity, it is transcendent: entities are discovered within it and can be discovered only if it has been disclosed. Understandingly coming back from the horizons to the entities within them is what is meant by letting entities be encountered. Both practical concern and thematic objectifying are ways of Being in the world and of discovering entities within the world. Indeed, precisely because *Dasein*'s temporalizing must come back to entities that are encountered, precisely because with its existence other entities are necessarily discovered, the fact of such discovery is not at our discretion. But what is discovered and disclosed, "on what occasion," in what direction, and how far, are matters for our freedom.

Theory and Practice: Analysis

The guiding understanding of Heidegger's discussion is that theory and practice belong to Being-in-the-world. This means that the structures of world are prior to both theory and practice, and that theoretical discovery is made possible by our projecting a world. World itself, and man's discovery of entities within it, can then be understood to be based upon the "ecstatic-horizonal" essence of temporality. Consequently, neither practice nor theory is, as such, the most distinctively human realm, and this is true whether or not practice is fitting or vulgar, just or unjust.

Now, it may seem that if Being-in-the-world is primary, practical entities and natural entities discovered theoretically could both be made intelligible in light of the other, as long as they were grounded in Being-in-the-world. But this is untrue, given Heidegger's analysis, because practice and *such* theory discover entities with different kinds of Being. Such theoretical entities can cause neither the Being of practical entities nor how they present themselves when discovered in their Being, because Being and its modes are not subject to entities. Thus, whatever may be said about the order of causality among natural entities discovered scientifically, this order could not account for an entity as it is discovered in practice. The appropriateness of an entity toward its work and end cannot be measured by the standards in terms of which such theoretical entities present themselves. And whatever may be said about the hierarchical order of practice, it could not govern entities that are discovered in another mode of Being. The joint root of theory and practice, according to Heidegger, must be found in the temporalizing of

Being and of *Dasein*'s Being. But the surprising result of this claim, I am now arguing, is that it is precisely in terms of this "Being" that a gap, indeed an abyss, between such theoretical entities and practical entities reveals itself. And, as I will argue further, this gap casts doubt on all of Heidegger's analyses.

Perhaps Heidegger's discussion of the "sight" in practice and the practice in theory complicates our interpretation. For if a kind of practice belongs to theory, does not this practice enter the realm and the standards of the practical as such? Heidegger's remarks suggest that he himself has in mind a "practice" belonging to theory that is meaningless except as part of theory and that therefore belongs to the discovery of theoretical entities, not practical ones. This, for example, is how he might interpret the scientist's reading of meters. Must we not say, however, that the ontically trivial fact that scholars read meters is matched by the familiar political observation that the government wastes money in awarding grants for the production of such meters, and that this is a waste of money as measured in practice?

If Heidegger intends to raise the issues suggested by this observation, he explores them insufficiently. Perhaps they are unexplored because they offer nothing to ontological analysis. Heidegger argues that theoretical discovery of nature thematically objectifies: it projects entities upon the possibilities of pure discovery in their presence. The heart of such theory, therefore, is understanding presence-at-hand. But would not the question of the involvement in practice of such entities discovered theoretically be ontologically relevant? Heidegger obscures this issue somewhat by concentrating on mathematical physics and the nature it discovers. But if we consider the theoretical discovery of nature more generally—the discovery of nature among the ancients, for example—we find a theoretical presentation of entities that are of the most decisive practical importance. (Indeed, the culmination of mathematical physics in technology, which Heidegger himself brings to light in later works, indicates a connection between entities judged by the standards of use and entities made possible by discovery of what is purely present—a connection whose ontological meaning is not fully intelligible if such entities as discovered in theoretical natural science and as encountered in practice are different in their Being.) Similarly, we might say that practical entities present their own possibilities of connection to the theoretically observed natural entities, and that these connections could not properly be dismissed as ontologically irrelevant. Heidegger discusses the modes of tarrying alongside, of merely looking, of discovering the presence of the ready-to-hand; but these modes belong to dealing with and encountering the ready-to-hand. Moreover, he suggests without developing his suggestion that the sciences of practical entities thematize these entities but do not understand the entities to have a changed Being. But this presumably refers to the sense in which the scholar may categorize, say, types of implements when not dealing with them in a ready-to-hand encounter.

Of its own accord, however, does not practice demand theoretical inquiry into "nature" and the truth sought by this inquiry? According to our previous discussions of human possibilities, is not practice necessarily unstable and does it not, therefore, point to a more complete stability? The deliberating that Heidegger finds to be crucial in practical interpretation ultimately is governed by that for the sake of which deliberation is. But do not these ends present themselves to men and for men as inherently imperfect? Whatever the concrete causes of ontic recognition of this imperfection, every practical end, from the most common needs to the most uncommon wish for theoretical knowledge, from the fullest equality to the greatest peculiarity, is impossible to attain in the *full* desirability projected for it.[7] Something like the entities discovered in the nobility of their pure perfection is what practical activity itself seeks to be and seeks to be grounded upon. Indeed, it is precisely the deficiencies in practice, which are noticed in practice itself, that open the possibility of theoretical questioning.[8] These questions indicate a fundamental interpenetration between the natural entities pursued theoretically and the practical entities. Heidegger's analysis obscures this connection, but the connection is relevant both for

---

[7]Consider Plato's *Republic* and Aristotle's *Ethics,* among others.
[8]Consider Plato, *Republic,* Book 1, and Plato, *Laches.*

theory and practice themselves and for the issue of the Being of such entities.

I believe that such interpenetration is explicable because of the fundamental unity of the entities with which both practice and theory deal. The entities that theory, and here, especially, political theory or political philosophy, attempts to discover are precisely the justice simply, the freedom simply, the human excellence simply that shape all political practice. These ends present themselves in practice as ends for which we strive, ends that we can attain only imperfectly. This imperfection colors all the means and structures, all the entities, that are subordinate to these ends such that they too are never discovered simply. Every practical deliberation is uncertain by its own lights because it cannot perfectly bring about what it seeks in the material in which it seeks it: there are inevitable scarcities of opportunities and other resources. This is most evident in the scarce opportunities for the display of the highest political achievement, and in the fact that every courageous or moderate action of citizens occurs within a political community whose sufficiency of wealth is based on its explicitly or implicitly taking more than can be justified from current neighbors and previous inhabitants. Even the fortunate accidents, whereby a man is gifted with excellent abilities and his community with excellent resources and potentially excellent citizens, suggest the imperfection inherent in our actions, because they indicate the unjustifiable element inherent in any practical attempt to be just or otherwise excellent. Now, it is obvious that much elementary practical deliberation can occur as if such imperfection does not exist; and it is true that to be as much as it can be of that for which it strives a political community or practical man normally must operate within an artificial blindness to such problems. But the fact remains that fully self-confident, fully whole and enclosed deliberations, are based on artifice and that, therefore, the entities discovered in practice for practice are meaningful only concurrently with their imperfection. But this shows that the theoretical attempt to discover what is fully just, fully excellent, fully proper, is in a sense made possible by the imperfections of political striving itself and, therefore, that what is discovered as theoretically natural need not be entities whose meaning and intelligibility is fundamentally different from those freed by practice. I am arguing, thus, that what accounts for the possibility of ontic connection of the theoretically natural and the practical, at least for the immediate material of political and ethical philosophy, is the similarity of their intelligibility, that is, of their "Being"; but this is again to suggest that Heidegger's Being may be otherwise accounted for.

Here we might consider whether our questions are based on a mistaken understanding of man as a "real" entity. But I have argued that we can understand man's peculiar finitude without conceiving him as ready-to-hand, present-at-hand, or as *Dasein*. One might also complain that our discussion of this issue has concentrated one-sidedly on arguments more appropriate to ancient than to modern political philosophy. But this one-sidedness follows from our previous attempts to show that the alternative analyses of the phenomena on which Heidegger concentrates, which both begin to meet his questions and offer means of clarifying what is doubtful in his discussion, are found in a repetition—not slavish imitation—of the ancient analyses, conducted with a view toward Heidegger's problematic. In general, the modern analyses are both more subject to his questions and less successful in dealing with what is obscure in *Being and Time* because they indeed depend on a misconception of man himself as a ready-to-hand or present-at-hand entity. This is evident from the moderns' original understanding of man as an enterprise and through their grounding of analyses upon natural laws and satisfaction of desires; it culminates in the contemporary understanding of the crucial political issues as issues of value. In any event, I doubt that Heidegger's analysis could allow the possibility of these ontic connections between the practical and the theoretically natural which we have been discussing; I believe that the alternative location that I have proposed for the union of practical and theoretical possibilities permits us to understand these interconnections properly.

It might then be argued that we are ignoring the connection and distinction between authenticity and inauthenticity, and that we are overlooking Heidegger's discussion of man's proper end and finitude: sufficient unity is found in *man's* Being and his temporality, not to speak of Being and its Temporality. Indeed, we ourselves were hardly able to discuss the question of the relation between practically discovered entities and natural entities discovered theoretically without discussing man's possibilities.

We may begin to consider this argument by considering the authenticity and inauthenticity of theory and practice. Heidegger remarks that theory can arise from the existent*iell* resolve to pursue *Dasein*'s potentiality for disclosing the truth. Yet, he discusses the temporality of theory in terms of inauthentic awaiting and making-present. Is theory authentic or inauthentic? Why does Heidegger not claim that theoretical resolve is grounded in anticipation and the moment? Presumably, theory may begin in resolve, but it projects the *Dasein* of the theorizer upon man in his inauthentic possibilities. This surely can uncover what is genuine, the factual truth of entities in their presence-at-hand, but it would not uncover even present-at-hand entities in the way that they could be freed for a fully authentic resolve. Indeed, science or scholarship need hardly even begin in existent*iell* resolve but may still attain genuine results. What these possibilities suggest is that theory as such is not necessarily authentic or inauthentic, and that the world in which theoretical entities are discovered is not constituted exclusively by authentic existence. The question of the interconnection of theoretical and practical standards and entities thus cannot be answered by locating theory in an inevitably authentic disclosure. And practice, too, may be authentic as well as inauthentic.

This leaves the problem of interconnection unresolved, in Heideggerian terms; indeed, the problem is complicated, if we remember the analysis in Chapter 4 of the obscure connections between the authentic and the inauthentic. It is precisely Heidegger's discussion of the change from practice to theory that fails to explore sufficiently how the theoretical and the practical are presented in their interdependence and interconnection. And this is true both for the entities discovered circumspectively and theoretically and for the presentation of man's potentiality for practice and for pure discovery of Nature. For what has been said here concerning the entities *discovered* by theory and practice is mirrored in the question of the propriety and integrity of

the theoretical and circumspective activities themselves. Theoretical activity not only discovers entities whose intelligibility is
similar to the intelligibility of what we discover in practice, but
it can also present itself as an alternative excellence: the con-
templative life is itself the just or excellent life. But this may
place a particular theoretical endeavor in conflict with practical
ones because of the pretense to completeness required of political communities, and because of the very insufficiencies, or
finitude, of the theoretical attempt.

Consider, for example, the *Apology of Socrates*. The theoretical
quest is commensurable with the formative possibilities of ordinary justice or statesmanlike excellence because these are all
similarly intelligible as quests to be the perfection they imitate.
But when we measure, we can discover no order correct in every
time and place because theoretical excellence, although it may
more beautifully imitate what both politics and philosophy seek,
depends on the necessities and the examples of excellence provided by the political order; and although it depends on the
political order, it threatens to corrupt both those citizens most
necessary to this order and the veil a political community must
draw down upon itself. This problem exemplifies what appears
to be an essential ontic disharmony among certain ways of life, a
disharmony grounded in the very principles that account for
their similar intelligibility and the concrete interdependence of
the entities meaningfully discovered on their basis.

Let us continue to explore these issues by further analyzing
Heidegger's discussion of theory. Heidegger intends to suggest,
as we have noted, that the ready-to-hand utensils of the domestic
and work world present themselves to scientific economics in
their purely objective possibilities of being discovered, but,
nonetheless, they are understood to have the Being of what is
ready-to-hand. Here we encounter the entire question of the
ontological status of the thematizing of entities that, in Heidegger's understanding, are ordinarily discovered circumspectively,
or as *Dasein* discovers himself—that is, those not discovered by
natural science or, perhaps, a political philosophy oriented to
nature. For an economist would not, in Heidegger's understanding, comprehend his objects to have a changed Being; yet he

would understand Being differently from the way he projects it in his concrete concerns. How is it possible for, say, usable entities to be released in pure presence from out of the scientific world and still be understood in their readiness-to-hand, where Heidegger presumably means neither the projection of, say, economic laws (for the Being of these laws would be presence-at-hand) nor the development of the kind of presence revealed in concern itself (such as the conspicuousness or obstinacy of factory equipment)? We might say that the scientific thematizing of such entities projects a prior understanding of Being as readiness-to-hand that frees ready-to-hand entities then projected upon Being as presence-at-hand and freed for discovery in this way, but not in the kinds of presence discovered in their being used. But Heidegger does not explicate the specifics of this possibility here. And, in any event, all this can occur only within the still unexplored understanding of Being-as-such.

My discussion raises an additional series of related questions. Heidegger intends his analysis of thematizing to cover the whole variety of sciences, not merely mathematical physics. Among these he has mentioned, or will mention, historiology, economics, mathematics, biology, psychology, literature, and theology, and he has indicated that Plato and Aristotle's work was also decisive for the sciences, although the precise meaning of sciences for the Greeks is unclear. We have questioned the connection between theory and practice, in general, and the status of political philosophy, in particular. But what is the relation between the entities discovered through the thematic objectifying of any area, and the entities prescientifically discovered in that area? And what is the connection between the requirements for scientific thematizing of an area and the rules and guides for ordinary activity and behavior within that area?

Concerning the first question, it is surely easier to see the connection between theoretically and prescientifically discovered entities within a single area than it is to make sense of the connections, at the level of entities, between the purely present natural and the practically useful. But the connection is by no means fully transparent. Are the discoveries of, say, theology necessary, useful, or proper for what is discovered in faith as faith? Heidegger himself is extremely cautious about this problem in a lecture on phenomenology and theology delivered in 1928.[9] We might raise a similar question concerning poetry and the scholar's study of it. In general, indeed, the issue is whether an entity experienced prescientifically allows itself to be experienced objectively in a manner that permits the prescientific entity to retain its powers, and consequently, allows the thematically discovered entities a possible connection to it. If the science simply transforms its entities, then we return to the problem of the meaning and possibility of such a gulf among theoretical and practical entities; and we would then need to explore the meaning of entities that cannot be thematically objectified without destroying the possibility of encountering them. If objectifying does not simply transform its entities, then, given Heidegger's analysis, the possibilities of the interconnections remain in the dark for several and, in a sense, all sciences.

For our second question—that of the relation between the requirements for scientific thematizing within an area and the ordinary rules and guides for practical behavior within the area—the issues are related. It is by no means evident that the faithful as faithful require or can permit the theologians: it is unclear that the theologian as theologian can retain the basic prescientific experience of his objects. That is, it is entirely possible that a science's activity is disharmonious with the activities permitted and required in the very area it seeks to thematize; and this problem is exacerbated when we consider the relations among the variety of sciences and their problematic realms. But if this disharmony exists, which set of demands takes precedence? Indeed, can Heidegger's analysis even allow us properly to ask this question?

Heidegger is, of course, aware of these issues. Beyond what we

---

[9]For a discussion of the gods in Heidegger consider Vincent Vycinas, *Earth and Gods* (The Hague: Martinus Nijhoff, 1961), especially pp. 174-223. For a discussion of theology in Heidegger see, among others, Heinrich Ott, *Denken und Sein* (Zollikon: Evangelischer Verlag, 1959). For an interesting discussion of theory and practice in *Being and Time* consider Gerald Prauss, *Erkennen und Handeln in Heidegger's Sein und Zeit* (Freiburg: K. Alber, 1977), and the review of it by Reinhold Aschenberg in *Philosophy and History* 11:2.

have already considered, notice his overall attempt to distinguish validity in the sciences in general from standards of validity in mathematics and physics—that is, his attempt to distinguish thematic objectivizing from simply considering all entities to be suitable objects for natural scientific objectification, his upcoming considerations concerning the connection between tradition and the historiological study of it, and his general attempt to distinguish human existence and Being from presence-at-hand and the sciences that study present-at-hand things. It might not be too much to say that his work as a whole is as much motivated by an attempt to save the prescientifically encountered entities from science as it is by the attempt to ground the sciences properly. For political science, this places Heidegger's analysis among those that attempt to describe those elements of human activity that cannot be grasped through a version of natural scientific methodology. Nonetheless, he hardly treats the issues we have just discussed even though they clearly appear to be ontologically relevant in their concreteness, dealing, as they do, with issues decisive for the problem of the a priori way in which we encounter entities.

This leads to our final problem in this series: on what basis are we to grasp the articulation, ordering, and ontic factuality of groups of entities and their respective sciences? First, how permanent is the articulation of areas of entities? Second, how precise is the connection between the numbers of modes of Being and the number of areas of entities? As long as *Dasein* is, is there a single articulation of the totality of entities that is always generally equivalent, with any change, beyond mere change in the "amount" of entities discovered, dependent on the manner and extent to which these areas are projected on their Being? We may perhaps make this assertion on Heidegger's behalf, as long as we consider the privative modes and therefore the "lack" of entities in these modes to belong to Being and thus to be implicated in the totality of entities any *Dasein* can articulate. Thus, we might suggest roughly that, for Heidegger, historical, artistic, and political (ethical) entities belong to human existence, along with the possible entities so far discussed in Heidegger's explicit treatment of the structures of care; nonhuman entities involved with man's "ends" belong to readiness-to-hand; the space of geometry, the numbers of mathematics, and the characteristics of matter such as motion and "time" belong to presence-at-hand; and the living entities belong to Life understood as a privative mode of *Dasein* itself. We leave open the question of the gods and of man's ends understood as Being for their own sake. If this summary is correct in general, then, needless to say, Heidegger has not made the specific elements clear. Particularly unclear is the prescientific status and articulation of those "things" that we can understand to have been projected on pure presence-at-hand, the relation of these things to the Nature that surrounds us, and the relation of this to Platonic-Aristotelian "nature." But if we must see the prescientific articulation as fundamentally changing, Heidegger has not clearly brought this out either. The importance of this issue is that we cannot sufficiently discuss the question of the interrelation of the sciences and the realms of entities unless we know the status of such entities within the totality of entities, and the historical status of the totality itself. What can properly be the relation of theology, faith, and law if their relative completeness and independence vary?

But is such an issue *ontologically* relevant? I suggest that it is for three reasons. First, we cannot completely clarify the meaning of Being as conditioning the possibility of entities unless we clarify the *range* within which Being permits the articulation of entities. Second, some understanding of the totality of entities must belong to Heidegger's own thematic access to Being, and *Dasein*'s Being, because he approaches man through the phenomena of death and anxiety, that is, through particular phenomena of completeness and negation. Third, this issue is relevant for Heidegger's upcoming ontological discussions of history and the "people."

This question is also important for the problem of the status of "nature." If the "natures" of Plato and Aristotle are not identical to the "nature" of natural science, how are we to understand the distinction? We might consider them to have discovered different entities from natural science, either by beginning from an identical thematizing or by thematizing different everyday entities to start with; or we might consider Plato's and Aristotle's "natures" to express the concrete characteristics of the modes of *Being* on which entities are thematized. In the latter case, a "nature" is a description *at* the ontological level of, say, the Cartesian or Kantian discussion, whereas the "nature" of natural science presupposes a prior, implicit, ontological projection. But then we see that the question must also be raised of the "historical" status of the different concrete philosophical arguments, and, consequently, of the differences among sciences and entities discovered on their basis. Heidegger has not yet uncovered the ground of the possibility of genuine concrete differences at this level. This problem leads to the next topic.

[3]

Heidegger's Enterprise as Thematic Understanding: Discussion

Heidegger's discussion of theory forces us to consider the possibility of his own thematic understanding of Being. He uses the term "thematizing" to describe his activity, the same term he uses to characterize scientific discovery of entities as purely discoverable objects. Consequently, we might say that his discussion of the genesis of thematic ontology from the everyday would be equivalent to his discussion of the change from practical concern to the theoretical discovery of Nature. But the issue cannot be so simple, because the changed understanding of Being relevant here is not change in the prethematic projection of modes of Being but a change from any prethematic projection to the thematizing of Being-as-such. Theoretical discovery of entities may be said to arise from the potentiality of discovering entities in their truth, a discovery that exists practically as well as theoretically. But what transformation makes possible fundamental ontology? Indeed, there is a prior question. Heidegger distinguished his fundamental ontology from previous metaphysics, or ontology, in his introduction, and I have just briefly alluded to such previous philosophy. But, apart from the question of the status of the philosophers' differences, we may ask: what transformation makes possible any shift from the theoretical and practical discovery of *entities* to the explicit treatment of the Being of these entities? Here I might suggest that if previous onotology has failed to uncover the gap between Being and entities, it has always, ultimately, treated Being itself as an entity, the highest and most general cause. Consequently, the explicit concern with Being is treated as an extension of the theoretical discovery of entities, and fails to disclose the radical split between Being and any possible entity. Heidegger has indicated this argument in his discussions of Descartes, Kant, and the traditional importance of pure intellectual intuition for philosophy, and we will consider this issue once more when we discuss his plan for the "destruction" of the history of ontology. But this makes the status of Heidegger's own fundamental ontology itself even more problematic. Presumably, we could say that fundamental ontology merely seeks to thematically disclose what all *Dasein* discloses—Being.

Yet, Being is everywhere projected unthematically: that is, its hiddenness, and the hiddenness of the world as the context belonging to *Dasein* that lets entities be encountered, appears to be of the essence of Being understood as the condition for the discovery of entities. Consequently, explicitly disclosing Being cannot simply be radicalizing man's understanding of Being, because the Being understood in this comprehension hides itself as Being. Indeed, it is tempting to suggest that man's care could not make the fundamental ontological thematizing of Being possible because the Being it understands is "there" only as hidden. Precisely man's ability to disclose prevents the full lighting of Being-as-such, not merely in the sense that our possibility of discovering entities is also the possibility of covering them up but also in the sense that Being can never be released as an "object" for pure thematizing.

But perhaps this is so for inauthentic existence, not authentic care? Indeed, authentic care is precisely that resolute understanding in which we are disclosed to ourselves as no entity. Cannot the Being that makes the authentic situation possible then be followed up?

The attempt explicitly to understand Being-as-such is not necessarily authentic, and Heidegger indicates that authentic care does not guarantee that the entities released in an authentic situation are grasped genuinely, although it is unclear whether what is not genuine is grounded in inauthentic relapse or can belong to authenticity itself. Still, *Dasein is* authentically disclosed when he reaches back to and projects himself upon his full finitude, the impossibility that constitutes his end, and his responsibility for, and lack of power over, his world. He projects himself upon his not being an entity who deals only with other entities, and, presumably, the Being that lies a priori in this understanding *is* Being-as-such, projected apart from any entities. But how could such Being become the proper object of thematizing? Obviously, Heidegger could have developed this question only after he explicated the meaning of Being; the discussion would likely have been an analysis of the ontological possibility of phenomenology. But if thematizing makes present and awaits, how could it ever release Being—one of whose modes is care—as an object? We might then suppose that Being-as-such can be objectified only within an authentic *situation,* that it can properly present itself only within the moment of vision, and not within the inauthentic present. Presumably, this is what Heidegger intends when he refers to his own hermeneutical *situation.* At best, the freeing of Being-as-such in light of its meaning is authentic thematizing. But, then, we must wonder whether Being can become an object for pure disclosing in any form of thematic objectification, because Being-as-such is not an entity. Indeed, we wonder whether the Being projected authentically must also remain hidden as such in order to enable entities, and particularly *Dasein,* to be freed in their authentic possibilities. If this is so, authentic existence also needs the obscurity of Being as Being, or even of the Situation as Situation. But, then, the authentic status of explicit fundamental ontology is complicated. And these complications are further exacerbated because Being must be projected upon Temporality if its comprehensibility is to be clarified. Indeed, the question of the ontological status of the explicit analysis of Temporality, the very question of the status of the inexplicit horizon for thematically understanding Temporality, remains unresolved.

[4]

The Horizons of Temporality: Discussion

This leads us to our final topic, Heidegger's analysis of the horizons of temporality. Why does Heidegger discuss horizons in addition to ecstasies? What does this discussion tell us about the interpretation of Temporality? And what more can we say about the relation between the transcendence to world and the transcendence to Being?

To say that temporality "horizons" is to say that it is by Being self-limiting. The horizonal temporalizing of temporality is the "closedness" by which man is open for entities, interpreted at the temporal level. It expresses the "inside" of the circle or spiral as which ecstatic *Dasein* leaps over entities and "to" which it leaps: it constitutes the "wherein." Both the openness of temporality and its closedness are thought from man's finitude, are thought as the meaning of the entity, man, who is most his own as the discloser of Being when anticipating his impossibility and resolving upon his guilt. Now, temporality is man's *meaning,* but because this meaning is not apart from him, temporality cannot be conceived as more perfect than man or his Being. Temporality's authentic characteristics, as the meaning of *Dasein*'s Being, are its self-limitations, its openness and closedness conceived solely in relation to the understanding of Being, and not in relation to Time's dependence on some other thing—say, an eternal Being of which it is the moving image. We thus cannot properly conceive temporality's finitude as yearning or as defensive enclosure; the ecstatic and horizonal characteristics of temporality are not deficiencies but its proper essence. Temporality temporalizes only as the finite presencing of the unity of the ecstasies and the horizons without being dependent on any thing, even the highest entities or most general features of entities, which are comprehensible only within its temporalizing. On the other hand, the fact that Heidegger's discussion of temporality's characteristics projects it upon *Dasein*'s transcendence as the discloser of Being points once more to the unique connection between temporality and the comprehension of Being, to the fact that the temporal meaning of man is thought here in relation to man's understanding of Being and not in a manner that projects it apart from *Dasein*. Presumably, as I have suggested, such a connection between Time, *Dasein,* and Being would only be strengthened were Temporality to be revealed as the meaning of Being-as-such.

Heidegger's failure to publish the portion of *Being and Time* that was to have explicitly considered Being (not merely *Dasein*) in relation to Time forces our discussion of his understanding of Being's Temporality to be largely speculative and questioning. The recent publication of his 1927 lectures, whose title may be translated as the *Fundamental Problems of Phenomenolgy,* however, does contain material relevant to the Temporality of Being. Even here, however, he did not develop most of the analyses decisive for the variety of problems we have noticed.

Heidegger projected the work in three parts. First, there is a "phenomenological-critical discussion of some traditional theses about Being." This develops much of the material that was to have comprised the second part of *Being and Time,* the "destruction" of the history of ontology. I will discuss this in Chapters 6 and 7, when we will consider Heidegger's analysis of history. In addition, this part contains versions of the analyses of Being-in-the-world, assertion, and truth that I have explicated on the basis of *Being and Time.* The second part was to have discussed the "fundamental-ontological question about the meaning of Being in general," the fundamental structures and ways of Being. Of this part, Heidegger completed only the first chapter, "the problem of the ontological difference (the difference of Being and beings)." The bulk of this chapter consists of an analysis of temporality, in particular, an analysis of the temporality of understanding, which I have discussed on the basis of *Being and Time,* and a discussion of the ordinary understanding of time, which I will discuss on the basis of the final published section of *Being and Time.* But the chapter also contains an analysis of Temporality and Being, highlighted by a "Temporal Interpretation of the Being of the ready-to-hand," which discusses "Presence [*praesenz*] as the horizonal schema of the ecstasy of making-present [*Gegenwartigens*]." In addition, it contains brief remarks on the ontological connection between science and philosophy and on "Temporality and the a priori of Being." The final three chapters of this part, however, were not written. They were to have discussed "the problem of the fundamental articulation of Being" (essence, existence), "the problem of the possible modifications of Being and the unity of its manifoldness," and "the truth character of Being." The third projected part, also unwritten, was to have had four chapters: "the ontical ground of ontology and the analytic of *Dasein* as fundamental ontology," "the a priority of Being and the possibility and structure of a priori knowledge," "the fundamental parts of the phenomenological method: reduction, construction, destruction," and "phenomenological ontology and the concept of philosophy."[10]

Let me now explicate the new material on the Temporality of Being. From its title we may see that it develops what Heidegger already indicates in *Being and Time*, namely, that the *horizonal* essence of Temporality is decisive for Being-as-such. Indeed, Heidegger described the first part of *Being and Time* as "the Interpretation of Dasein in terms of temporality and the explication of time as the transcendental horizon for the question of Being."[11] And we now have some understanding of what he means by a horizon. But the immediate question that arises is this: how is the connection of Being to Time's horizoning to be differentiated from the discussion of ecstatic-horizonal temporality that we just completed? The point to keep in mind is that Heidegger has not yet shown Temporality to be that which frees Being-as-such and its modes. For, while temporality's horizons enable *Dasein* to await, make present, and retain itself and other *entities* in their possibilities (their Being), we have not yet seen how, or, indeed, whether, Temporality allows the understanding of this Being-as-such. Heidegger briefly discusses this, for readiness-to-hand, in the *Fundamental Problems*. What is ready-

[10]Martin Heidegger, *Die Grundprobleme der Phanomenologie* (Frankfurt am Main: Vittorio Klostermann, 1975). All quotes are from pp. 32–33. Because this discussion has not yet been translated, my paraphrase will be quite literal, if inelegant.
[11]*Sein und Zeit*, p. 41.

to-hand can become unhandy: readiness-to-hand and unhandiness are variations of the fundamental phenomena of presence (*Anwesenheit*) and absence, which, in general, can be called Presence (*praesenz*). How is "Presence" distinguished from the temporal characteristics we have already discussed? Presence is the condition that makes understanding readiness-to-hand possible and therefore, must not be confused with the "now" or succession of "nows" that belong to present and ready entities within the world, for the ready-to-hand entity can be discovered only if readiness-to-hand has previously been understood. In fact, all the vulgar determinations of time that, say, the ancients used to distinguish entities, the "temporal," changeable, entities that partially are and partially are not; the entities beyond time, that is, the eternal, the always; and the timeless entities such as numbers and pure space—all these deal with the innerworldly time of entities. But these entities can first be revealed only on the ground of original Temporality. Indeed, that time-determinations function as naïve ontic classifications of entities is itself an indication of the authentic meaning of Temporality, and how such Temporality makes ordinary time possible will be Heidegger's theme in the final chapter of *Being and Time*.

But not only is Presence different from the now, it is also different from the present (*Gegenwart*) or making-present, even the moment of vision, for Presence is not characterized by the ecstatic structures of ecstatic temporality. As we have seen, the ecstasies are not simply raptures such that they are carried toward nothing or are undetermined: to each ecstasy there belongs an horizon that first fully determines its structure. Making-present, authentically or inauthentically, projects what it makes present upon something such as Presence. The ecstasy of the present is the condition for the possibility of *Dasein*'s projection in terms of Presence. As such, the ecstasy has a schematic "draft" of toward where it goes outside of itself, and it is Presence as an horizon that chiefly determines the wherein of the out to. The present projects itself ecstatically in terms of Presence. Presence, therefore, is not identical with the present but is the fundamental determination of its horizonal schema.

Making-present understands itself as such in terms of Presence, and the present, as a rapture, is a Being open for encountering what has been understood in terms of Presence: all that is encountered in making present has fundamentally been understood in Presence, that is, in the horizon to which the present has already been carried, and it has been understood *as* Present, that is, in terms of presence (*Anwesenheit*). Readiness- and unreadiness-to-hand signify modifications of Presence, and thus the Being of entities encountered within the world is presencial. But this means that we understand Being in terms of "the primordial horizonal schema of the ecstasy of temporality,"[12] and "Temporality is temporality with a look back in terms of its unity with its horizonal schemata" as the condition of the possibility of an understanding of Being.[13] In general, temporality, in the unity of its three ecstatic-horizons, is the condition of the possibility of all understanding grounded in transcendence; temporality is the primordial self-projection simply. The result of this discussion, therefore, is that "the readiness to hand of what is ready to hand, the Being of these entities, has been understood as Presence which Presence, as unconceptually understood, is already revealed in the self projection of temporality." "Readiness-to-hand formally says Presence, presence [*Anwesenheit*] but a Presence of its own type."[14]

For Heidegger to complete this discussion, he would need to explore the other two horizons and the interrelations of the three; he would need to develop the concrete possible modifications of Presence; and, presumably, he would need to repeat the entire analysis of *Dasein* in terms of Presence and its modes. All this goes beyond what he published in *Being and Time* or discussed in the *Fundamental Problems*. In the discussion before us, for example, he does not develop the Presencial meaning of readiness-to-hand as opposed to the Presencial meaning of presence-at-hand; he does not explore the detailed

---

[12] *Grundprobleme,* p. 436 (italics omitted).
[13] *Grundprobleme,* p. 436.
[14] *Grundprobleme,* p. 439 (italics omitted).

connection between the understanding of world and the under-standing of care; and he does not argue the status of care in terms of Presence.

I will return to certain issues concerning Temporality and Being and explicate additional material from the *Fundamental Problems* in Chapter 7. Here, however, we must recognize that none of the issues raised in this and previous chapters has yet received its fullest treatment within the confines of the pub-lished portions of *Being and Time*. We therefore turn to Heideg-ger's next chapter, his discussion of *Dasein*'s "historicality," in order to grasp his most complete analysis of man's possibilities, man's temporality, and man's connection to a people. Indeed, the additional material now available on the Temporality of Being does less to clarify the issues with which we are concerned than does the discussion of history.

6. Heideggerian History and Heideggerian Politics

We might suppose that Heidegger's analysis of man's temporality is complete. But, according to Heidegger, it is not. First, however adequate his ontological projection of *Dasein*'s end as death, he has not grasped *Dasein*'s other end, his beginning. Consequently, he has also failed to grasp the manner in which man stretches along from birth to death, and he has discussed the existential structures only with reference to static situations. Second, this insufficiency makes it impossible adequately to understand the meaning of man's everydayness. For the temporal analysis of existent*iell* everydayness has neglected the way in which man lives today by Being stretched along, because the analysis has immobilized *Dasein* in particular contexts. Now, we cannot consider such "stretching" to be equivalent to a calendrical enumeration of days, because man is, at root, not an entity in time whose time can be counted in the manner in which one understands things that are in and subject to time. Precisely what is missing in the analysis, therefore, is a discussion of the temporal meaning of man's everyday temporality, his everyday "historizing" or "happening" (*Geschehen*).[1] Neither has *Dasein*'s authentic happening, his authentic stretching, been explored.

---

[1] The English translators sometimes translate *geschehen* with the neologism "historizing" to remind us of Heidegger's connection of *geschehen* and *Geschichte* (history). This connection should be kept in mind, but I will confine myself to use of the more ordinary "happening." What I call happening would sometimes sound more idiomatic as "occurring," but "to occur" is used to translate *vorkommen* and refers to present-at-hand things.

[1]

History: Exposition

(§72–75) The way in which *Dasein* stretches between birth and death—the connectedness of life—might seem to be characterized properly as a sequence of experiences in time. This characterization leads us to consider as actual only the experience present-at-hand *now*, with the others being no longer or not yet actual: man hops from one now to another and is the sum of the momentary actualities of experience. We then believe that what remains constant in all this is the selfsame self who is in time and has the experiences. But when we interpret the self in this way, we are conceiving it inappropriately as something present-at-hand. If we then attempt to say that man's life is a series of experiences fitted into a "framework" constituted by the birth that is no longer and the death that is not yet, it becomes impossible to say how this framework remains present-at-hand when only the current experience is actual. Therefore, to understand properly the connectedness of life, we must see how birth and death *are* on the basis of man's Being. Man exists as already dying and as factically born, and he exists "between" them on the basis of his Being as care: the movement in which man stretches himself must be rooted in the temporal unity of his Being. The name for this movement is *Dasein*'s "happening." The question, then, is ontologically to understand historicality by clarifying the temporal conditions that make happening and its structure possible; and the aim of Heidegger's analysis is to make clear that *Dasein* is not temporal *because* he stands in history, but, rather, that he exists historically and *can* exist historically because he is temporal in the basis of his Being.

To begin to clarify historicality (*Geschichtlichkeit*), we must first develop the ordinary understanding of history (*Geschichte*). The dominant significations—all of which are to be distinguished from the historian's study of the past, which Heidegger will discuss later—are these: history is what is past and either no longer affects the present or continues to have its effect. History is something an entity has as it develops or declines, or even as it is epoch making and determines a future: in this sense history means a context of events drawing through past, present, and future. History is the totality of entities in time, the spiritual or cultural entities as opposed to the natural ones. History is whatever has been handed down to us.

The result of these significations is that the past is the central element in the concept of history: history is the happening of man in time, dominated by those past happenings with one another that have been handed down. But how does this happening of history belong to man? Man is ordinarily regarded as the subject of events and circumstances. But does some present-at-hand man become historical by becoming wrapped up in these events, or are circumstances and events "ontologically possible *only because Dasein is historical in his Being?*"[2] Heidegger examines this idea by considering the manner in which past entities are past. For what precisely is "past" in, say, the ancient equipment that is preserved in a museum and, through this preservation, is present now? What is it that these articles of equipment are no longer? It cannot simply be that they are decaying, for they continue to decay now, and it cannot simply be that they are no longer used, because something is past even in heirlooms presently in use. Rather, what is past is the world within which man encountered them: they are past as equipment within the world even though they are now present in the museum. But a world *is* in the manner of *Dasein;* therefore, it can be no longer only in the manner in which *Dasein* is no longer. *Dasein*'s past is not the no-longer-being of a thing. Rather, a man who no longer exists *is* as having-been. The antiquities of the past are past because they belonged to "the world of a *Dasein* that has been there."[3] That is, it is man who is primarily historical, not the other entities. These entities, whether equipment or the environing nature, are world historical because they are what they are by belonging to the world.

This still leaves the possibility that man first becomes historical by no longer being there. But if the temporality at *Dasein*'s heart temporalizes a having-been only as something futural, how can

[2] *Sein und Zeit,* p. 379.
[3] *Sein und Zeit,* p. 381.

this be so? Is not *Dasein* historical in his full existence? We must understand man's historicality in its ontological constitution if we are to resolve this question.

Because man's Being is grounded in temporality, Heidegger's ontological discussion of historicality proves to be "a more concrete working out of temporality."[4] Temporality was found to be the basis of anticipatory resoluteness; therefore, the first locus for the temporal discussion of historicality is the possibility of authentic happening. Now, the existential analysis does not tell us what we resolve upon in any particular case because we can disclose this only in a particular resolution. Moreover, the existential analysis does not attempt to project the general concrete possibilities of man upon authentic existence because the intention is merely to sketch the possibility of authentic disclosedness. Nonetheless it is necessary to ask from where in general *Dasein* can draw his possibilities. For although anticipatory projecting of myself upon death, upon the unoutstrippable possibility, guarantees authentic *wholeness*, I cannot gather my concretely disclosed possibilities from death itself.

The discussion of the past points to the taking over of my thrownness into the world as that which discloses the horizon from which the possibilities are grasped. In his thrownness, *Dasein* is submitted to a world of entities and exists with others. He is usually lost in the "they," understanding himself in the average possibilities freed in today's public interpretation. An authentic understanding cannot simply extricate him from these well-known yet ambiguous possibilities; rather, it resolutely seizes a possibility only for or against the interpretation that has been handed down. When *Dasein* resolutely comes back to himself, he discloses the current possibilities of authentic existing in terms of the heritage that he takes over: he hands down to himself the possibilities that have come down to him. The less ambiguously a man understands himself in relation to death, the less does he merely accidentally choose the possibility of his existence. That is, the more man is authentic—the more Being free for his death gives a man his goal—the more he is pushed to the

---

[4] *Sein und Zeit*, p. 382.

possibility of his existence, pulling back from all the comfortable possibilities into the simplicity of his "fate." Fate is Heidegger's term for the authentic happening in which *Dasein* hands himself down to himself in a possibility both inherited and chosen.

Such fate exists only in the freedom for death, only in man's letting death become powerful, and in man's understanding himself in the "superior power" of his finite freedom. This freedom *is* only in *Dasein*'s having chosen this choice, but it is in this freedom that man "takes over the powerlessness" of abandonment and "clearly sees the accidents of the disclosed situation."[5] Therefore, Heidegger can say that fate is "that powerless superior power which puts itself in readiness for adversities," because in Being fateful, in authentically handing myself down to myself, I must at once anticipate death and resolutely take over my own Being guilty.[6]

Fateful *Dasein,* as all *Dasein,* is essentially in a world with others. This means that his happening is always a "co-happening." The authentic happening of the community or people is called destiny (*Geschick*). *Dasein*'s fateful disclosing has already been "guided in advance, in our Being-with one another in the same world and in our resoluteness for definite possibilities."[7] Fateful happening is, thus, always determined by the happening of the community or people that runs in advance of any man and cannot be conceived as something constructed from the mere occurring together of separate subjects. "*Dasein*'s fateful destiny in and with his 'generation' makes up the full authentic happening of *Dasein*."[8] This power of destiny itself becomes free "only in communicating and in struggling."[9]

This discussion of fate makes clear that fate can exist only on the basis of temporality. For *Dasein* to exist fatefully, he must be futurally free for death and able to let this shattering against death throw him back against his "there." Only then can he hand down to himself the possibility he has inherited, and be in his

[5] *Sein und Zeit,* p. 384. My translation (italics omitted).
[6] *Sein und Zeit,* p. 385.
[7] *Sein und Zeit,* p. 384.
[8] *Sein und Zeit,* pp. 384–85. My translation.
[9] *Sein und Zeit,* p. 384.

(present) moment. This is to say that authentic temporality is the condition for the possibility of authentic historicality.

Because the meaning of authentic historicality can be seen most clearly as the taking over of what has been handed down, we can develop the argument by elaborating authentic having-been. When resoluteness projects itself upon a specific existen-*tiell* potentiality, it can do so only because temporality makes it possible for such a potentiality to be explicitly gleaned from the way in which *Dasein* traditionally has been understood. The explicit handing down of, the explicit going back to, a possibility of the man who has been there is called the "repetition" of this possibility. Such repetition does not require explicit knowledge of the origin of the repeated possibility, nor does it mean that one discloses a past of *Dasein* in order to actualize it again. For the repetition of a possibility is grounded in resoluteness, and this means that the repetition is always a "reciprocative" rejoinder to the possibility that has been there, a rejoinder made in the authentic present. It is therefore a disavowal of that "past" we see working itself out "today." That is to say, we cannot understand repetition to repeat possibilities when they are held in inauthentic understanding. *Dasein*'s repetition of a possibility is the possibility of choosing his hero; and this becoming "free for the struggle of loyally following" the "repeatable" is grounded in resolve.[10] Indeed, "if everything 'good' is a heritage and the character of 'good' lies in making possible authentic existence, then the handing down of a heritage constitutes itself in resoluteness."[11] But this means that *Dasein*'s repeating, his explicit existence as fatefully bound up with his heritage, his resolute handing down of himself to the disclosure of the moment, is based on the ecstatic openness of temporality. Because the central ecstasy in temporality is the future, man's historicality is basically grounded in the future, not the past. But the dominance of handing down and repeating in historicality makes clear why, in authentic historicality, having-been comes to the fore.

The present discussion, according to Heidegger, leaves unre-

[10] *Sein und Zeit*, p. 385.
[11] *Sein und Zeit*, pp. 383–84. My translation.

solved the following questions: how could such fateful happening constitute the connectedness of man or help us understand such connectedness? Is man's connectedness merely a sequence of resolutions? Or is the question of connectedness based on an inadequate interpretation of Being whose roots lie in man's inauthentic historicality?

Heidegger's discussion of *inauthentic* historicality develops the understanding of world history that he already sketched. *Dasein*'s historicality is the happening of a world because man is always in the world. The entities within the world are world historical only in a secondary sense, but our projection of our Being upon these entities makes us understand our historicality as world historicality; and our understanding of Being as presence-at-hand makes us experience and interpret the world historical as something present that comes along and disappears. *Dasein* therefore considers his history in relation to the many opportunities, circumstances, and affairs he awaits; and from this fallen dispersion the question arises how man himself can be "connected" and connect his experiences. But this means that the question of connectedness is grounded in irresoluteness and is an inappropriate way of uncovering the wholeness of man's happening. Authentic historicality, on the other hand, is the happening of anticipatory resoluteness, the "repetition of the heritage of possibilities by handing these down to oneself in anticipation."[12] And *here* we can see that the question of connectedness does not properly arise because the whole of existence is stretched along in such historicality: resoluteness against distraction *is* the steadiness of self with which fate incorporates birth, death, and what is between. In fateful repetition *Dasein* brings himself back to what has been; but this "birth" is caught up in *Dasein*'s coming back from the unoutstrippable possibility of death. Indeed, such resoluteness is *Dasein*'s loyalty to his own self. But, at the same time, a resoluteness that is ready for anxiety is "a possible way of revering the sole authority that a free existing can have"; it is a way of revering the repeatable possibilities of existence.[13]

[12] *Sein und Zeit*, p. 390.
[13] *Sein und Zeit*, p. 391.

We might still say that such reverent constancy exists only with an act of resolve, and "acts" of resolve are actually experiences only as long as they last. To claim this, however, is to misinterpret resolve and to forget the meaning of repetition. For resoluteness has already gone before every possible moment of vision that may spring from it. As fate, it is freedom to give up a definite resolution on the basis of the demands of some possible situation: *Dasein*'s resolute steadiness is not formed by joining moments but arises from the unity of ecstatic temporality, which has already been stretched along.

History: Analysis

We may begin our consideration of historicality by distinguishing Heidegger's analysis from the familiar argument that man is essentially historical because he is determined by his age and his time. Such arguments misconceive man as an entity in time, subject to the principles of historical movement, whether or not these are understood to lead to a final result. Heidegger is not an Hegelian or Marxist and does not believe himself to be an historicist. His discussion of man's historicality is intended to be a discussion of historicality as belonging to man's Being when Being has the noncausal status he attributes to it. Man's *Being* is authentically or inauthentically historical, and, consequently, his understanding of Being is historical, but this does not mean that man is somehow caused by the efficient or material causality of an "age." Rather, historicality spells out the meaning of his temporality: it is the manner in which possibilities present themselves to *Dasein*. Historicality does not mean the becoming or changing of an entity in time but is the ground of the kind of not-yet distinctive to *Dasein*. Presumably, even if there are permanent possibilities for man's guidance, possibilities either eternal or there as long as and whenever man is, Heidegger would still believe these possibilities to be historical in his sense. Whether historicality *can* in fact free all decisive possibilities is a question I will address shortly, but here it is necessary to protect Heidegger's argument from premature identification with historicism.

The peculiarity of Heidegger's concept of historicality comes to light if we recognize that it is *not* intended to be dependent on the existence of historians or on the modern experience of historical and cultural variablity. Heidegger's argument is meant to suggest a structure belonging to all men, even those least obviously historical, and the oblivion of authentic historicality is, if anything, greatest in an age such as ours, replete with "history" yet dominated by the immediately present. Indeed, the historicality of which Heidegger speaks is constitutive of old communities immersed in tradition even if the formal discussion of "tradition" is a categorical discovery of the modern historical consciousness. Moreover, Heidegger's analysis of historicality does not necessarily connect historicality to the thematic or unthematic concern with antiquity or "past" ages. His discussion of the *Dasein* who "has been there" does not determine anything about the length or distance a past event must have in order to become historical. Such determining would belong to the ontic consideration of the concrete characteristics of historical things; moreover, it would be considering them as they are presented inauthentically.

By locating Heidegger's discussion of historicality at the ontological level, we set the stage for developing the problems we have already raised, now in relation to this new discussion of historicality. But here a prior problem emerges. What is the *precise* connection between historicality and the other ontological characteristics of *Dasein*? Historicality is a possibility that may be existent*ielly* seized and developed in many ways, but this characteristic does not differentiate it from other possibilities. Further, as a possibility, it is conditioned by the three ecstasies of temporality, but this does not differentiate it from any other existential characteristic. Rather, historicality appears to be somehow broader or more general than any particular existential structure. In particular, it is care when caring is considered from the point of view of movement or stretching, caring when an act of care is considered to belong to a "moving" whole of *Dasein*'s type. Heidegger's discussion of historicality elaborates his analysis of temporality because it spells out how having-been and Being futural make possible what is between guilt and dying.

Authentic Resolve and the Choiceworthiness of Ends: Analysis

The outstanding positive result of Heidegger's analysis of historicality concerns his discussion of fate. His discussion develops the ontological answer to the question: from "where" do possibilities come? We remember that every world is constituted by that for the sake of which man is. Ontologically, what is decisive about these ends is both how they are disclosed and whether they constitute significance authentically or inauthentically. Consequently, their substantive content is *not* ontologically relevant as such. Nonetheless, all concrete existent*iell* possibilities must be disclosed to us as somehow belonging to existence. And if existence is historical, the possibilities must be historically disclosed. Both authentically and inauthentically, possibilities come to light in a reaching forward that reaches back, as this is framed by dying and guilt. Authentically, our concreteness is disclosed as fate. Even the most permanent and powerful of human possibilities—say, the philosophic life itself—can be chosen only as and because it is presented in the fate and tradition I project. That what I can be can be mine only as traditional means that my possibilities are subject to all the covering of tradition, but were they not traditional, they could not be mine in any way. Authentic resolve on death shatters the obfuscation of tradition but never in a way that lets an everpresent standing possibility emerge authentically. Rather, an authentic possibility comes to govern from out of the sheer openness of dying and guilt. I disclose it in its intelligibility to myself in my pure ability to disclose. A potentiality for Being can *be* only as "mine" because it cannot be except through the individualized openness of thrownness and guilt. Consequently, an authentic possibility can be only by coming to light for me as I am "there," and I am always "there" historically. Whatever I might later say to distinguish transitory and conventional elements in my ends from permanent and essential ones, authentic possibilities, according to Heidegger, *are* only in my fate, only in my concrete historical disclosure.

It is tempting to say that any man who seizes his fate would necessarily take leave of all reverence and obligation because what is can be revealed fatefully only to *this Dasein*. Consequently, any man would be his own final court of appeal. But, according to Heidegger, fateful choice, like existent*iell* resolution, cannot properly be conceived as arbitrary willing because it concerns the way in which possibilities are presented to *Dasein* and not their validity within that presentation. Indeed, Heidegger speaks of fateful resolve as the self's loyalty to himself and his reverence for the repeatable possibilities of existence. This means that loyalty and reverence are still experienced by authentic man, indeed that authentic *Dasein* experiences these in their proper, ownmost, or authenic Being. But, then, does not Heidegger elevate self-loyalty above every other loyalty? This is surely not his intention, if the "self" of self-loyalty is understood as the "I" opposed to "we," the individual as opposed to the collective subject. Rather, the self to whom I am loyal is the self I disclose for my repetition as discloser of my own Being, that is, it is the "I" of authentic identity.

By locating reverence at the heart of authenticity, Heidegger intends to indicate that the possibility of experiencing what is monumental and heroic belongs to man as the authentic discloser of Being and is not merely reducible to interpretative error arising from man's misunderstanding of himself as present-at-hand. This is also the point of his later short discussion of Nietzsche. Whatever we may say about the fate of Kantian moral standards, eternal standards, unchanging rank orders of human possibilities and values, Heidegger attempts to describe not merely inauthenticity but also authenticity in a manner that would permit some such possibilities of guiding authority to come to light. Precisely among the other goals of Heidegger's analyses of human existence is the finding of the source of high (and low), of authority to be revered, in man's authentic disclosing of Being. Although Heidegger's intention is more manifest in his discussion of the gods in his later works, just as the split he intends between his thought and metaphysics is more manifest, it is clear enough here.[14]

---

[14]Consider Leo Strauss, "Philosophy as Rigorous Science and Political Philosophy," *Interpretation*, Summer, 1971.

Indeed, Heidegger now experiments with the understanding that everything "good" is a heritage and that authentic existence is itself "good." The quotation marks indicate Heidegger's earlier connection of good to present- and ready-to-hand entities and his separation of authenticity from moral evaluation. His point here is to suggest how what is good—that is, what is authoritatively guiding—is freed by Being presented in the authentic repetition of possibilities. Ontologically, his argument unites the possibility of goodness and the possibility of Being one's own. My authenticity (my "ownness") becomes concrete in the fateful handing down of my heritage, and that heritage's possibilities, repeated authentically, are the sole authority revered by my existence. The presentation of such possibilities, in turn, is inevitably connected with the full disclosure of a self who is continually framed by the individuating nothingness of guilt and dying. The goodness of resolve is thus the authentic ground of reverence for tradition; presumably, it is also the authentic ground for whatever "goodness" is presented in possibilities misinterpreted as ends that fulfill and satisfy.

Now, it is clear that authentic possibilities, whatever their content, disclose situations and moments that could not imply an unalterable course of action: resoluteness is not to be confused with stubbornness or blindness, and any particular decision may disclose possibilities leading us to give up the original resolve. It is also clear that an authentic fate does not, and perhaps cannot, present possibilities and situations that are themselves unchanging rules and regulations. Beyond this, however, we may wonder what more we can say about the guiding possibilities freed by authenticity. Is it not true, for example, that everything "bad" is also a heritage that can be repeated fatefully; or need what is bad be inauthentic flight? Can Heidegger's analysis fully make intelligible the manner in which "good" possibilities display their choiceworthiness?

We must understand fateful resolution to free both "good" and "bad" in at least one sense: any particular world releases both the serviceable and the detrimental; and, consequently, a situation frees instrumental good and bad in accord with a man's authentic possibility. But when the for-the-sakes-of, the human possibilities themselves, happen fatefully, can they be both "good" or "bad"? Does revealing possibilities in authentic repetition as my own and our own by itself disclose a difference between good and bad "ends"?

The issue here arises from the fact that, traditionally, the ways of life that guide men by being choiceworthy and authoritative, by being "good," are found in his nature or in his reason—that is, in his essential possibilities. Such natural possibilities are then *opposed* to the particular and peculiar circumstances of any man, that which exists as his own—his own body, his own traditions, his own conventions. But, for Heidegger, a man's "possibilities" are released through seizing what is most his own, his own death as it released from the heritage of his people. Thus, precisely as we are attempting to distinguish Heidegger's analysis from historicism or conventionalism, precisely as we are attempting to consider his analysis at the level of Being, there emerges once more the difficulty of conceiving the traditional political philosophical problem of the choiceworthiness of the various ways of life. For all ways in which we can speak intelligibly of guidance, direction, and authority, such that these are not ultimately relative, apparently depend on the kind of universality in possibility that Heidegger denies for man. This is even true of the non-absolute Aristotelian prudence or the Platonic measure of the fitting, for in the last analysis these rely on an understanding of what is natural in the humanly noble, the humanly just, and the humanly good. Heidegger's discussion of fateful resolution cannot simply be identified with what sooner or later becomes arbitrary convention, but if "goodness" is grounded in what is not permanently possible, is it not finally reduced to the arbitrariness of one's own?

We may ask this question more forcefully by examining whether the intelligibility of guides and standards must indeed be rooted in permanent natural possibilities. When, following our usual practice, we consider the classical defense of the superiority of the theoretical life or the classical defense of the political supremacy of the man of great soul, we see that such defense is conducted in terms of self-sufficiency, comprehensiveness, and what is attractive or stunning. Philosophy is the most self-sufficient, most comprehensive, and most noble of human possibilities, and it is so because it treats the most self-sufficient, comprehensive, and beautiful—the cosmos, or Being itself. The man of great soul is the most free, most comprehensive, and most unique of political men. This understanding does not equate such ways of life with the perfections to which they are oriented or see political and theoretical excellence simply as instrumentalities to other ends. Rather, statesmanship and philosophy are characterized by an openness, or imperfection, whether or not this openness is grasped properly, as it is not grasped properly by political men. But this imperfection is comprehensible as such only on the basis of the perfection for which it strives. Moreover, the desirability—and undesirability—of other ways of life is intelligible in relation to greater or lesser imitation of the overarching political and philosophic possibilities. For Heidegger, however, all such philosophy and politics is dependent on the *Dasein*—the openness to Being—of the philosopher or statesman; and all classical defense of philosophy or politics is conducted in relation to a sufficiency and comprehensiveness that misinterprets man's existence.

Now, Heidegger's own discussion of authenticity is conducted similarly but, in his view, with ontologically appropriate meaning. Death is the end that constitutes a whole whose beginning is guilt; man's Being a whole—man's Being in his self-sufficiency, comprehensiveness, and uniqueness—is his fateful repetition of possibilities disclosed as stretching between guilt and death. The terms of Heidegger's discussion therefore remain the formal terms in which guides, standards, and rank orders traditionally have been comprehended. Perhaps, then, it is difficult to account for the full intelligibility of authoritative "good" in *Being and Time* only when considering the classical connection of nature and possibility?[15] We might then suggest that the comprehensiveness and sufficiency of authentic Being is of the sort that we know as the life history of the self more or less within the development of the people. But, even apart from the root rela-

[15]Consider Plato's *Laches.*

tivism of such analyses, human "selves" guided by what is implicit in their personal life history are entities who have not been conceived appropriately as *Dasein*. From Heidegger's perspective, all philosophy of life, even when returned to the Hegelian context from which it springs in opposition, considers man as a subject and "business enterprise." This is also true for the wholeness of the Hegelian thinker and his time. Consequently, although Heidegger's connection of authentic "possibility" and radical "ownness" belongs together with the traditional terms of discussion in political philosophy, this does not mean that such ontological intelligibility can allow these terms their traditional function.

The wholeness of a man who is authentically framed by death and guilt is the wholeness of man as discloser of Being. His comprehensiveness is equivalent to the a priori comprehensiveness of Being and world, as that which must first be understood if entities are to be released for any concrete use or function. The historicality of a people, and my authentic fate within that destiny, include my possibilities and run ahead of any particular concern. But such a priori comprehensiveness is precisely *not* the a priori comprehensivenss of the powers of the soul, whose fullest development and order requires the fullest possible orientation to the permanent cosmos. It is, rather, a comprehensiveness that can no more be understood in the nexus of formal and final causality than can Being itself. Therefore, although Heidegger's discussion of authentic fate makes use of terms like wholeness and self "constancy," these terms do not serve the function of a metaphysic of "ethics" or of political philosophy because they belong to the fundamental-ontological characterization. In general, Heidegger's analysis of authenticity neither originates nor employs a conceptual structure that constitutes or gives rise to a "new" ethic or to a new defense of the old. More than this, it obscures the intelligibility of questions about the concrete comprehensiveness and clash of possibilities, as we will see again in the following section.

We may still wonder, however, whether Heidegger's ontological discussion of authentic fate can in some way guide choice, and how to conceive its validity or invalidity if it is not completely neutral. Let us, therefore, turn from authentic wholeness itself and once more consider the authentic situation coordinate with the seizing of fate. The situation wrests genuine possibilities from the fallen public: it frees man's possibilities in their authentic Being and therefore frees possibilities in their a priori temporality. If such possibilities are developed in their genuine disclosedness we may say that we are authentic. Presumably, man's authentic disclosing of his possibilities permits the freeing of other entities in *their* ownmost readiness- or presence-at-hand because the Temporal meaning of all Being must also have its primordial and derivative (ordinary) modes. In this sense, the authentic possibility can be a for-the-sake-of, an "end," that constitutes a world or situation; the authentic possibility therefore guides or orders entities. But how can *Dasein*'s authentic possibilities ultimately provide guidance if no one authentic possibility can, as such, be more choiceworthy than another? To free a possibility authentically is precisely not to free it as belonging to a proper way of life insofar as the propriety of ways of life is finally defended in the traditional terms we have discussed. Rather, it is to free it as belonging to man's a priori transcendence to Being and, consequently, *as* belonging to that Being. This means that the issue of "rank order" of possibilities, the issue of the choice of a way of life, rests with the inauthentic public: the "goodness" Heidegger finds in authentic possibilities does not appear to enable us to discriminate among them. Authentic fate is a transformation of the averageness and impersonality of "our" possibilities. But the public world is precisely the world where authentically historical possibilities are leveled on the basis of misinterpreting man as an object. The theoretical interpretation of man's Being then formulates itself in the terms of eternal needs, eternal powers, and objective fulfillment that Heidegger seeks to overcome. But, apparently, authentic resolve on one's fate can at most newly disclose possibilities in the ranking they have for the "they." Obviously there is no guarantee of the genuineness of any specific ranking, either in the current public or in the philosophical interpretations; and, according to

Heidegger, the dominant philosophical interpretations from Plato through Nietzsche and Scheler are misconceived.

Destiny: Analysis

We may develop these issues still further by considering Heidegger's discussion of the people's "destiny." For Heidegger, the people is the authentic analogue to the public; people or "generation" is an ontological term. Consequently, questions about the *ontic* limits and range of a people—questions, for example, about whether "people" corresponds to the legal political community, whether it encompasses the broader nation, whether a generation is twenty years or thirty years long—are, from Heidegger's perspective, ontologically inappropriate. Authentic man's situation is necessarily a "popular" situation, just as inauthentic *Dasein*'s everyday activities belong to the public world.

Nonetheless, I believe that Heidegger's use of "people" or public in fact depends upon a commonsense understanding of its concrete range. Let us consider first the analogous case of the individual. The authentic *Dasein* is the Being of the "individual" whose death and life history have ordinary meaning. However much Heidegger's understanding of authentic Being, and, indeed, of inauthentic Being, shows the inadequacy of the ordinary ontic discrimination, only this ordinary *ontic* separation of individuals enables him and us to hold in advance the entity whose Being as "*Dasein*" he is interpreting. Similarly, although "public" is meant ontologically, the public equipment, the public norms and rules, the "public" interpretation of possibilities and the destiny of the people are apparently intelligible as the Being of an entity roughly equivalent to the specificity and developing history of a politically organized linguistic community. By "people" Heidegger means the Greeks or his generation of Germans but also Germans as "Germany" facing these political decisions. But this suggests unclarity, for the linguistic community and its chief political organization are not as such ontically identical. Indeed, this was notoriously true of Heidegger's own Germany. We may wonder, therefore, whether Heidegger's discussion is distorted by his failure sufficiently to consider the ontic presuppositions that enable the ontological discussion of the people's destiny to be intelligible.

Yet, is not Heidegger's entire enterprise precisely the attempt to specify what we presuppose man is whenever we deal with or study him? That is correct. But in ontological analysis we must also presuppose, at least to begin with, concrete characteristics of the entity whose Being we are interpreting. For although Being is not the cause of entities, and although Heidegger seeks to understand Being without grounding it in its utility for understanding entities, he argues that Being is always the Being of entities.[16] And here our very unclarity about the entity that *is* as public or people indicates that Heidegger has not sufficiently developed the ontological status of the limits and specificity of the people.

It is, therefore, tempting to ask how a people can have a destiny if "it" is not guilty and cannot die; and, further, we may wonder how a people can resolve, or want to have a conscience. What could be the analogue to these phenomena at the level of the people? The people's destiny is freed in communicating and struggling; that is, it is wrested from fallen public discourse. This apparently makes "destiny" subordinate to fate, not in the sense that destiny is pieced together from individual "fates," but because the popular destiny within which fate is possible is first freed by the anticipatory resoluteness that uncovers an individual fate. Does this then mean that the authentic self's self-loyalty is equally a loyalty to his people's destiny? That would appear true, because there is no fate without destiny. But if there is no public anticipatory resoluteness analogous to the individual's anticipatory resoluteness, how may we understand the ontological ground of public responsibility? How may we understand the Heideggerian ontological ground of making "good" laws, or of properly directing the people? Presumably, these laws arise as part of the destiny revealed in the individual grasping of fate. But for what *entity* is the seizing of destiny a guide to the

---

[16]*Sein und Zeit*, p. 6. Also consider L. M. Vail, *Heidegger and Ontological Difference* (University Park: Pennsylvania State University Press, 1972).

situation, if it is unclear what the unit is that we first of all consider to be as an ontological people or public? What is the "state" to which statesmanship (understood as authentic discovery of the possibilities of the people) applies? Heidegger fails to develop the coherence or lack of coherence between the people's destiny and the individual's fate within that destiny. (This failure is especially evident if "people" is considered to be connected to the state.) The whole of possibilities as they belong to one *Dasein* is framed by death and guilt, but Heidegger leaves unexplored both the whole of possibilities as it is in the public and the precise connection of the individual and political situations freed within the fated possibility.

To say these issues are unexplored is not to say they could not be developed. But Heidegger's failure to examine the concrete unit that *is* as a people would make this developing particularly problematic. For his omission leaves unclear how any particular possibility finds its place within potential destinies. That is, we cannot say whether the authentic possibilities concretely pursued by *Dasein* can all equally be freed in the people's destiny, or how the various potential destinies affect one another. Thus, when the entity that is as people or public is left unclear, it becomes difficult to understand the relation between concrete political standards and laws and the activities or ways of life that are authentically meaningful. Heidegger's concern in *Being and Time* and other works is structured, among other things, by the problems we associate with the Nietzschean uncovering of nihilism and the "decline of the West."[17] But is the relevant public or people the "West," is it our German or European destiny, is it the lingering philosophical epoch of the Greeks or the moderns, is it the public connected to a transpolitical art or profession? The formal discussion of public or popular destiny need not be limited to or necessarily imply any of these. But can the way in which "one's" possibilities or "their" possibilities are transformed into my possibilities and our possibilities be identi-

---

[17]Consider Stanley Rosen, *Nihilism* (New Haven: Yale University Press, 1971). For a discussion of the people and historicality also consider Werner Marx, *Heidegger and the Tradition* (Evanston: Northwestern University Press, 1971).

cal for any of these entities that could be a public? That is not possible, for the concrete coherence of these publics is doubtful. The political horizons of a particular community are necessarily closed to the full possibilities encompassed in the destinies of "publics" whose possibilities lie beyond politics. The narrowness of political communities, for example, conflicts with the breadth of more universal religious, scientific, and artistic communities. But if possibilities are presented in destiny, which destiny guides my fate? And if no particular destiny guides my fate, then Heidegger's analysis has not freed the intelligibility of the complexity of choice that *Dasein* faces.

Yet, is not Heidegger guided precisely by the need to understand complex existent*iell* choice ontologically? Yes. But the vagueness of the ontic referent of the public or people makes it difficult to grasp the concrete presentation of the fundamental possibilities *as* choiceworthy, because the implied inclusiveness of "destiny" at any time hides the exclusivity or contradictory nature of traditionally presented possibilities at any time. This obfuscates both the attractiveness of—and the clash among—possible ways of life or guiding possibilities in general. It is not clear how Heideggerian destiny can present possibilities in a manner that would allow their ontic development in any but an arbitrary way. Moreover, this problem is not merely "ontic." The unexplored nature of the kind of totality belonging to a people's destiny makes it impossible to state a wholeness in destiny that is comparable with the wholeness permitted by dying, and this then leaves the status of the wholeness of tradition and possibilities unclear. The thrust of my argument, therefore, is not merely that Heidegger's analysis obscures both the problem of choice among ways of life and the manner in which certain ways are both limited and presented as possibilities within concrete communities. For what if the rest of his analysis is proper? Rather, I argue that the finitude or limit of man that Heidegger seeks to ground by understanding man's Being as *Dasein* is obscured by his very analysis, and that he does not present with sufficient clarity the possible totality of finite destiny.

But perhaps this difficulty is an artifact of Heidegger's discussion of the people's destiny. For it is the individual's authenticity

that first appears necessary to free the destiny to which he belongs, and it is ultimately neither destiny nor the individual's fate
but the Being projected in authentic understanding that is the
home of totality. We have, however, already discussed the
obscurity of the relation among possibilities within an individual's anticipatory resolve. Beyond this, we must also remember
that the resolute individual wrests his fate from the averageness
of the public possibilities of the they-self. He casts the ordinary
possibilities on the possibility of radical nullity, thereby freeing
them as *Dasein*'s. But if an authentic fate cannot be except as a
transformation of the public possibilities, the status of the public
is decisive. Still, the public is constituted primarily by the they-
self, by the choice of the "they" as the hero for the sake of whom
Dasein is. Consequently, we might now argue, the transformation
of the public into a people with a destiny is explicable as the
transformation from individual inauthenticity to authenticity,
and the totality and order of the people's possibilities can be
understood as the authentic anticipation of death because the
totality of the inauthentic public has been understood previously
in the misinterpreted totality belonging to the public self. But
the sense in which a particular self could be a "complete" public
self is mysterious. Any particular posibility and mood, and the
entities discovered with this, are implicated in the they's ambiguity and averageness, and in this sense Heidegger claims that
one self can represent the others in the everyday public. But
concretely, no self is all possibilities; therefore, the concrete inclusiveness of the public possibilities cannot be equated with any
particular self. But then we see once more that the precise manner in which the public contains the totality of possibilities it
presents is unexplored. How compatible, how open and how
closed, how amenable to contradiction and ranking, are the possibilities insofar as they are presented as possibilities? What is the
possible order and extent of the possibilities—that is, to what
degree does their "goodness" as possibilities in Heidegger's
sense allow this issue to be meaningful? Once we have seen that
the issues of compatibility and extent are central to the presentation of possibilities *as* possibilities, we can then observe that
Heidegger's discussion of averageness, curiosity, and ambiguity

does not show how these ontological characteristics could free the totality of the public's possibilities.

By choosing authentically, the fateful man transforms the public into a people, a public that is authentically historical. Presumably, such a people stretches along as *Dasein* stretches along and has the self-constancy appropriate to man. Perhaps, then, the people's totality *can* be reduced directly to the self's totality, and the question of the range and extent of possiblities can be handled through this reduction. But no particular self has the totality of concrete possibilities that the people presents. More, the correspondence between the "totality" of a people's destiny and the "totality" that the authentic individual gives his possibilities by freeing them all in their nullity is even weaker than the correspondence between the average presenting of possibilities by the public and by the particular they-self. This correspondence is weak because Heidegger discusses nothing "popular" that is analogous to individual death and guilt, whereas inauthentic man and his public may both be captured by inauthentic conceptualizations of wholeness and totality. Consequently, the problems raised by Heidegger's ambiguity concerning the status of the possible totality of a people's destiny, and his ambiguity concerning the concrete entities that "public" and "people" ontologically ground, are not false problems.[18]

[2]

Heidegger and the Nazis: Discussion

Although Heidegger's analysis of authenticity does not result in concrete standards or a concrete rank order of human activities, and although authenticity is itself neither a "value" to be chosen nor the equivalent of the "formal" moral personality associated with Kant, we may still ask whether there is something common to the concrete guidance that all authentic *situations* may reveal. In particular, we may ask about concrete connec-

---

[18]I have not completed discussion of these problems. We will return to them—more concretely—in the next section, and discuss them once more in the conclusion.

tions between a people's destiny and an authentic man within that destiny. Here, two examples present themselves. One is Heidegger's own thematic enterprise as he pursues it. The second is his activity as rector of Freiburg University during part of the first year of Hitler's regime and his speeches from that period. We have partially explored the first topic and will continue to discuss it after we have considered Heidegger's understanding of the connection between historicality and historiology. The second topic is difficult for several reasons beyond its ugliness. First, it cannot be clear that Heidegger's understanding in 1933 and 1934 is equivalent to his understanding in *Being and Time*. In particular, the discussions connecting statesmanship, work, and Being in the *Introduction to Metaphysics* and *Origin of the Art Work* might be considered the most relevant texts. Second, there can be no guarantee that Heidegger's actions and speeches stem from a genuine resolution. Nonetheless, these events are useful in understanding the inclusiveness of a people's destiny and the possibilities of guidance that emerge when concrete issues are considered in the light of their Being freed and transformed by resolute choice.

Heidegger's most complete public statement concerning his activity as rector appeared in an interview given in 1966 and published, as planned, after his death.[19] Heidegger says that he took the rector's position at the urging of the faculty; he had serious doubts up to the morning of his institution, because he knew he would have to compromise himself. He resigned in 1934, after less than a year in office, over governmental interference with the selection of faculty deans. He denies encouraging book burning and denies forbidding his teacher, Husserl, a Jew, access to the philosophical library. Heidegger says that he forbade the hanging of "Jewish Posters" and asks his readers to consider his speeches of the time in the context of the time. He speaks of his concern for one of his Jewish students, Helene Weiss. He explains that he was absent from Husserl's funeral because of illness. He appears to place responsibility for his

[19]*Der Spiegel*, May 31, 1976. The interview was conducted on September 23, 1966.

break with Husserl on Husserl's wife and on a public discussion of his (and Scheler's) thought by Husserl, and he apologizes for his "human failure" in not expressing gratitude to Husserl once more before Husserl's death. He points out that his seminars were attended by informers during the Nazi regime and that his successor was considered by the Nazis to be the first National Socialist rector; they believed Heidegger to be the most dispensable of Freiburg professors, and he was, therefore, drafted into the people's militia in 1944. Finally, he claims that those who heard his 1935 lecture on metaphysics would have understood properly his remark on the "inner truth and greatness of the National Socialist movement" without benefit of the parenthetical explanation written in 1935 but not presented then ("the encounter between global technology and modern man").[20]

Heidegger does not claim, however, that he took the rector's position solely or even primarily in order to protect the university from the Nazis. Rather, he indicates that he had reflected about the political situation, and, especially, about the university situation, in the years just before 1933, and that he had discussed possibilities of university reform with several other faculty members. Heidegger used the opportunity afforded by the rectorate and the new regime to attempt these reforms, but he was unsuccessful, lacking support both from the education ministry and from his own faculty. The precise direction of these reforms is unclear, although Heidegger remarks that he desired greater student participation. The reforms seem to have been part of an overall attempt to revitalize German scholarship.

Heidegger's activities hardly demonstrate that his understanding of Being necessarily leads to Nazism, because the depth and extent of his support for the regime was not sufficient to sustain this claim. Nor, however, is it true that his philosophical activity was wholly without consequences, because his various remarks about labor service, military service, and, most obviously, scholarship and the university in his 1933 and early 1934 speeches are grounded in the attempt to root them in their

[20]Martin Heidegger, *Einfuhrung in die Metaphysik* (Tubingen: Max Niemeyer Verlag, 1966), p. 152.

original soil, that is, in Being and in man as transcendent to Being. From this perspective, scholarship itself is freed as an activity—is possible as an activity—only on the basis of the destiny that belongs to the people. The "new teaching" means "becoming master over [the unknown] in conceptualized knowledge and becoming secure in one's sight of the essential. It is out of such teaching that true research awakes. It is bound up with the whole because it is rooted in the people and bound to the state."[21] This destiny, moreover, is equally capable of freeing other activities, although scholarship occupies the central place, at least for the scholars. There

> will flourish the threefold commitment and service of the German student body, once in the community of the people through the labor service; again to the honor and destiny of the nation through army service; and a third time in commitment to the spiritual order of the German people through the service of learning. These three binding ties are alike original and necessary to the German essence. The German universities will only attain power if the three forms of service unite in overwhelming strength, if both teachers and students in their will to essence place themselves side by side in the struggle.[22]

> We have on the one hand the new Reich and on the other the university, that must take its tasks from the Reich's *Daseinswillen*. There is a revolution in Germany and we must ask ourselves, "Is there a revolution also in the university?" No. The fighting is still in the skirmishing stage and has so far mounted only a single attack—the formation of a new life in the Hitler labor camps—in the educational circles close to our college. They have taken from

---

[21] From Guido Schneeburger, *Nachlese zu Heidegger* (Bern, 1962), p. 75 (from *Heidelberger Neusle Nachrichten*, July 1, 1933, reporting what Heidegger said, among other things, in a lecture to Heidelberg students on "the university in the new Reich"). See Dagobert D. Runes, translator, *German Existentialism* (New York: Philosophical Library, n.d.), pp. 23-26. Translations from Schneeburger are my own.

[22] From Schneeburger, pp. 54-55 (from the *Freiburger Zeitung* May 23, 1933, report of Heidegger's Rector's address, "The Self-Assertion of the German University"; see Runes, pp. 18-20). The full text of this address is available separately: *Die Selbstbehauptung der Deutschen Universität* (Breslau: Korn, 1933).

us those educational tasks to which we hitherto thought we had sole claim.

There is always the possibility that the university may suffer death through forgetfulness and kiss goodbye any educational power. But it must be incorporated anew into the community of the people and bind itself to the state. The university must become once more a force in education that may educate the leaders of our state from knowledge to new knowledge. The goal requires a threesome: (1) knowledge of the contemporary university; (2) knowledge of the current dangers for our future; and (3) a new courage.[23]

In general, then, Heidegger attempted to revitalize science and scholarship by locating them in their source, the disclosing of Being; and such a locating results in uncovering the unity to which scholarship belongs. In support of German withdrawal from the League of Nations, Heidegger told his fellow scholars that "the people is winning back the truth of its *Daseinswillen*, for truth is the manifestness [openness] of what a people makes secure, clear, and strong in its action and knowledge. From such truth springs the genuine will to science. And this will to science determines the claims to knowledge. And from there the boundaries are finally set, within which genuine questioning and research must ground and preserve themselves. From such origins, science arises for us. It is bound up with the necessity of the self-responsible *völkischen Daseins*."[24]

Although it is true that Heidegger cannot be understood as wishing to subordinate scholarship to ordinary political institutions, these remarks, placed in the light of our previous discussions, show that the "resolute" freeing of scholarship in its genuine possibilities ultimately masks the split between particular political activity and the simple pursuit of knowledge, the split that is the chief theme of the tradition of political philosophy. That is to say, Heidegger does not discuss any root ontic discontinuity between these activities and opens the prospect of a specific and full interconnection here and now. And this at the same

---

[23]Schneeburger, p. 74.
[24]From Schneeburger, p. 149 (see also Runes, pp. 29-33).

time that he leaves largely in the dark the possibility of the concrete relations between what is discovered practically and theoretically, and the possibility of the concrete intermingling of practical standards and theoretical activity.

Knowledge and possession of knowledge, as national socialism understands these words, do not divide the classes but bind and unite the *Volksgenossen* and *stände* in the one great will of the state.

To us work is the title for every regulated deed and act that is done with responsibility to the individual, the group, and the state and so is of service to the people [*Volk*].

Science is only the stronger and therefore more responsible way of that knowledge that the whole German people must demand and seek, for its own historical-political *Dasein*, if, in general, this people wills to securely place its duration and its greatness and preserve its future. The knowledge of genuine science is not distinguished in its essence from the knowledge of the farmer, the lumberjack, the miners, the craftsman. Knowledge means knowing one's way around the world in which we are placed communally and individually. Knowledge means to be growing in resolve and performance of the task given each of us respectively whether this task is now ordering the fields, felling the trees, mining, questioning the laws of nature, or placing history out in the power of fate. Knowledge means: to be master of the situation in which we are put.[25]

Heidegger's argument does not rely on any of the traditional categories of political judgment; as I have argued, it could not. The scholar is to discover the possibilities of scholarship through resolve and destiny, not through longing to know and the fulfillment of his abilities. This cannot be equated with irrationalism if we consider seriously Heidegger's claim to have uncovered a dimension that makes possible both rationalism and

[25]From Schneeburger, pp. 201, 202, 201 (from an address of Heidegger to newly employed workers in Freiburg as reported in *Der Alemanne,* February 1, 1934. Italics omitted. See Runes, pp. 37-42). Consider Chapter 5 above, section 2.

irrationalism, the correct and the incorrect, correspondence and lack of correspondence. Moreover, Heidegger's discussion of, say, Nietzsche, even in *Being and Time*, not to speak of his Nietzsche lectures of the 1930s and 1940s, makes clear that his interpretations vary from Nazi "ideology" and "German" science. But is it, then, merely an accident that Heidegger's discussion of resolve, people, destiny, and struggle (*Kampfen*) is so reminiscent of the Nazis? In one sense there is nothing in this similarity that distinguishes Heidegger from other historically oriented German publicists—there is nothing essentially National Socialistic about "will" and "people." Even though Heidegger does not argue that man's Being is willing, or that man is determined by his people and his time, Heidegger's ontological formulations of authenticity use these terms, among others, in a transformed way, and he is, therefore, able to accommodate his rhetoric. On other occasions Heidegger might have emphasized anxiety, conscience, guilt, and the "not"; in fact, he claims that the thought in his rector's speech, for example, was at the heart of his inaugural address, *What is Metaphysics?*, in which anxiety and the "not" were central. Indeed, it is the emphasis on "nothing," already fundamental in *Being and Time,* that leads many scholarly and political critics to claim that Heidegger is a nihilist. The central question concerning Heidegger and the Nazis, therefore, must be the ground on which Heidegger believed that the new regime, or the situation giving birth to the regime, afforded an opportunity for the rebirth of the university, and even for people as a whole. How, if at all, can the situation in 1933 be understood as awakening the possibilities arising from the resolute projection of Being? Why, at the least, did Heidegger's thought not lead him to see the atrocity of Nazism from the beginning, or to oppose it in active resistance?

As an answer to the primary question, I suggest these considerations. Heidegger's attempt authentically to free scholarship in its Being connects scholarship to the people and to the nonscholarly in a manner radically different from not only the classical understanding but also the usual liberal understanding. The goodness or choiceworthiness of scholarship is freed in its genuine ownness for me and for us in a manner that uncovers its unity with this common ground or soil. It is neither an independently cosmopolitan nor independently private activity; nor is it one that becomes useful as technology even though its genuineness is concretely connected to the worker. The Nazi regime was clearly opposed to the liberal democratic division of spheres and activities. Was it possible, then, that this regime was rooted in authentic politics—that is, politics that freed its tasks and assignments in relation to German destiny? At least, could it be turned in this direction, given its departure from adherence to everyday codes and standards? Such thought appears to be underlie Heidegger's actions insofar as these are not merely an attempt to preserve the university in unfavorable circumstances. Indeed, we must say that Heidegger's attempted renewal of scholarship does not take place simply within a radically undetermined situation, but that the rejection of liberal democracy and the apparent rootedness in the people—that is, the apparent National "Socialism" of the Nazis—can be understood to belong to authentic political resolve, and that this would not be true of every political alternative.

> This will, to complete the condition of work in a correct condition of knowledge, this will must be for us: inner certainty and never wandering belief. For in what this will wills we only follow the surpassing will of our leader. To enter his following means: to will imperturbably and undeviatingly [*unausgesetzt*] that the German people grows in its unity as a work people, finding again its simple worth and genuine power, and procuring its duration and greatness as a work state. To the man of this unheard of will, our Fuhrer Adolph Hitler, a threefold Sieg Heil.[26]

But it is difficult to be more specific than this. Moreover, the very finitude of *Dasein*'s possibilities makes it impossible that any particular regime could be permanently valid authentically. For this reason it is folly to try to derive from Heidegger a "political philosophy" in which this means a theory of *the* best regime. In the interview mentioned above, Heidegger indicates that

---

[26]From Schneeburger, p. 202.

"democracy" is unlikely to be the proper political response to the present domination of planetary technology, but he offers no alternative and disclaims the possibility of his thought's uncovering effective alternatives. He also suggests in later works, particularly "Overcoming Metaphysics," that the dominance of technology directs the manner in which statesmen or men of practical affairs come to light, namely, as "leader natures." To explore this idea, we would need to discuss Heidegger's interpretation of the Being of technology. That would take us beyond *Being and Time,* although the meaning of Heidegger's interpretation cannot be grasped without understanding *Being and Time.* Moreover, Heidegger explicitly distinguishes his later interpretation of technology from what he meant in 1935, and the precise place of technology in *Being and Time* itself is unclear. Technological entities can be understood to come to light primarily either as ready-to-hand or present-at-hand and, more importantly, technology does not enter into the forthcoming discussion of the history of ontology; but in later works it comes to light as an epoch of Being. For our discussion here we may suggest that the technological entities are those discovered on the basis of the greatest forgetfulness of the rootedness of man and entities in the Being projected by *Dasein*'s care, and, in particular, in the greatest lack of authentic historicality.[27]

Be that as it may, and assuming the genuineness of Heidegger's resolve, political judgments that come from the resolute seizing of fate in destiny can and did lead to an understanding of both the unity of activities and their rebirth that permitted loyalty to the Nazi regime. That this is not a trivial observation becomes clear if we ask ourselves whether, say, Kant's or Locke's or Aristotle's understanding of the place of philosophy and the "sciences" would ever have allowed such a judgment concerning the proper political situation that is implicated in the seizing of the possibilities of thought. We cannot simply argue that such comparisons are irrelevant because Heidegger's activity is wholly

---

[27]On technology, consider William Lovitt's introduction to his translation of Heidegger's *Die Frage Nach der Technik* in *The Question Concerning Technology* (New York: Harper & Row, 1977).

other than that of these philosophers. First, such an argument, even if correct, cannot discharge the responsibility for attempting to consider the political meaning of Heidegger's thought. Second, Heidegger's situation of the university within the people is not merely and, indeed, not primarily a situating of his own thought, but of science and scholarship in general. Third, it is the history of philosophy that constitutes the specific tradition within which Heidegger will soon locate himself in *Being and Time*.

We must not neglect the fact that Heidegger resigned his position in 1934 and began a period that cannot be called a period of support, even if we do not wish to call it a period of opposition. But if we are to understand this activity in the light of Heidegger's attempt to reawaken authentic possibilities, we are not permitted to "reduce" it to moral revulsion. Rather, we might say that Heidegger came to understand that the Nazis did not draw their understanding from destiny, that they could not be turned in that direction, and that authentic scholarship in the properly assertive university was not compatible with Nazi dominance. But this is not to say that the situation with regard to the universities has improved—quite the contrary, according to the 1966 interview.

Heidegger's speeches during the Nazi period also help us to illustrate the issues I have raised concerning the concrete scope of the "people." By the "people" in these speeches, Heidegger means something more than the organized Reich at any time, because he distinguishes state and people and, in one speech, notes the existence of the eighteen million Germans outside the Reich. But the National Socialist revolution, and Hitler in particular, expresses the German *Dasein*. Consequently, Heidegger can write: "The Fuhrer himself and alone is the current and future German reality and its law."[28] This does not resolve our issues, but it indicates that the full authentic fate of the German individual is within a destiny that receives concrete expression in the political existence of the people. At the least, there is a possi-

---

[28] From Schneeburger, p. 136 (from an article published under Heidegger's name in the *Freiburger Studentenzeitung*, November 3, 1933).

bility of political resolve coordinate with popular destiny, which resolve makes ontic sense in a people's political union and political independence. Heidegger therefore supports Hitler's determination to withdraw Germany from the League of Nations. The other peoples, as well, are to exist in manly independence. But Heidegger does not discuss whether one may belong to more than one people, especially if it is true that a people is a politically resolute unit. At the most, the political resolve of the leaders of a politically independent people takes the lead in shaping destiny; that is, only if there is a politics oriented in Being, in the essential, can there be resolute work and scholarship, not to say philosophy (ontology) and fundamental ontology. Scholarship and science aid politics in its resolve, although it is more evident here that science must be anchored in a destiny belonging to political resolve than that politics requires science.[29]

Our discussion has suggested one way in which the destiny disclosed in authentic disclosure frees possibilities ontologically so that, as such, they offer a type of concrete guidance and do not merely free the specifics of the situation. I have argued that Heidegger's activities and speeches are suited to a certain unity, coordination, or agglomeration of possibilities that is not simply neutral and that is not abstract or formal but can occur here and now. In particular, the split between thinking and politics becomes disguised and certain kinds of separation of activities become improper. An authentic fate within a destiny that is at least coordinate with a political unit apparently need not find itself in basic or immediate conflict with the other authentic human pos-

[29]For Heidegger's political activity during this period also consider, among others, Alexander Schwan, *Die politische Philosophie im Denken Heideggers,* Ordo politicus Vol. 2 (Cologne and Opladen, 1965); Jean-Michel Palmier, *Les écrits politique de Heidegger* (Paris: Editions de l'Heine, 1968); François Fedier, "Trois attaques contre Heidegger," *Critiques* 234; and Beda Allemann, "Martin Heidegger und die Politik," in *Heidegger, Perspecktiven Deutung Seines Werkes,* Heraus, Otto Poggeler (Cologne, Berlin: Kiepnauer und Witsch, 1970). Further discussions of Heidegger's politics may be found in Karl Lowith, *Heidegger: Denker in Durftiger Zeit* (Frankfurt am Main: S. Fischer, 1953); the exchanges between Lowith and Alphonse de Waelhens in *Les temps modernes* 3-4; Otto Poggeler, *Philosophie und Politik bei Heidegger* (Freiburg: K. Alber, 1974); and Karsten Harries, "Heidegger as Political Thinker," in Michael Murray, ed., *Heidegger and Modern Philosophy* (New Haven: Yale University Press, 1978).

sibilites, and, concretely, each can come together with the others in institutions such as the Nazi labor camps, universities, and military training groups. Yet, the institutions in which they come together cannot be understood as devoted to thinking first of all but to the people's political expression first of all. But I have not claimed that these guides are particularly specific, ontically, or that authentic resolve is itself defensible by an external standard. Indeed, as I argued earlier, the status of the "new courage" in relation to ordinary standards is problematic, and the present discussion does not overcome these problems any more than it explores the status of the relation between what is freed by the new courage and what previously has been freed inauthentically.

I believe that the result of my discussion of Heidegger's support of the Nazis is consistent with my previous analyses. When I have argued that Heidegger's analysis of authenticity, understanding, and significance does not permit the fully intelligible freeing of the political conflicts among ways of life; when I have argued that his discussion of *Dasein*'s possibilities leaves unclear the status of these possibilities as they are in themselves, or can be for what is not man; and when I have argued that his analysis obscures the possibility of the interconnection between the theoretical and the practical, I have stressed primarily the implications of these facts for the status of Heidegger's own understanding of man and Being. And I have attempted to develop alternative ways of understanding these phenomena while still capturing those phenomena that reveal man's finitude. Here we see that the concrete result of considering, on the basis of authentic fate and destiny, political alternatives, the proper course for an enterprise such as scholarship, and the relation of scholarship to other activities in a particular place and time is to mask these differences, and, indeed, to make it difficult to see how genuine scholarship, genuine work, genuine political action, could be disharmonious. Heidegger's political judgment is therefore at once immoderately restrained and immoderately assertive. It is immoderately restrained because the situation of workers and scholars is judged solely in the light of this people and destiny and not in the light of such possible activities as they are intelligible beyond their Being fated. It is immoderately restrained also because the differences in order and dignity among the human possibilities are too quickly merged. But it is immoderately assertive because the limits these very differences place on political action and the effectiveness of philosophic understanding are not freed in their concrete effect. And it is immoderately assertive because the distinction between this people and the others in their concrete political expressions is made too significant. Ultimately, Heidegger's political judgment is immoderate because the grounds of moderation—the imperfection of human activities in the light of their own ends—are not freed; this is true even though such immoderation need not have the precise results always that it did in 1933. Proof of this immoderation is Heidegger's year-long support of a regime—however one attempts to excuse this support—whose intention to murder all Jews was already manifest.

We will turn now to Heidegger's discussion of the connection between historiology—that is, the scholarly study of history—and historicality. This will aid us in our attempt to discover whether any directives or guides can issue from authentic resolve other than what is relative to the particular authentic situation. In addition, it will help us grasp more fully the meaning of science and advance our consideration of the status of Heidegger's explicit questioning of Being in relation to the authentic destiny in which scholarship and other possibilities can be freed.

7. *Time and the Study of History*

On the basis of his analysis of historicality, Heidegger now turns to historiology. The intention and limits of his discussion are similar to the intention and limits of his previous discussion of science: his purpose is to uncover the authentic possibilities of a science by projecting its idea upon man's Being. Heidegger's interpretation of historiology, therefore, does not abstract a definition from what historians do today, because even if today's historiology represents historiology's authentic possibilities, which is doubtful, the discovery of an abstract concept of historiology is itself dependent on the inquirer's already *existent* understanding.

Heidegger's discussion of historiology attempts to be a fully developed understanding at this existential level, based on his understanding of *Dasein*'s Being in general and his historicality in particular. In this sense, we may distinguish Heidegger's discussion from our contemporary analytic philosophy of history, which projects historiology upon an ontologically uninterpreted idea of science, abstracts it from the practices of historians, or projects it upon an understanding of human being that remains caught in the comprehension of man as present-at-hand, even as it recognizes the need to grasp what is distinctive in human being. Heidegger develops this last point by attempting to connect his thought on History to, and distinguish them from, those of Dilthey.

[1]

Historiology: Exposition

(§76) Historiology examines historical entities. It thematizes them; that is, it projects what is prescientifically familiar upon its "specific Being" and in this way bounds off a realm of entities, methodologically manages the way of access to them, and outlines the conceptual structure for interpreting them. But historiology can thematize the past only because the past has already been disclosed. Consequently, the object of historiological research has the Being of *Dasein* who has been "there": historiology has its ontological roots in historicality. Moreover, because when man is no longer "there" his *world* is also no longer "there," historiology can be world historical: world historicality is the condition that makes it possible for present-at-hand remains and records to turn into material for understanding the *Dasein* who has been. When such materials are understood with regard to their historical worldliness, they then become historiological objects: by interpreting them we give definite character to the world that we have already projected. It is the historian's historical existence that allows his Being toward the *Dasein* who has been, and this is then the ground for his considering past materials, not vice versa.

Because historiology is grounded in man's historicality, its true object must conform to the authentically historical disclosure of the past. Authentic historical disclosure is the repetition in which we understand the authentic possibility of the man who has been. Consequently, the fundamental theme of historiology is the possible, not the factuality of the present-at-hand. Indeed, because man *is* only in existing, his "factuality" is the facticity found in his resolute projection, and what has been authentically "is the existentiell possibility in which fate, destiny, and world history have been factically determined."[1] Therefore, the more concretely historiology understands factical having been in its

---

[1] *Sein und Zeit,* p. 394.

possibility, the more historiology discloses the "quiet strength of the possible."[2]

If this is the meaning of historiology, then we see as mistaken the question whether historiology reveals universal laws operating in individual events or merely seeks to put individual events in a series. The theme of historiology is neither one time happenings nor the universals that somehow float above these happenings. Rather, it is the possibility that has been existent factically. A repetition of a possibility, an authentic historiological understanding of it, is not its being turned into a "supertemporal model." In order for the power of the possible to reach one's existence, it must come toward that existence futurally. It can do this only if what has been is disclosed by authentic historicality as a resolute fate, only if historiology's objects have already been met in the "factical existentiell *choice* of *Dasein*'s historicality."[3] In this sense, indeed, fateful repetition guarantees the "objectivity" of historiology because "the objectivity of a science is primarily ruled by whether it can bring to our understanding the entities which thematically belong to it uncovered the primordiality of their Being."[4] The universally valid standards demanded by ordinary common sense to govern objectivity are less possible as criteria of truth for authentic historiology than for any other science precisely because of the nature of its theme, namely, the possibility of existence that has been.

Because history is handed down in such a way that it always exists in an interpreted form, historiology can usually grasp what has been only through traditional history. It therefore holds itself in "varying closeness to its authentic theme." Concretely, this necessity of a traditional interpretation means that the historian who attempts to look straightaway at an era's world view does not thereby demonstrate an authentically historical understanding. Moreover, the great interest in the most remote cultures in our age hardly proves that our age is authentically

[2] *Sein und Zeit*, p. 394. My translation.
[3] *Sein und Zeit*, p. 395.
[4] *Sein und Zeit*, p. 395. My translation.

historical, and the very emergence of the problem of historicism associated with this contemporary interest indicates how historiology itself may alientate man from his authentic historicality. Indeed, although historiology is founded on historicality, authentic historicality does not require historiology.

Heidegger concludes by briefly considering Nietzsche and Dilthey. I will summarize his discussion of Nietzsche, which attempts to show that Nietzsche's division of historiology into the monumental, antiquarian, and critical is rooted in historicality as Heidegger understands it, a historicality whose ground is "*temporality* as the existential meaning of the Being of care."[5] When *Dasein* is authentically futural he resolutely discloses the possibility he has chosen, and in resolutely coming back to himself he is open in repetition for the "monumental" possibilities of existence. But such historiology is also antiquarian because, in the repetition that makes a possibility one's own, the possibility is also opened of "reverently preserving the existence that has been there in which the seized possibility has become manifest."[6] Finally, such historiology is also critical. The present discloses the authentic "today" in the moment of vision, a today interpreted in resolute understanding. This means that one is "painfully loosening oneself from the fallen publicness of today": authentic historiology is a critique of the present.[7]

[2]

The History of Ontology: Exposition

Heidegger's discussion of historiology raises the problem of his own activity as a kind of thematic historiology. We have already explored the issue of the connection between the people's destiny and the scholar's authentic historicality. Here, let us consider the concrete historical possibilities that Heidegger presents

[5] *Sein und Zeit*, p. 397.
[6] *Sein und Zeit*, p. 396. My translation.
[7] *Sein und Zeit*, p. 397. My translation. For Heidegger's later understanding of Nietzsche, see his *Nietzsche*, 2 vols. (Pfullingen: Neske, 1961).

to himself and the manner in which they must become thematically transparent in historiology. For Heidegger understands his
own activity as requiring such historical transparency. Consequently, *Being and Time* was to have had a second part, devoted
to a "destruction" of the history of ontology. He briefly outlines
this part in the second chapter of his introduction to the work: I
will explicate it now. In the analysis following this explication, I
will, among other things, question both the historical status of
Heidegger's own "characteristics" of Being and the sense in
which this discussion contributes to understanding the finite
wholeness of Being itself.

(§6) The inquiry into the meaning of existentiality and Being,
Heidegger says, makes it clear that man is historical. But this
means that the inquiry is itself historical; we must therefore
consider its history in order fully to possess its possibilities. But
in his average Being, man falls both to the world and to the
tradition that he takes hold of. Indeed, man's possibilities of
Being are regulated and disclosed by his traditional way of interpreting himself, and the tradition prevents him from furnish-
ing his own guidance in choice and inquiry. Tradition transmits
by concealing things because it converts what it transmits to
self-evidence, thereby closing the original sources and making us
forget that what is transmitted originates in these sources. In
this sense tradition conceals our very historicality from us. It
does so in ontological understanding as well; the sources of its
basic concepts have been forgotten. Greek ontology shows that
man understands himself and Being in terms of entities within
the world, and this ontology has determined philosophy until
today. Indeed, even when domains of Being such as the subject,
the I, reason, spirit, and person come into view in the course of
history, the Being of these entities remains uninterrogated and
they are understood in ways that, fundamentally, employ the
traditional Greek categories. To make Being's own history
transparent, therefore, the traditional concealments must be dis-
solved: we must destroy the traditional content of ontology "by
taking *the question of Being as our clue*" in order to come upon the

experiences in which the first ways of determing the nature of Being were achieved.[8] This, Heidegger claims, is neither a vicious relativizing of ontological standpoints nor a negative eliminating of tradition but a grasping of the tradition's positive possibilities.

Heidegger planned this destruction for the decisive stages of the history of ontology, and, because the question of Being has been shown to be connected essentially to Temporality, the destruction was first of all to have raised "the question whether and to what extent the Interpretation of Being and the phenomenon of time have been brought together thematically in the course of the history of ontology, and whether the problematic of Temporality necessary for this has ever been worked out fundamentally or ever could have been."[9] The first stage to have been discussed was Kant: Kant went part of the way toward investigating Temporality, but it can be shown how he shrank back from uncovering it. For he both neglected the general question of Being and failed to provide an ontology of *Dasein*—that is, what would be called in Kantian terms a preliminary ontological analysis of the "subjectivity of the subject." His failure is rooted in his taking over of Descartes's position. Consequently, Kant's analysis of time is oriented to the ordinary understanding and he fails to question, let alone to work out properly, the connection between "I think" and Time.[10]

Now, Kant's failing to provide an ontology for man is an omission that is decisive in Descartes as well. For in Descartes's radical "I think [therefore] I am," the meaning of the Being of I am is undetermined. Therefore, the second stage of the destruction interprets the "*cogito sum*"; and the purpose of this interpretation is to show why Descartes "had to neglect the question of Being" and why he believed that the certainty of the thinking "I" made unnecessary a discussion of man's Being. Nonetheless, when we consider Descartes's *Meditations*, we see that the thinking I is ontologically determined in a sense, for Descartes con-

[8] *Sein und Zeit*, p. 22.
[9] *Sein und Zeit*, p. 23. My translation.
[10] On this topic consult Charles Sherover, *Heidegger, Kant, and Time* (Bloomington: Indiana University Press, 1971).

siders the I to be a created entity. He thereby takes over medieval ontology. But createdness in the sense of something's being produced "is an essential structural moment of the ancient conception of Being."[11] The third stage of the destruction would therefore be an attempt to uncover the meaning and limits of Greek ontology, and this would require interpreting the soil of Greek ontology in the light of Temporality. Here Heidegger planned to show that the Greeks interpreted the Being of entities in terms of entities within the world—that is, Nature—and that their understanding of Being is obtained from time. Outward evidence of this is the Greek understanding of Being as (*par*)*ousia,* whose ontological-temporal significance is presence. For when entities are grasped in their Being as presence, they are understood with regard to a mode of time, namely, the present. Moreover, man's Being is delimited as the rational animal or, more precisely, as the living entity "whose Being is essentially determined through the potentiality for discourse," and discourse becomes the clue for obtaining the structures of Being of the entities we encounter.[12]

As such "logos" is interpreted, the possibility of a radical grasp of the problem of Being grows, and Aristotle radically grounds and subsumes the Platonic dialectic; discourse understood as *noein* is the awareness of something present-at-hand in its pure presence-at-hand, and this has the Temporal structure of making-present. Authentic entities are, therefore, conceived as presence (*ousia*), but neither Aristotle, Plato, nor Parmenides understood the ontological function of time—or the ground of its possibility. Time itself was grasped as an *entity* whose Being is comprehended within the horizon of an understanding of Being naïvely oriented to time. Thus, Heidegger planned to show the limits of Greek ontology by interpreting Aristotle's discussion of time in the *Physics,* and this in turn would have made clear how Kant's discussion of time and contemporary discussions of time fall within Aristotle's structure. This, finally, would have shown that the basic orientation of ontology remains Greek.

---

[11]*Sein und Zeit,* p. 24. My translation.
[12]*Sein und Zeit,* p. 25. My translation.

The History of Ontology: Analysis

Heidegger's discussion indicates that the projected destruction of the history of ontology would have shown how Temporality was taken for granted as the horizon for the meaning of Being, and how the meaning of Being was itself taken for granted. His discussion does not attempt to demonstrate that his own understanding of Being is a new and final stage in the history of philosophy but, on the contrary, attempts to show that thematic ontology becomes increasingly oblivious of its primary sources up through Kant, and beyond. Kant's distinction is the uncovering of man's transcendent and moral personality that, when fully oriented to Temporality, begins to lead to the Heideggerian understanding of *Dasein* and Being. But according to Heidegger, even Kant takes the meaning of Being for granted, as *Being and Time* as a whole makes clear.

Not only does the destruction not claim to uncover a new stage, it does not appear to encompass a "historical" account of Temporality itself or of Heidegger's own discussion of Being. Let us develop this argument. Heidegger's fundamental ontology is intended to bring to light the essential structures of Being, and we have discovered certain structures of this Being— readiness-to-hand, presence-at-hand, and care—even though the full Temporality of these modes, and the most general meaning of Being, do not come to light explicitly in *Being and Time*. But it is clear in Heidegger's later works and lectures, in the *Fundamental Problems of Phenomenology*, and, here, in the discussion of Aristotle, that some sense of presence is the meaning of Being that has guided philosophy. But the precise sense in which Temporality makes this presence possible and, more, the precise sense in which presence makes all the modes of Being possible, is hardly developed explicitly beyond what we have already discussed. Moreover, the precise implications for the projection of Being of the distinction between authentic and inauthentic time is neither developed nor discussed in *Being and Time*, or in the contemporaneous works. Presumably, if Being has a "presencial" meaning, it has an authentic and inauthentic presencial meaning. We may suggest that Being as Presence would authentically mean Being understood in the horizon of a Presence correlated with the moment of vision (*Augenblick*); and, here, the horizonal interplay of the future would have to be decisive. Being would not itself mean purely presenting but something like historically-factically standing forth in its moment. Indeed, a possible German term to bring this out would be *ereignis*, event, a "historical" term with resonances of *eigen*, own, to remind us of authenticity and "properties" (*Eigenschaften*), and with an archaic connection to *eraugnen* to remind us of the *Augenblick*. *Ereignis* does become a fundamental term in Heidegger's later work, but not to "name" Being, when Being is understood from the horizon of an authentic present where horizon and authenticity are simply projected as they are in *Being and Time*. In any event, something like this authentic understanding would apparently necessarily have been held in advance of Heidegger's own "destructive" enterprise. Moreover, although previous philosophers have failed to see both the significance of Temporality and the primordial meaning of Temporality, this presumably need not mean that their ontological understanding is "wrong." This is so, first, because an understanding may be drawn from a proper look at Being, even if what is understood is insufficiently or erroneously conceived thematically (for example, Kant's understanding of man as an end in himself, or the Aristotelian understanding in the *Ethics* of truth and of the proper time or proper occasion connected to prudence), and second, because even if the understanding is fundamentally inappropriate, it may still reveal the Being of a region of beings within limits, much as an inauthentic understanding of entities can still discover what is correct. But this then forces us to wonder whether ontology, which fails to understand properly the Temporality of Being, can be reformed on the basis of the proper understanding. Or, are the decisive stages of ontology all drawn from an unthematic glimpse at authentically given presence?

Does not this entire discussion raise the question whether Heidegger's fundamental ontological structures are themselves historical, and how they are historical if they are? This issue points in two directions. First, how precisely is the historicality or, better, the incompleteness, the finite openness, of the structures of Being to be understood in and for the structures as such? For Heidegger, any philosopher's ontological understanding is dependent on his projection of *Dasein*'s Being and therewith of Being-as-such, and the finitude of Being's Temporal meaning can in this way be grasped as grounding the existent*iell* possibility of philosophy, just as it can be grasped as grounding all other activity. But are the structures of Being historical in and of themselves? This question is relevant for all activities, but it would appear to be particularly relevant for philosophy, which believes itself to be discussing what most fully is. According to our previous discussions, we would be inclined to say that Heidegger's Being is indeed historical in and of itself, not as an entity in time but as the moving ground of the totality of entities, projected in advance of any concrete possibility. But to say this is still to consider Being's "historicality" from the perspective of *Dasein*'s historicality and not from its own finite openness. That is, it is not yet to grasp Being's "facticity" from Presence, presumably authentic Presence. For if Presence is the authentic horizon for Being, then must not the "whatness"—the "content"—of presence (Being) be finitely open or incomplete as such, that is, as thought from Temporality? Or does the fact that the possibilities of *philosophy* happen in a destiny in no way show that Being itself is destined even if there is Being only as long as there is *Dasein*?

Second, in what specific way is Heidegger's own enterprise, Heidegger's own fundamental ontology, historical? If his is the first explicit uncovering of the horizon for Being's meaning, his activity cannot simply be understood as reawakening or "repeating" traditional ontology. Rather, it uncovers that which makes possible the possibilities of ontology; in this way it also uncovers that which makes all activities possible. But this suggests that Heidegger's own activity is possible only on the basis of the situation with regard to Being that comes to light in current science and philosophy, namely, the fullness of the forgetfulness of Being in the activity devoted to truth about what is. But if this is so, are not the structures Heidegger uncovers themselves historical both up to now and from now on? Cannot the structures of care, presence-at-hand, and readiness-to-hand be overcome, and overcome not simply because of correctable inadequacies but because of the nature of what *Being and Time* is about— Being in its temporal meaning? Could not Heidegger's entire argument that Being, world, and time are projected in advance of every activity, including philosophy, be overturned? Indeed, would not this overturning be possible for the articulations of Being, for example, the belongingness to Being of the fact that every entity is as *what* it is and *that* it is, as well as for Being's modes—care, presence-at-hand, and readiness-to-hand? What occurs once the oblivion of Being as the horizon for entities is capable of being thematically known both as oblivion and in its structures? Heidegger's own thought might not be finite in the manner of previous philosophy but would it not come together with the finitude belonging to Being itself?[13]

In order to pursue this argument we must, at the very least, distinguish such a possibility from the argument that Heidegger's thought, and Being, are *in* time and therefore temporal. Again, Heidegger's Being cannot be subject to ontic causality, and thought of Being also cannot be subject to ontic causality. But the truth of Being in relation to beings is not eternal, and, according to Heidegger, the eternal has meaning only within the horizon of Being's having been projected on the finite Temporality that frees authenticity. So-called "infinite" time belongs to the ordinary understanding, and this understanding is not the primordial understanding.[14] It is with this in mind, therefore, that all questions concerning the completeness and permanence of the structures of Being must be asked.

The problems we have raised are not thematically treated in *Being and Time* and the contemporaneous works. Indeed, they point in the direction of Heidegger's later investigations. Nonetheless we may attempt a step or two on the basis of *Being and Time* and certain arguments from the *Fundamental Problems*.

---

[13]Consider here, among others, Otto Poggeler, "Heidegger Heute," in *Perspektiven* (translated in Ballard and Scott); Joseph J. Kockelmans, "Heidegger on Time and Being," and Charles E. Scott, "Heidegger and Consciousness" (both in Ballard and Scott).

[14]Consider *Sein und Zeit*, Div. 2, chap. 6.

Let us begin by stressing the relation, for Heidegger, of the problems of finitude, nothingness, and completion. Recall, for example, that man's Being a whole is essentially connected to his possible impossibility, his orientation to the "not" at the basis of his Being. Recall as well that a whole of equipment is first lit up by tools that are lacking or unserviceable. Heidegger develops this argument in relation to the presencial meaning of Being itself in the section of the *Fundamental Problems* in which he discusses the Presence of readiness-to-hand. Everything positive, including the Presence of readiness-to-hand becomes especially clear through privation, and the ground for this circumstance lies in the "essence of temporality and the negation rooted in it."[15] Ready-to-hand entities are unobtrusive, and are accessible in their unobtrusive Presence when our dealings with them are undisturbed. These dealings are disturbed when, for example, we come to a stop because a tool is lacking: such a lack means the being not-handy of something already ready-to-hand. But what makes possible the discovery of something lacking, given the fact that we do not have access to the not-ready-to-hand? "The own-most way of discoveredness of the not handy in a specific mode is missingness."[16] What, then, is the ontological possibility of the missing? Missingness is not a not making present, a not letting be encountered: it is not the opposite of finding because we are discussing our access to the nonhandy. In truth, its essence "lies in a determined mode of making present."[17] For we can find something to be lacking only when we let entities be involved, only when we are awaiting a whereto and making-present what is serviceable to that. Missingness is "an un-making *present* as a determined mode of the present in unity with an awaiting and retaining of what is available."[18] It does not spring from *no* horizon but is a modification of the horizon of the present—it is a modification of Presence. In particular "to the ecstasy of the un-making present that makes possible missingness belongs the

[15] *Grundprobleme*, p. 439.
[16] *Grundprobleme*, p. 441.
[17] *Grundprobleme*, p. 441.
[18] *Grundprobleme*, pp. 441-42.

horizonal scheme of *Absence.*"[19] The modification of Presence to Absence, however, can be interpreted fully only in reference to the modification of presence as Not (*Nicht*); and here we would then need to discuss fully how nullity (*Nichtigkeit*), the essence of not, can be interpreted only in reference to the essence of time. But Heidegger does not go beyond this here, and, indeed, points back to the connection of man and Being, presumably to the connection of the finitude of temporality and the finitude of *Dasein,* as the ground for further development.

This discussion indicates the essential connection between Presence and Absence, or Being and Nullity. In this sense Being is finite, because Nullity and Being belong together. But such finitude speaks directly neither to our question about the historical incompleteness of Being's having its modes and articulations nor to our question about the possible relation of this incompleteness to explicit thought about Being. We may further develop this problem, however, by considering the finitude of Temporality. Primordial temporality is explicitly said to be finite, but, as we noted in our discussion, its precise differentiation from the temporal projection making anticipatory resoluteness possible is unclear. Indeed, we questioned whether Heidegger had thought through Temporality's essential connection to Being from Temporality itself. We can see now that Heidegger attempts to consider Temporality's horizonal essence strictly in reference to temporality. The various ecstasies in their very going out go out *to,* and that to which they go out is their horizon. The meaning of temporality need not be further grasped in terms of a wider horizon; temporality "is" as temporalizing its own "in terms of." The continuity of the projections "understanding of entities, projection in terms of Being, understanding of Being, projection in terms of Time, has its end in the horizon of the ecstatical unity of temporality. We are not able to ground this more originally here; we must, moreover, enter into the problem of the finitude of temporality. In this horizon every ecstasy of time, that is, temporality itself, has its end. But this end

[19]*Grundprobleme,* p. 442.

is not other than the entrance and exit [beginning and con-
clusion] for the possibility of all projections."[20] Here we meet the
following issue. Although we may begin to see how Presence and
Absence belong together in Temporality, Heidegger does not
develop their possible belonging together in Temporality's own
finitude: he does not develop how the horizon "horizons" finitely and *thus* frees a possible Presence and Absence. We may
question in particular whether Heidegger has truly thought
through the finitude of the interplay of horizons. How are the
horizons themselves finite that the ecstasies go toward? Man's
authentically Being futural is essentially connected to his own
impossibility. If temporality's finitude and wholeness is strictly
analogous to *Dasein*'s, what is the equivalent "death" of temporality, how is it "present" as "absent?" That is unclear. But if
Temporality's finitude is not analogous to *Dasein*'s, how can it be
grasped more concretely? Developing such questions would appear to lead in the direction of Heidegger's thoughts concerning
belonging-together, the giving and withholding of time, the
bringing into one's own as bringing into what is withheld—that
is, the thoughts in his more recent works.

Let us return to the question of the possible completeness of
Heidegger's understanding of Being and Time. Clearly, the
finitude and negativity of which we have been speaking are
of a peculiar order. Why would they alone demand the impossibility of a complete understanding such that no new modes and
articulations of Being, or no new dimensions of Time and its
relation to Being, could be revealed? The difficulty of fundamental ontology—the fact that we are bringing to light what
ordinarily is in the dark, and bringing it to light in the meaning
of its darkness—increases the likelihood of falling short, but this
danger is not the precise issue here. Can fundamental ontology
be a complete science, can it be one that cannot be overturned in
its fundamentals as long as it is pursued, and is it possible in a
situation less inclusive than Heidegger's situation? Here we may
be tempted to draw an analogy from the sciences, in which unchanging facts can be discovered but in which there is no need to

[20]*Grundprobleme*, p. 437 (my parenthetical remark).

presume that these facts are complete or that they have been placed on a final ground. But the reason for this is, on the one hand, the multiplicity of actual entities to be scientifically thematized and, on the other, in Heideggerian terms, the varying possibilities of grasping the Being that we project a priori to these entities. The explicit projection of the meaning of Being, however, is the projection of the possibility of what is itself the source of the possibility of entities. Being is a priori to what is as a priori. Consequently, cannot the elements of Being be grasped fully and explicitly in terms of Temporality?

At the least, these considerations lead to the suggestion that we cannot decide the issue of the stability of fundamental ontological truths on grounds identical to those on which the question of metaphysics and its history is to be decided (and that this issue is also not identical to the issue in the sciences). Moreover, the peculiar finitude at the ontological-temporal level is such that the "thatness" of the modes and articulations of Being (that is, their belonging together with "nothing" in a manner similar to the unobtrusive presence of what is ready-to-hand) must be "there" as a condition of possibility and as conditioned in its possibility. Therefore, the question of the "thatness," "whatness," and permanence of understanding of the modes of Being is different even from the issue of the connection of facticity and possibility in *Dasein* himself. For temporality's temporalizing and Being's making-possible is not an existent*iell* choice or an act of resolve. But, then, Heidegger's treating his fundamental ontology as a kind of scientific thematizing is peculiar, because the historical and objective self-presenting of its themes would in fact need to be different from the possible presentation of entities thematized in their Being. For all these reasons, the place of Heidegger's fundamental ontology within destiny is obscure because the relation of the finitude of Temporality and Being to the historical finitude freed in destiny is so problematic that Heidegger's own enterprise does not furnish an example for specifying the guidelines, if any, that emerge in a destiny.

If we retreat from this horizon of fundamental ontology back to the implications of traditional philosophic ontology as an existential possibility, we are faced with a similar fact. Heidegger's discussion in *Being and Time,* and his procedure in the *Fundamental Problems,* does not show in any great detail how ontology is a historical repeating of possibilities, although he unmistakably intends to show the continued dominance for the moderns of what the Greeks uncovered. Consequently, his analysis also does not help directly with the problem of destiny, our original reason for pursuing it. But his discussion raises a further difficulty, which we have mentioned previously in relation to Aristotelian ethics and Kant's moral teaching. For what is the precise status of the results achieved by the other philosophers? Heidegger attempts to show how their results are drawn from an unthematic taking for granted of Being as Presence, of Temporality's own function, and of care as man's mode of Being. He also appears to suggest that explicit ontological results after the Greeks proceeded by projecting the tradition begun by the Greeks, with an ever greater covering of the roots of that tradition. At the same time, the difference of man from other entities—man as subject, person, spirit—comes increasingly to the fore but is not wedded to an increasing broadening of the ontological tradition as such. Moreover, he also believes himself able to show that certain ways in which entities always present themselves, most obviously in philosophical analysis but in practical activity and science as well, can be rooted in Being as Presence, or in Temporality. To some extent he begins to show this, in the *Fundamental Problems,* for the characteristics of essence and existence, and for the appearance of entities in the horizon of grounding and causing. But what does the content of the various philosophies tell us about Being, and how can the variety in this content be judged at its own level?

This is a difficult matter because it is not clear precisely what the content of the traditional philosophies is about. We are tempted to say "Being," or entities in their Being, and although this is not incorrect, it is misleading, because we have also noted that, according to Heidegger, the philosophers have not discussed Being in his sense but, rather, they have discussed the highest entity(s) and most general characteristics of entities. To discuss an entity in its Being amounts to examining that entity in reference to the highest and most general, as this reveals itself as, say, essential characteristics that cause the entity to be what it is. If we call this "the beingness of entities," we may then say that, for Heidegger, this beingness is itself freed in terms of Heideggerian Being and is peculiarly revealing of this Being because it is how to Be comes to light in the fullest sense. At the same time, it is a peculiarly grave covering of Heideggerian Being, precisely because it appears to be that Being: the philosopher's activity is in this manner blind to the gulf between beings and Being because the philosophers believe they know what Being is. And this blindness would be true, for Heidegger, even where philosophy remains an open search. The variety of philosophic epochs can therefore each find a root in Heideggerian Being, and the leading doctrines of an epoch can be grasped as the chief way in which Being covers itself in its opening of entities.

Such considerations, immanent in *Being and Time,* become important in Heidegger's later works. Indeed, I might go as far as to claim, for Heidegger, that the apparent contradictions between, say, Kant's and Aristotle's ethical teachings and their grounds are contradictions only when the magnanimous man and moral person have been freed in their Being—that is, that these are not contradictions at the level of Being. Moreover, I could argue that this root harmony exists whatever the exclusivity or intermingling of the philosophies and their results in "ages" in time. Both correct and incorrect statements about entities and circumspective deliberation about entities free these entities in their meaning. Similarly, the meaning of the philosophers' disputes is beyond these disputes themselves even if the connection between Being's own finitude and these disputes is left unresolved.

But this cannot be the simple end of the issue. First, the questions asked about the sciences' relation to nonscientifically freed entities could also be asked of the philosophic understanding of these entities (in Heidegger's sense). Similarly, they could be asked of the philosopher's own activity, in relation to other activities and to his people. Second, to whatever extent the freeing of man's possibilities in the light of his openness to Being gives positive guidance, the philosophical grounding of possibilities can be more or less amenable to this authentic gift of man. In the light of Being, then, would not the differing results of the philosophers need to be judged differently? Third, Heidegger sometimes treats Kant and his successors as if they highlight new or different domains of Being, such as "spirit" or person. If this highlighting is not merely synonomous with the changed content of their discoveries, then does it mean that the later philosophers are necessarily more complete, in their accounting for entities, than the earlier ones? Or is Kant as different from Aristotle "morally" as the natural science he grounds is from Aristotelian nature? How, from their own perspective, are we to understand the openness of the philosophers, their apparent disputes among themselves? Does not the way in which each thinker implicitly or explicitly overcomes earlier and later thinkers speak against Being's presenting the matter for the philosophers' discussion in a neutral manner? Must we not say that Heidegger's Being, in fact, is fully a priori to only one philosophic possibility (such as Nietzsche's)? Or does this implicit or explicit overcoming merely confirm the single root of the equal philosophical possibilities?

We may develop this point by considering the related issue of whether Heidegger's Being could free the possibility of entities grounded philosophically in unchanging generalities and orders. As we have noted, the question of validity in the sciences is not simply equivalent to the question of validity in philosophy, or in the theoretical in general, and, therefore, Heidegger's allowing the scientific discovery of what is binding for every possible assertion about an entity is not directly relevant to our issue. Indeed, how could any metaphysical statement properly be binding for one who perceives the possibility of philosophical variety? This issue depends, among other things, on the status of the differences among the philosophers. But if each is *sui generis* in his interpretation of the Being of entities, must not those interpretations that fail to leave a place among entities for the decisive new philosophic endeavors be concretely incorrect in certain, and in a sense all, respects? Would we not need to say in advance, for example, that understanding entities in terms of eternity misjudges them? But if certain philosophic statements *are* unchangingly binding, how can Heidegger's *Dasein* and

Being in fact fully free the possibility of philosophy? We may suppose that Heidegger's understanding of inauthentic time allows this freeing. But then, would not the authentic grasping of the possibility of philosophy make fully binding philosophic assertions impossible? If so, has Heidegger properly grasped the Being in terms of which philosophy is freed?

If Being is understood to free the possibility of the variety of philosophies, yet if, at the same time, each philosopher's activity is *not* considered to be *sui generis* but his assertions are considered to be equally measurable as correct and incorrect, then this weakens one of the important reasons for believing with Heidegger that there is a Being and Temporality that is not explicable in philosophically metaphysical terms. It might still be possible that Heidegger's Being has been overlooked without then requiring that this Being be the condition for the meaning of the full variety of philosophic structures. More likely, however, our argument would require that the function of Heidegger's Being, such that it is the source of the meaning and light whereby entities can be understood, be conceived as a result of the effectiveness—that is, the attractiveness—of the highest things. I have made this suggestion, and have argued further that philosophy's seeking to know what most fully is, the unchanging entities in their unchanging characteristics and order, is its attempt to be this order, is the philosopher's imitation of what is. But precisely if the philosopher is finite, he must fail, and this means that his discourse fails to capture all it seeks to capture. Briefly, how can we grasp in its own terms this failure of discourse from the side of what he seeks—that is, what eludes us and why? We suggest that to be knowable is not the full being of what the lover of knowledge seeks to know. Rather, its comprehensibility is its power of attracting human discourse in a human soul, but this discourse and soul need not be. What the philosopher seeks to know is what is independent, self-sufficient, and unique and, therefore, what *is* whether or not it is known or—in a sense, if there is no discourse—knowable. To know such a being fully is not to possess it fully, not to capture all its characteristics, some of which are to shape material that we make intelligible only by referring to "chance." Moreover, perhaps what the seeker of knowledge seeks allows discourse or knowledge only up to a point because the attractive independence of what he seeks to know does not allow a fully correct discussion all at once: perhaps every discourse must be partial; perhaps what is can offer its wholeness always only in imperfect images; perhaps it can never be presented as it is fully apart from some one of its aspects. But this reservation need not invalidate the possibility of some assertions that could not be disputed correctly. At the same time, it would clarify the inevitability of dispute.

In this way we might begin to explain the finitude of philosophy (and the connection and difference between "to be" and "to be true") differently from Heidegger, and do so in accordance with our other arguments. In any event, our discussion cannot be conclusive, and not merely because of its brevity. But we may summarize the analyses in this section by remarking that Heidegger himself has not sufficiently clarified philosophy's relation to his fundamental ontology or the relation of the pursuit of his fundamental ontology to man's possibilities within what is common.

[3]

Ordinary Time: Exposition

Heidegger's analysis of history attempted to show that man's historicality is temporal in its roots, thereby confirming and expanding his discussion of temporality in general. He completes both his elucidation of temporality and the published portion of *Being and Time* by analyzing the origin of the ordinary concern with, and conception of, time. The analysis is also important for our purposes because it clarifies and expands Heidegger's discussions of world, the public, Nature, and the infinite.

(§79–81) What is the temporal basis of our concern with time? Man is concerned with entities within the world; this concern is grounded temporally in a making-present that awaits and retains. In man's planning, reckoning, and preventing, he audibly or inaudibly expresses this awaiting as a "then": something will happen "then." He expresses his retaining by saying that this eluded us on that former occasion (*damals*); and he expresses his making-present by saying "now." We recall that making-present takes the lead in ordinary concern; we can thus see that what basically lies in the "then" is the *now* not yet, and what lies in the "on that former occasion" is the *now* no longer. The horizon for the now is "today"; for not-yet-now, "later on"; for no-longer-now, "earlier."

Further examination of these three expressions reveals that every "*then*" is a "then when," every "*now*" a "now-that," and every "on that former occasion" an "on that former occasion when"; that is, the three expressions have a relational structure that Heidegger calls "datability." Man expresses a now-that when he concernfully addresses things, because he is expressing his Being-alongside them when he deals with them. For *Dasein*'s addressing entities is made possible by his making-present; and his awaitingly retentive presentation interprets itself in his addressing—our temporality is always familiar to us, and our immediate familiarity with it is as we interpret it in ordinary concern. Indeed, that temporality is the source of time is confirmed by the fact that "now," "then," and "on that former occasion" are datable. "Now" is always understood as now-that; the door slams, for example, because "now" interprets a making-present of entities and is therefore dated in reference to entities encountered in *Dasein*'s temporally rooted disclosedness. This, of course, is not to say that we thematically understand the unity of temporality when we "give" time, or that we necessarily conceive or even know primordial temporality.

Datability is one structure of time. The second is "spanned-ness." When a man awaitingly makes present, he understands an "until then," because he understands what he awaits in reference to the "now" in which he makes it present, and the "then" (or not-yet-now) in which he awaits it. We express this until-then as "during." Indeed, we grasp enduring or lasting in light of the understanding of "during" that first arises in everyday concern: such lasting is the time that becomes manifest in our interpretation of ourselves; we comprehend time as a span.

Now, because man's existence is Being-with others, he usually holds himself in average public intelligibility. Thus, we understand the now-that and the then-when in their everyday public expression. This publicness of time is its third structure: rather than knowing time as his own, *Dasein* utilizes the time with which "one" reckons and does so especially when he specifically concerns himself with time.

Indeed, one directs oneself according to public time in a manner that makes it clear that everyone can come across it. Public time is not equivalent to dating in reference to the environment; on the contrary, this dating takes place within the horizon of public "time reckoning." Astronomical and calendrical time calculation is the kind of time within which ready-to-hand and present-at-hand entities are encountered, and its ontological basis is not the quantitative procedures that go with it but the temporality of *Dasein* who reckons with time. When man is submitted to what is within the world, he awaits his own potentiality for Being in a manner that reckons in and with "whatever has an *involvement* for the sake of this" potentiality.[21] Such concern requires sight for its circumspection and it is the day's brightness that gives this sight. When a man discloses his world, he also uncovers Nature, and, as thrown, he is therefore "surrendered to the changes of day and night."[22] *Dasein* thus dates his concern in reference to something both connected with brightness and involved within his environment. The ready-to-hand sun and its place in the sky is available environmentally to all and, like the public environment, we discover it along with our current world of equipment. The measure that arises from time is the day, which is itself divided according to the regular passage of the sun; *Dasein*'s happening from day to day and dividing the day arises from his finite awaiting of "thens" in light of his concern. *Dasein* therefore has a "natural" clock that is discovered with and necessitated by his thrownness, and this means that the temporality at the root of our thrownness is the condition making possible the natural—and, ultimately, the more handy artificial—clocks.

The time with which we concern ourselves is made public

---

[21] *Sein und Zeit*, p. 412.
[22] *Sein und Zeit*, p. 412.

when it is measured. To further uncover the ontological meaning of such time, we must consider how what is dated shows itself when dated through reckoning. Here we see that the "then" dated in concernful awaiting is explicitly or implicitly expressed in a statement such as "then in the morning it is time for work." This means that the time that we concretely interpret in concern is understood as time *for* something: the then, the now, all the modes of interpreted time, are as such appropriate or inappropriate. This structure of appropriateness, in which time is always the right or wrong time for something, exists because public time makes manifest the structure of significance that constitutes the world's worldhood. As time for something, public time manifests the relation of "in order to," and thus can be seen in its essential world character: public time is world time. In sum, each everyday structure of time, each everyday now-*that* and then-*when* is preconceptually understood as datable, spanned, public, and belonging to the world.

If we now think about the activity of reading off the time from clocks, this structure becomes even more evident. The time is not in the clock, nor could we find it merely by observing the pointer's changing position. Rather, our looking at the clock is guided by our "taking" time: implicitly or explicitly, we say it is *now* eight o'clock, now is the time for awakening. When we regulate ourselves by time, we are essentially saying "now," where the now has been interpreted in its structural content. Precisely because this is so obvious, we do not note it, or know it explicitly. But the now that we "say" discursively articulates the making-present. Indeed, because of this priority of making-present, the measuring in which time is read off from the clock is also expressed by the now, and time is publicly encountered for everyone on every occasion as a universally accessible "*present at hand multiplicity of nows....*"[23]

The discussion of time, Heidegger continues, makes it clear that time is neither subjective nor objective. It is not objective because it is not a present-at-hand entity; it is not subjective because it is not a Being present-at-hand that occurs in a subject.

[23]*Sein und Zeit*, p. 417.

245

Rather, as world time, it is both the condition for the possibility of any entity within the world and the condition for the possibility of the Being of the existing self. It is neither inside nor outside of anything present-at-hand, and it is "earlier" than subjectivity or objectivity because it is the condition for any earlier and later: world time belongs to the temporalizing of temporality.

Now, when time is made present in its movement by being counted, it is nows that are counted, nows that will immediately no longer be and have just not yet been: world time is ordinarily seen as now time. For everyday understanding, time shows itself as a sequence of nows that pass away and come along but are constantly present-at-hand, a flowing succession of nows, the "course" of time. This ordinary *interpretation* of world time can be ontologically understood by comparing it with the essential structure of world time. We then see that the whole understanding of temporality becomes distorted. The datability of the now, such that it is essentially now-*that,* and the significance that belongs to the now, do not become accessible when time is understood as "pure succession." They are covered up in the ordinary interpretation such that the now loses these relations and the ecstatic-horizonal constitution of temporality is leveled.

This covering of the fundamental structure, and this misconception of time as something present-at-hand, is exacerbated by the conceptual characterization of time developed in ordinary interpretation. The sequence of nows is thought to show its constant presence in each now, precisely as each now is already vanishing: time is believed to continue without interruption and to have no gaps. It is further considered to be "infinite," endless on both sides, because every "last" now is already no longer, already past, and every first now is just now, not yet now in the "future": one can never think time to its end, and it is therefore believed to be infinite. But the thesis that time is infinite, the principal thesis of the ordinary interpretation, is possible only when we have leveled the full meaning of the "now" as datable, significant, and "having a location of the same kind as *Dasein*'s." Everyday man therefore looks away from his finitude and, consequently, does not recognize authentic futurity or any authentic temporality. Indeed, the entire basis of world time in *Dasein*'s temporality is covered up precisely by the understanding of time that belongs to man's average Being. This ordinary interpretation is justified within limits, but it cannot provide the basic horizon in which time must be interpreted. Rather, temporality, not ordinary time, is primordial.

After analyzing Hegel's conception of time, Heidegger concludes the published portion of *Being and Time* by asking whether time manifests itself as the horizon of Being.[24]

Ordinary Time: Analysis

An exhaustive analysis of Heidegger's discussion of ordinary time would take us beyond our task. Therefore, let us confine ourselves to the following points.

I must emphasize the connection between ordinary time and world. We can understand ordinary time to be freed by temporality because it specifies the structure of significance that belongs to world. In this sense, the chief clue to ordinary time is the datability of that with which *Dasein* is concerned. Now, this datability is always connected to the appropriate and fitting time. Consequently, such time is prior to simple counting of merely present-at-hand nows in much the same way that the ready-to-hand in general is prior to the present-at-hand. Even the sun, the chief entity by which time is measured, is first discovered as an entity for public dating. Only then does the sun become uncovered as present-at-hand, and only then does a clock become used and time become measured in such a way that measuring means that "a standard which has presence is made present in a stretch which has presence," where the standard itself is conceived to be present-at-hand. This makes clear that in *Being and Time* the "natural" order of the seasons, of the day, of the visible heaven, is not superior to or more comprehensive than world, and that the generality that allows the sun to serve the measuring function it serves is ultimately within the world and the

---

[24]On time, consider Hans Georg Gadamer, "On Empty and Ful-filled Time," translated by R. Philip O'Hara, from *Die Frage Martin Heideggers* (Heidelberg: C. Winter, 1969) in Ballard and Scott.

world's public character as a characteristic of *Dasein*. Ultimately, as Heidegger has already indicated in his discussion of Reality, Nature is a "real" entity: it is not Being. Although Nature is not present simply as ready-to-hand or as a natural thing, any intelligibility of the "Natural" order is first freed within the world.

Now, it is unclear whether Heidegger believes that the way in which the sun serves as a present-at-hand measure exhausts the sense in which nature can be something other than ready-to-hand or a present-at-hand thing. If it does exhaust it, then we may say that he has overlooked the sense in which the physically "natural" order is itself a model of regularity and sufficiency that attracts human order. If he has not overlooked this, it remains difficult to discern how such attraction, and how the peculiar measuring that occurs in attempted imitating, is congruent with the other characteristics of Heideggerian presence-at-hand.

Our discussion of time measuring leads us to see a related area in which Heidegger's discussion of ordinary time is insufficiently developed. For, although Heidegger explores the leveling of significant time to time as ordinarily understood, he does not explore the precise connection between the more or less thematic discussions of the "appropriate" time—say, Aristotle's in the *Ethics*—and those theses at the basis of the ordinary and the theoretical understanding. Similarly, he does not analyze the related Aristotelian understanding of measuring excess and deficiency (or the Platonic understanding in the *Statesman* of the two types of measuring) in his own analysis of time measurement. He does, however, argue that Aristotle's definition of time as that which is counted according to the earlier and the later genuinely grasps ordinary time; but it fails to see its derivation from Heideggerian temporality. This leads us to wonder whether the entire question of time measuring may not be more subtle than a leveling of significance to presence-at-hand, and whether there may not be a more fundamental commensurability between the counting of nows and the enumerations of practical activity than Heidegger's discussion suggests. Here again it may be suggested in his behalf that the root connection is found in temporality as it frees *Dasein*'s Being. But then I would argue that Heidegger's primordial temporality can be accounted for in a manner similar to that in which we have disputed certain of his other arguments. In particular, I would suggest that *Dasein*'s temporality as that which frees authentic anticipation of death is itself ultimately rooted in man's striving or yearning to be what attracts him. Then, the genuine movement of man would be his striving, and ecstatic temporality in Heidegger's sense would become intelligible in light of the aim of this striving. In this sense, even the physically "natural" order of the heavens reflects the self-sufficiency and comprehensiveness that men seek to imitate, without itself being beyond time. The proper understanding of the intelligibility of ordinary time within this perspective, and, perhaps, an elaboration within this perspective of Heidegger's ontology of the presence-at-hand of things as freed for modern natural science, depends on clarifying the problems of counting and measuring.[25]

[25]Consider here Jacob Klein, *Greek Mathematical Thought and the Development of Algebra* (Cambridge, Mass.: MIT Press, 1969).

Conclusion

We have now finished our study. I have attempted, first, to clarify the intention and significance of Heidegger's analyses; second, to consider and illuminate the status of certain ethical and political possibilities in the light of these discussions; and third, to question Heidegger's general analysis in the light of these issues.

Concerning the first attempt, I believe we have seen clearly the precise manner in which Heidegger's discussion of man explores him in his distinctive openness to Being: we have attempted to consider Heidegger's conceptual discussion of man as an ontological discussion and to differentiate his understanding of Being from traditional understanding. In particular, I believe we have newly clarified several areas: the status of temporality as both ecstatic and horizonal, the place of Temporality as the horizon of Being, the historical meaning of Heidegger's own exploration, the connection between Heidegger's existential discussion and the possibility of philosophical questions, the status of theoretical as opposed to practical understanding. In claiming this, of course, I do not also claim fully to have solved these problems. Moreover, I also believe we have seen more clearly the relation of existential and temporal structures to concrete ontic and existent*iell* differentiations; the precise status of *Dasein*'s death, guilt, and finitude; the meaning of, and connections between, authentic and inauthentic *Dasein;* and the relation between Heidegger's discussion of *Dasein*'s historicality, temporality, and existential structures.

Concerning the second attempt, I will say that the first positive result of Heidegger's analysis is to show the inadequacy of any attempt to describe human affairs through the means of natural science or what imitates natural science in its leveling of man to mere presence-at-hand. For then what is missed is precisely the utility of the useful, the affective character of moods and what is released through them as fearsome or desirable, and the holistic character of ends as ends. Any political, ethical, or economic matter is implicitly grasped in its meaning as human before any other treatment of it, and other treatments and their results are therefore founded on this intelligibility. But precisely because this intelligibility is not self-evident, it cannot be treated as if it were self-evident. Because the results of social science find or lose their significance in reference to this level, they must ultimately be based on the explorations at this level.

The second positive result concerns the implications of Heidegger's analysis of human finitude for the problem of moral rules and regulations, that is, for the problem of moral absolutes. The fact of human openness, and the fact that any human action carries its particularity with it, speaks against the possibility of rules and regulations that can be unalterably true in every situation. By illuminating and clarifying these facts, Heidegger forces any thought that seeks to anchor choice in something permanent to consider the difficulty, indeed the impossibility, of finding a genuine anchor in the kinds of "absolutes" that are, in our day, believed necessary for the task. In the same way, his analysis of the status of human being clarifies the errors that ground the attempt to reduce morality, or choice in general, to a question of values. Whatever the criticism of Heidegger, he illuminates the ground on which any effort to steer a proper course between unconvincing absolutism and reductionist relativism must begin, and he himself attempts such a course.

As a third positive result, Heidegger clarifies the intelligibility of practice *as* practice apart from theory. In doing so, he forces us to avoid the simple and subtle forms in which the practical is submerged in the theoretical, and this accomplishment is useful even if we finally defend such a submersion. Practical deliberation is not equivalent to theoretical affirmation; practical discovery is not a less conscious version of theoretical questioning; practical truth is genuine, and not undeveloped science. This attempt to develop the independent status of practical activity is a decisive step in rescuing the dignity and intelligibility of what is ordinary or extraordinary but not theoretical. Moreover, Heidegger's understanding of the significance of the practical environment and the significance of entities freed within that environment force scientific and theoretical activity to lose their status as activities that simply can be taken for granted. The grave peculiarity of theoretical activity becomes more clear, and, in general, Heidegger's analysis begins to restore the sense of wonder that theoretical activity can happen at all. The questioning of the ontological possibility of theory releases the uniqueness and even the charm of both the simple and remote by cutting through the habitual and customary encrustations that cover them. Beyond any questions concerning the specific quandaries of political philosophy and political practice, beyond any problems of how to begin an adequate theoretical account, Heidegger focuses our attention upon the root peculiarity of the fact that there can be such a thing as theoretical activity at all. This fourth result of Heidegger's analysis also retains its force even if we finally disagree with it, because Heidegger so clearly clears the ground on which such disagreement can take place. In doing so, he presents an interpretation that, to say the least, is hardly less compelling than the alternatives.

In a fifth positive result, Heidegger cogently discusses the status of history and historical possibilities and cogently differentiates thematic historiological research from other scientific enterprise. More radically than his predecessors or successors, Heidegger elaborates the historical as historical—human possibilities, and the repetition of these possibilities, conceived from finitude with no reliance on what is eternal or on entities that transcend man. Moreover, his analysis of man's fate within the destiny of the people enables him to clarify the strange combination of contingency and inevitability with which possibilities are first presented. Consequently, he is able to uncover both the contextual (or systemic) nature, the interconnection, of what we can choose and the impermanence of these contexts. His analysis of the historical essence of the people, and his analysis of the public in general, forces any genuine consideration of human affairs and political possibilities to come to grips with this horizonal or cavelike aspect of the human.

This brings us to our third goal in conducting this study: to question Heidegger's general analysis. The preceding points do not mean that Heidegger's analysis of human Being permits us to understand the possibility of political entities or of political and moral issues with complete clarity, even in his own terms. Guided by our concerns, we have, for example, examined more fully than does Heidegger himself the implications of the connections between authenticity and inauthenticity, the connections between the scientific and prescientific freeing of entities, and the status of the ontic unit that is as a people. And we have discovered that these implications are by no means clear. More than this, we have discovered that both these implications and his analyses as they stand do not allow the full intelligibility of what is political. Indeed, our questions have led us to wonder about the being of what Heidegger himself calls Being and about the possibility of what he considers to be as *Dasein;* and we have considered whether the phenomena that most clearly seem to require interpretation as *Dasein* may be accounted for in other ways. But in making these arguments, and in considering the status of politics, morality, and the interconnections of human possibilities, we have only, as it were, examined in another way the topography of the area to which Heidegger has led us. I will now conclude by summarizing, and in some cases briefly developing, these arguments.

I argued, first, that political entities—such as justice, glory, courage, moderation—cannot genuinely be interpreted as ready-to-hand in Heidegger's sense, and that they are most fruitfully grasped, in his terms, as possibilities of *Dasein.* But I further argued that these possibilities need not come to light as belonging to man exclusively and, indeed, that their attractiveness for man derives from a perfect possession of them beyond finite man's capacity. Insofar as what attracts man can be for its own sake or can be for a god, Heidegger fails to clarify the status of these possibilities. But insofar as such entities transcend man, who is attracted by the very self-sustaining perfection of perfect righteousness or a revered god, such possibilities *as* man's cannot be examined apart from their greater status. Consequently, Heidegger's analysis of man's possibilities, and, especially, of the possibilities that come to light as the virtues of statesmen and citizens, is imperfect.

But does not this argument require us to consider man as a tool or a present-at-hand thing, and has not Heidegger shown that the human as human cannot come to light in this way? Here I reach my second argument, namely, that the phenomena on which Heidegger bases his interpretation of human finitude as *Dasein*'s finitude—as the finitude of man as transcendent to "Being"—can be understood as revealing a finitude congruent with the connection between man's possibilities and the possibilities of what is beyond him. I have argued that practical and philosophical activity can both be understood as finite precisely in reference to the fact that the intelligibility of human activity is finally rooted in the perfection that men seek to imitate; I have held that the phenomena of openness, striving, imitation, can be interpreted in the light of this perfection without interpreting man as present-at-hand in the natural scientific sense, as a tool, or as an entity that can be perfectly fulfilled. Moreover, I have argued that the phenomena of the prior intelligibility of entities with which we deal concretely, phenomena that Heidegger interprets in terms of *Dasein*, can be grasped sufficiently by this alternative analysis.

But in what way is Heidegger's analysis faulty? What phenomena that he discusses recommend alternative interpretation? Beyond my discussion of the uncertain status of what I called the "noble entities" in *Being and Time*, I suggested, among other things, that Heidegger's discussion of wholes and Being a whole failed to clarify sufficiently the very questions of the interrelations and clashes among activities that we might have expected to be clarified in a discussion of existential wholeness. Heidegger's analysis does not make clear the grounds on which the political and philosophical ways of life are both intelligibly interrelated and split. Moreover, the propriety of explicit inquiry into Being is not and cannot be developed sufficiently. I found these problems to exist both in his analysis of "*Dasein*'s" wholeness and in his discussion of historical possibilities and the people's destiny. Furthermore, I argued that Heidegger's discussion obscures the status of the possible ontic interconnection between what is discovered practically and theoretically. And I tried to indicate that the similar intelligibility of what is discovered practically and what is searched for theoretically in political philosophy better permits us to account for these interconnections; that the similar status of practical and theoretical pursuits as imperfect imitations of more perfect justice, self-sufficiency, and comprehensiveness better allows us to account for the necessity of their clashes, whatever the concrete political community; and that this analysis better permits us to understand the possibility of rank order among possibilities without reducing man to readiness-to-hand and without claiming that theoretical activity is simply independent of, or always more urgent than, just practice. Finally, I argued that Heidegger's analysis of the freeing of possibilities by the people leads to a mistaken understanding of the separation and division among these possibilities that is congruent with his speeches in 1933 and 1934, that the uncertain status of the dominant entity that is as a people contributes to this problem, and that the practical effect of treating the political community as a people in Heidegger's sense is the immoderation that I described.

Because Heidegger does not adequately grasp the proper sense in which human activities are and are not whole, he overlooks the concrete way in which it is the political community that is the proper entity first to serve the "ontological" function of being a public. Consequently he also ignores the proper sense in which the political community in general—and as such a public—is and is not whole. I have sketched these arguments in the preceding chapters; let me now summarize and elaborate.

The political community is a whole by being oriented to the ends that complete it and, consequently, by organizing what belongs to it. This organizing is not simply an intelligible freeing of means in relation to an overarching end, because the community itself reaches or embodies its end—insofar as this can be reached or embodied—in its structure and in its distribution of goods, that is, in its ordering, ranking, and placing. For the material matters with which politics deals, any individual's pursuit of a particular possibility necessitates his participation in these ends *as* they belong to the political community. For example, the justice or pride of the statesman is found in relation to the distribution of concrete goods commonly produced and commonly enjoyed and in the honor received from other men. Therefore, although we may speak of the individual projection of these ends, the end itself is attained, insofar as it can be attained, in its forming of the community and, therefore, in the individual participation in the community.

This comprehensiveness of the political community—which arises from its comprehending a sufficiency of bodily goods, of virtuous dealing with these goods, and of human discourse as praise and blame in relation to these virtues and these goods—enables the political community to be an image not only of this or that perfection but of the whole of things in their perfection. In this sense, the decisive political entity is justice, with justice as the name for the end that forms a whole; and this is why I have generally used it as my example rather than employing glory or the virtues that first present themselves less completely. Such wholeness, however, is necessarily imperfect because the political community cannot fully embody the justice it seeks; it cannot do so because, as I suggested, the very place in which it seeks perfection is too fleeting, disordered, and narrow to allow it. There are human possibilities beyond political embodiment, and beyond the praise and blame of political speech; the urgency of here and now prevents the full adhering to the rank order sought by politics; and the very material of political life, the resources and circumstances on which even the best political life depends, are provided by accident or force and can never be justified fully by the community's own lights. For these reasons, no political community genuinely embodies the perfection for which it strives, or even embodies it to the degree possible for human beings. The essential openness or disputability of any political entity as a whole thus comes to light not only in the possibility of activities that transcend it but also in disputes about the proper meaning of justice itself. This disputability is further apparent in the pretense to authority of ends that are less complete than justice itself—say, pleasure, a liberty indistinguishable from license, or the goals that characterize a merely traditional society and result in the narrowing of the possibilities of virtue and distinction that arise from the statesman's speech and deed. Even injustice is, from this perspective, a failed or mistaken perfection. It is this incompleteness of the political community, combined with the intelligibility of its end and the other ends in the light of a fuller perfection, that allows us to understand both the possibility of the fundamental disputes within it and the interconnection between the practical and theoretical ways of life.

But it is for these reasons as well that any political community acts behind a veil of authoritative opinion. Moreover, the serious attempt to perfect political life requires a certain blindness or dedication, an assertive self-enclosure of the community, by its rulers for the community. Consequently, the essentially disputed issues of the proper ordering of human possibilities are first of all seen by men within this enclosure. Further, the political community is the home of the greatest possible perfection within the inescapable material of the human body and the powers of intelligence and speech as they are concerned with the goods of the body. No lesser community allows a sufficiency of resources or opportunities for excellence. Even further, it is unclear that the possibilities of perfect sufficiency, and, especially, perfect wholeness, could begin to be imagined were it not for political life, and it is unclear how even the theoretical life would be possible were we not first presented with the necessity of being accurate and reliable in practical affairs. Consequently, political orders can normally be treated moderately despite their pretensions. More than this, we are then able to see how the concrete political order, the particular regime in the particular place and time, controls the first intelligibility of human possibilities. We can see how the function Heidegger ascribes to the people or public is a function of the concrete political order, how it can present possibilities as they are first for us only because its wholeness, its completion, and the ends for which the political man strives imitate what is first as such. Nonetheless, precisely because the political order is incomplete, it cannot simply dominate what it presents. But this incomplete primacy of politics does not then require that there be an endless series of peoples or of possibilities to be repeated, for the possibilities of political justice are limited, as limited perhaps as the traditional classification of forms of government; and this is true of the possibilities of theoretical excellence as well.

I believe, therefore, that the function of "*Dasein,*" and, consequently, of Heidegger's "Being," can be understood sufficiently in what for him would be "ontic" or "metaphysical" terms, and that these terms enable us better to grasp the status of moral and political possibilities as a whole. Of course, this argument is disputable even if it is correct. For this reason, more conclusive remarks would be unjustified. But that is not to say that they could never be just.

Afterword

When I began to study Martin Heidegger nearly fifty years ago, my goal was to explore the meaning of *Being and Time* for political philosophy. I wished to discover what it might offer for clarifying the grounds on which the basic concepts and alternatives of political philosophy rest. Would a close reading of it help us understand the questions of justice, freedom, the common good, natural rights, virtue, human happiness, and the philosophic life? These questions are as important today as they were then.

To study these issues by exploring Heidegger was a much less obvious path then than it is now, but it was not unique or unprecedented.[1] *Being and Time* was understood to be the heart of the 'existentialism' that was still a dominant approach in the 1960s and 1970s, especially in the humanities. And although existentialism did not have the obvious political salience of the other dominant approaches, Marxism and Freudianism, it certainly focused on the question of humanity, and to be human is to be political. Besides, the chief existentialist, Jean-Paul Sartre, was an aggressive Marxist, and Albert Camus' works were staples of what was then 'contemporary' political theory. Moreover, several of Heidegger's first students became leaders in contemporary political thought—Hannah Arendt, Herbert Marcuse, and, above all, Leo Strauss. As a student of a student of Strauss, I learned that one should study thought by considering its powerful fathers, not its

---

[1] I footnote in the book several works that examined the implications of Heidegger's work for political philosophy and politics.

sons and daughters, however clever. So it seemed reasonable to explore the political meaning of existentialism by exploring its source in Heidegger. Strauss had written (and I came to think) that the best way to study serious thinkers is to comment on their important works, step by step, and to read them as if what they argued could be true. Although such analyses might serve as the basis for other modes of presentation, one might also offer one's work as a commentary: this could be especially useful for a difficult and obscure work. Although there was no reason to think that Heidegger wrote esoterically, or that he intentionally hid behind masks, his work was certainly difficult enough. For these reasons, therefore, I thought that a commentary on *Being and Time* with a political-philosophical focus would be useful.

Strauss had claimed that Heidegger was the chief proponent of a radical historicism that challenged the possibility of permanent truths about the basic questions of political philosophy.[2] This historicism is intellectually more subtle than the notion that thought is relative to its time—that, for example, the Declaration of Independence's defense of natural rights was the passing product of old-fashioned Enlightenment beliefs. As a more subtle and enticing enemy of natural truth, Heidegger's historicism is also a more challenging and dangerous one. I had recently finished my dissertation on Plato's *Statesman*, and Heidegger's historicism was a central foe of Platonic or Aristotelian natural justice as well as of Lockean or American natural rights. So not merely Heidegger's grounding of existentialism and his influence on important contemporary thinkers but also the challenge of his historicism made it desirable, or indeed necessary, to study *Being and Time*.

The shadow that darkened the attempt to consider what Heidegger could offer to political philosophy was his association with the Nazis. One could believe that this association had little or nothing to do with his thought (because, say, he was a politically unsophisticated provincial), or, on the contrary, take seriously the relevance of the association for his work. I believed that the association was likely closely connected to his thought. The notion

[2]See Leo Strauss, *Natural Right and History*, University of Chicago Press, 1953, and Leo Strauss, *What is Political Philosophy?*, The Free Press, 1959.

that someone who wrote so deeply about human understanding, moods, our "being-with" others, everyday life, and authenticity would make political judgments that were naively or incompetently dissociated from these thoughts was ludicrous on its face. (Why would one take such a figure seriously?) But this association (whose full extent was in any event unclear) did not necessarily make all his thought incorrect. Considering Heidegger's thought on its own, but keeping this association in the background, and sometimes the foreground, of my analysis seemed both honest and prudent.

In 1981, when I completed *Heidegger's* Being and Time *and the Possibility of Political Philosophy*, most students of his work did not take the association seriously intellectually and, indeed, downplayed it altogether. In the ebbs and flows of attention to Heidegger's politics that occurred after the Second World War, we were in an ebb. The contrary views of Karl Löwith, for example, were not dominant. Heidegger's explanations of his association with the Nazis, chief of which were his assuming the rectorate of the university in Freiburg and speeches he made and actions he took in support of Hitler in 1933–1934, were accepted, if hesitantly. He portrayed himself as one who hoped that Hitler's ascension would be an auspicious moment for university reform; in any event, he claimed he needed to help save the university. The interview he gave to *Der Spiegel*, published after his death in 1976, was treated by some as the final word. Move on—there is nothing more to see here. In contrast, I argued that Heidegger's thought and political action were connected, that his support of the Nazis was unsurprising although not in every situation required by his thought, and that his illiberalism never changed. I doubt that I convinced anyone who was not already sympathetic to my view.

It was not until information appeared later in the 1980s and 1990s connecting Heidegger to the Nazis in greater detail that it became hard for anyone to ignore or dismiss the association.[3] Although it was difficult to ignore the association, its link to Hei-

---

[3]See Victor Farais, *Heidegger and Nazism*, translated by Tom Rockmore and Joseph Margolis, Temple University Press, 1989, first published in Spanish in 1987; and Hugo Ott, *Martin Heidegger: A Political Life*, translated by Allan Blunden, Basic Books, 1993, first published in German in 1988.

degger's thought remained contentious. To comprehend this link depends on understanding not only Heidegger's thought but also discussions of man and politics in other thinkers. Political philosophy and political action, however, are often only minimally or peculiarly grasped by Heidegger scholars. Much of the attempt to explain Heidegger's link to the Nazis rests on taking for granted the truth of his claims to have overcome previous philosophy, or on accusing him of sliding back to the usual metaphysics he believes he has moved beyond. Oddly, despite the general denunciation of Heidegger's Nazism, one saw and sees little discussion of the proper intellectual grounds for condemning a regime that murdered vast numbers of Jews and others, and for supporting those who fought the regime and defeated it. Heidegger's views about man and being are rarely confronted unflinchingly by those who know him or seek to know him best.

Even attempts to claim that although Heidegger's association with the Nazis is connected to his thought, it is nonetheless an aberration that is not truly directed or determined by it, were increasingly difficult to maintain as lectures and seminar protocols from 1933 to 1935 became known. His discussions of the *Volk* (the people), of the *Führer* (the leader), and of the state are too pointed, too detailed, and too reminiscent of the style and content of Heidegger's other teachings to dismiss. They provide intellectual background for his already widely read Nazi-oriented speech on assuming the rectorate, and his messages supporting Hitler's actions, such as withdrawing from the League of Nations. The new material makes it very difficult to consider these speeches and messages as merely prudent, or to consider Heidegger's only goal to be educational reform. Taken together with things he said and wrote after the war, they make it hard to see his support for Hitler and his indifference to or encouragement of at least some elements of the awful fate of the Jews as a passing mistake, an intellectual aberration, or the short-lived weakness of a fearful man.[4] I also consider it a mistake to explain

[4]Consider the second Bremen Lecture, delivered in 1949: Martin Heidegger, *Bremen and Freiburg Lectures*, translated by Andrew Mitchell, Indiana University Press, 2012, p. 27, and first published in German in 1994.

his support for Hitler as based on personal anti-Semitism. This is merely another way to try to rescue Heidegger's thought from Heidegger's politics. Most of what he says and fails to say about Jews and "Semites"—that they are rootless, destructive nomads, that they are at one with the dominance of the technology that he abhors, that mechanized agriculture and the gas chambers are equal instances of technological destruction, and that internal enemies of the people (Jews? communists?) should be "annihilated"—is presented not 'personally' but, on the contrary, as integrated within his teaching and thought.

The now indisputable evidence of the serious connection between Heidegger's thought and actions has led some to wish to dismiss his thought altogether: his arguments are nothing but and were always nothing but Nazi propaganda. This view, pressed by Emmanuel Faye in 2005, has led to the most recent renewal of attention to Heidegger's politics.[5] It was Faye who brought to light Heidegger's continued collaboration with many academics sympathetic to the Nazis and emphasized the seminars and lectures from 1933 to 1935, several of which were not scheduled to be published among Heidegger's complete works and some of which have only recently come to light. Faye does not succeed in making his case that Heidegger's thought is Nazi propaganda through and through. Still, his arguments and, especially, the new evidence are damning enough that one wonders "whether we can disentangle the truer or more promising aspects of his philosophy from the more pernicious ones."[6] So the issue for many today is no longer whether one can ignore Heidegger's politics or separate it from his thought but whether the connection discredits his thought altogether.

[5]Emmanuel Faye, *Heidegger: The Introduction of Nazism into Philosophy*, translated by Michael Smith, Yale University Press, 2009, first published in French in 2005. The German publication in 2014 of several of Heidegger's notebooks, the so-called Black Notebooks, has further added to this renewed attention, especially toward Heidegger's view of Judaism.

[6]Gregory Fried and Richard Polt, Editors' Introduction, p. 1, in Martin Heidegger, *Nature, History, State, 1933–1934*, translated and edited by Gregory Fried and Richard Polt, Bloomsbury, 2013, first published in German in 2009. See also my review of Faye's book: Mark Blitz, "Natural Reich," *Weekly Standard*, February 8, 2010.

Heidegger's Importance

Before I present the material from the 1933–1935 seminars in detail, we should therefore remind ourselves of Heidegger's philosophical importance. The elements of this importance are most visibly displayed in *Being and Time*, although not only there, and I summarize and analyze them in my book. Most concern a novel and often immediately convincing discussion of what makes humans human. Oddly, Heidegger's discussion of man has not been a major element in the scholarship of the past thirty-five years. One reason is that the emphasis on man in *Being and Time* turned readers in the wrong, existentialist, direction. Heidegger himself meant to direct us to being: what is distinctive about human being is that our own being is an issue for us. We are therefore open to being as such, can understand its several modes, must deal with the entities that concern us in being's terms, and also inevitably misunderstand it.[7] We cannot help but recognize that we talk, think, and feel, meet our needs together with others and through what is not human, deliberate and choose, are always immersed in a here and now, and die. For Heidegger, we should first see each of these characteristics in terms of how we are open to being, how we implicitly deal with and are thrown among meaningful entities and understand being, the ground of this meaning. It is this radical discussion of human being, and not only or primarily of being as such, that was forceful and appealing in Heidegger's work and attracted people to it. The scholarship now focuses largely on the question of being because this is Heidegger's question and the source of his novel understanding of man, but it is his understanding of human being that is the first and in my judgment still the most powerful source of his attraction.[8] Much of his discussion struck and still strikes one as novel, deep, true, coherent, and overlooked by everyone before him, and it is in *Being and Time* that he carries out his analysis most comprehensively. What Heidegger says about man in other works is seen best as repeating and occasionally clarifying or extending *Being and Time*.

[7]I will use beings and entities equivalently, and (except at the beginning of sentences and when mentioning the book *Being and Time*) will not capitalize being.

[8]The other source, for scholars especially, is his illuminating discussion of a wide range of previous thinkers.

What is important in Heidegger's discussion of human being, or of *Dasein* (existence), the term he uses to name humans in our being and our openness to being? First is his novel philosophical emphasis on our ordinary immersion in ordinary things, our usual dwelling in our everyday world of use and activity. In *Being and Time*, Heidegger's example is the use of tools in a workshop. In his first lecture course in Freiburg in 1919 he discusses the immediate environment of his lecture, of seeing, dealing with, and approaching the lecture hall and the lectern. Such examples lead him to analyze the structures that permit things to present themselves in the implicit meaning and connections that allow us to deal with them in our everyday environment. Heidegger proceeds to bring out the difference between our ordinary context of time and space, which is connected to places and events, and the leveled-down space and time of the objects that we consider in physics and chemistry. These neutral frameworks have misleadingly become the clue to our understanding of being and human being. To open up the time, space, and other characteristics of the everyday world where things are ready to be used is thus to widen the context for ontology generally. It is also to remind us of, and then to examine, our human activity within the ordinary world. Heidegger's discussion uncovers, for political philosophy and generally, a way to rescue and understand practical action in its own terms as something whose being is not inferior to the being of the neutral material that we merely observe. Although I indicate in the book ways in which I think Heidegger's argument is limited, it is a telling and powerful first step in regaining the meaning (and independence from scientific analysis) of our ordinary experience, and, thus, of human being generally.

Discovering the character of the contexts in which we are ordinarily immersed is central to Heidegger's radical re-thinking. His discussion of worlds, however, is not only important in itself. He connects it to his radical re-understanding of the usual terms of reason, feeling, and bodily necessity.[9] Part of Heidegger's importance is his remarkable grasp of the meaning, possibility, power,

---

[9]Heidegger's argument, I should also say, attempts to be fully secular, and independent of theological demonstrations grounded in faith.

and function of moods and dispositions, language and discourse, and understanding and concepts. Heidegger re-thinks each of these characteristics from the standpoint of their essential connection to our openness to the intelligibility, meaning, or being that illuminates things, and how we fix entities in these meanings.

Much of my book describes these phenomena: here, I will only discuss moods. As with our other characteristics, their essence is found in the way they belong to the human revealing of beings, including ourselves, in their being. Fear, for example, reveals beings as detrimental for a possibility for the sake of which I am. Whether I find myself fearing the harmful or alarmed by it, terrified by what threatens or dreading it, depends on the humanly meaningful speed and direction with which the fearsome approaches me, and the importance and scope of the activity in which I am engaged. Fear is not an 'internal' feeling, because it is always connected to a world of my concern and to my possibilities generally. Nor is it caused by something 'objectively' independent from me. These ways of understanding can be related to 'fear' only when we first see fear in the way that I just described it, a mood that reveals beings, including myself, in their meaning, and that is not 'objective,' 'subjective,' or identical with the behavior or shrinking back that one sees in an animal or plant, let alone reducible to what is merely chemical. Fear, moreover, as is true of other moods, reveals an entire world of things that strike us in a certain way. Part of the significance of Heidegger's understanding is his enduring portrait of the presence and motions of experiences such as fear as we actually undergo them. (Whether his analysis captures how we best understand dealing with fear courageously is another matter, however, which I discuss in the book.)

After *Being and Time*, Heidegger does not change his analysis of dispositions, although he varies which ones he emphasizes. He becomes especially concerned to discuss the basic or foundational moods that, he believes, can show us our openness to and responsibility for being simply, and not only to this or that meaningful set of entities. These basic moods can become a ground of the authentic self-understanding in which we confront our own mode of being, and do not treat ourselves as if we are only a different kind of animal or physical object. Such moods are also central in what Heidegger considers to be the great acts of philosophic, poetic, or political founding. In *Being and Time*, anxiety is the central mood that he discusses. Later he examines the fundamental boredom in which the meaning or attraction of all things slips away, and (in his discussion of Hölderlin's poetry) what he calls holy mourning in readied distress.[10] In general, Heidegger's discussion of moods, in which we reveal entities in their being and our own being, is difficult to dismiss. This and his discussions along these lines of our other human characteristics are powerful and memorable.

Being

Although Heidegger's most evident philosophical significance is his novel and convincing understanding of human being, his central question is that of the meaning of being as such. What changes and does not change in Heidegger's thinking about being in the years that follow *Being and Time*? In my judgment, Heidegger's work remains unified because its central outline, direction, and question stay the same, and differentiate him from previous thinkers. The basic outline was clear when *Being and Time* was published: I quote in my book a passage from the 1927 course *The Basic Problems of Phenomenology* that presents this outline: "understanding of entities, projection in terms of being, understanding of being, projection in terms of time, has its end in the horizon of the ecstatical unity of temporality. . . . In this horizon every ecstasy of time, that is, temporality itself, has its end."

In the ensuing years some elements of the outline have become clearer and others more obscure. But it is primarily the interrelations among these elements that Heidegger developed further and elucidated or even modified. His evident outline was nonetheless unclear to some who first read *Being and Time* because its execution was broken off. Heidegger had planned two divisions with three parts each, but finished only the first two parts of the first division. The second division was to have explored or "decon-

---

[10]Heidegger discusses boredom in a 1929–30 lecture course that is published in English as *The Fundamental Concepts of Metaphysics*, translated by William McNeill and Nicholas Walker, Indiana University Press, 2008.

structed" Kant's, Descartes', and Aristotle's understandings of time. Despite its absence, one can recapture what Heidegger likely would have said by considering his summary in the sixth section of his introduction to *Being and Time*, and by reading *Kant and the Problem of Metaphysics* and courses and manuscripts which are now available in which he discusses Aristotle and Descartes. The (ostensibly) more difficult issue is the missing third part of the first division in which Heidegger intended to show that time is the horizon for the question of being. There is little in his courses before *Being and Time* that is helpful in filling this absence, and what is published in earlier sections of *Being and Time* and in the *Basic Problems* illuminates this third part only partially.[11]

Most characteristic of Heidegger's later approaches to discussing what in *Being and Time* he describes as the horizon for the question of being is his consideration from the beginning of the link or togetherness of being as such, human being, and temporality.[12] They are not given separately only to come together, but belong together from the start. Emphasizing and exploring this togetherness, rather than discussing temporality separately or independently, is a feature of Heidegger's later work.[13] It is one reason that this work is less conceptual or 'scientific' than what he wrote earlier. The belonging together of being and human being is the central fact that allows them to be as they are. It is also tells us that being cannot be without humans, that it requires man. Heidegger's German term for this belonging is *Ereignis*, "event," usually translated in Heidegger texts as "appropriation" because of the word's resonances and roots.

One can see almost immediately that if being needs man it can be no more permanent and eternal than man is. So Heidegger's being is not what one might usually think being is. This again

---

[11]We now even have a book of essays on the missing third part. The somehow comic but very Heideggerian absurdity of writing about what is absent, or about nothing, as it were, is not lost on the editor, and several of the essays are illuminating. Lee Braver, editor, *Division III of Heidegger's* Being and Time, The MIT Press, 2015.

[12]In summarizing some of the results of these approaches I will leave unremarked many of the evident similarities with *Being and Time*.

[13]This is not to say that Heidegger does not already have this togetherness in mind in *Being and Time*, as we can see from his discussion there of time's horizons.

suggests why his understanding of human beings turns out to be so novel, for we always are by being together with or open to a "being" that needs us in order to be, and which we need in order to be, but which differs from "being" understood as eternal or unchangeable.

It is, of course, difficult to catch sight of and remain within what Heidegger has in mind with being, and with its belonging together with man. For what one says is almost inevitably taken as a statement about the qualities or powers of an entity, or the predicates (such as enduring or causing) of a subject, namely, being. One might even wonder if what Heidegger is examining as being matters very much, or if it does matter why it deserves the name "being."

The reason why Heidegger's examination of being matters is that anything's being in a causal or any other sense—say, the power that defines this object as opposed to that—requires a clearing or dimension, a stage, in which it comes to presence. It is this clearing and, therefore, this presence that cannot be apart from man, who, as it were, holds it open and stands within it. This holding open and standing within, indeed, is the heart of our thinking or awareness. Being and entities are unintelligible, or have no meaning and cannot assume their powers and possibilities without man. But we do not control this presence and, indeed, always find ourselves already resident in some intelligible world, dealing with things in some characteristic way. Our understanding cannot avoid a circle in which we always see what we seek to know more fully within some prior intelligibility from which we can never 'absolutely' free ourselves. It is this circle, or, as Heidegger occasionally says, vortex around and in which we are always turning.[14]

The essential belonging together of man and being, and this clearing in which being takes place, are the background for what is intelligible. We largely ignore or overlook it because we turn to things. When we use tools we implicitly grasp the interrelations of the steps we must take to do the work at hand: we implicitly grasp the order of involvements—this here, for that—that allows

---

[14]I believe that this is the basis of the turns that Heidegger mentions in his work and that are a source of scholarly dispute.

a tool to be a tool. But in using the tool we do not see this background. Nonetheless, when Heidegger points out the structure of involvements we can understand it. In fact, the concrete order of work does become explicit when, say, a tool is missing or broken. So, our experience allows us sometimes to recognize an order of involvements and thus to observe and follow a 'formal' discussion of availability and manipulability. We can bring the background to light. But we seem to have no concrete experience of working within the clearing of being as such, nothing on which to draw that would then allow us to observe and discuss this deepest, most original background.[15] We do not even know how we can look at it at all, because this looking is inseparable from the background, and unlike describing the usability of things we have no broader dimension to which to appeal. Moreover, anything we see in its meaning or intelligibility is freed by us from the un-cleared vastness or darkness of all that we have not revealed, the untruth into which what we understand is always threatening to fall.

Nonetheless, what Heidegger has in mind can be grasped to the degree we have just discussed it, especially if we see how he worked to this origin. Heidegger moved to this beginning by inquiring about the single meaning that being or "is" has throughout its multiple uses. We differentiate what things "really" are from how they merely look or appear, from how they could be or ought to be, from their changeable and variable characteristics. The being of a house differs, say, from the color or size of any particular house. This being itself is nowhere to be seen: it is invisible. Such being, or true being, or the reality of things, is the object of philosophers and scientists. This being or truth, however, has many elements, modes, kinds, and characteristics. It is not only that there are many beings—many of Plato's ideas, say—but also that these ideas have several features: they are what we can know simply, they are unchanging and unmarred, they cover each thing that belongs to them, some fit together but others do not, and they are all connected to the rest, motion, sameness and differ-

---

[15]This is one reason that Heidegger always sought to make us aware of the fundamental moods that could take us away from immersion in entities and allow us to be mindful of being.

ence that Plato also thinks of as being. Aristotle discusses various categories—things as having qualities and quantity, say—and also things as having characteristic activities or ways of working, things as having natures, and things as being true practically, theoretically, artistically and so on. What, if anything, unifies all these meanings of being?

As we have seen, Heidegger begins his inquiry by examining the "factic" or everyday life of human beings, and his first central insight and argument is that the entities with which we ordinarily deal "are" as fully as the entities that we examine theoretically. The hammer's weight is too much or little for the job, not a neutral amount, its space is here where I can find it easily, not its neutral geographical coordinates, its time is when I need to use it, not a neutral hour we read from a clock. One cannot build up to such times, spaces, and weights from mere neutrality. Heidegger then examines our everyday environing world in ways I describe in the book and have briefly rehearsed here.

But why, in any event, do we always find ourselves among the entities of the everyday world? The reason is that we are the beings who need to determine our being. Our being is an issue for us; our being is ours to be; each of us is a who, not an instance of a what. That our being is an issue for us means that we are always ahead of ourselves, always "futural" in resolving our being. But in being for the sake of our possibilities we are also always among other entities in the world, always moving in significant environments that allow these other entities their being. We choose shelter, and things thus have meaning as tools. Indeed, we make our choices or decisions in terms of possibilities that already have a meaning, ones that we have inherited, in a world into which we have been thrown. (What could it mean to be or want to be an artist or statesman without some prior and ongoing sense of what these are?) Yet these past and present meanings come to light and are further determined only because we decide to be out for them, only because we are futural. This overall openness to and immersion in the being of beings is precisely why examining human being is central in understanding being, and the temporal extendedness inherent in our understanding and decisions is why we are essentially historical.

In *Being and Time*, Heidegger develops our "existential" characteristics, the structures that enable us to understand ourselves, after discovering and discussing them in his courses and lectures in the years that preceded his writing it.[16] Everything—anxiety, our dying, our immersion or falling into the things with which we deal and our misinterpreting our being as if we are a thing—turns out to be crucial for understanding us in our openness to our being and to being as such. Above all, Heidegger thinks that our temporality, understood in a way appropriate to man, as I just briefly described it, is the condition of the possibility of our own being and is basic for the question of being as such. Heidegger's first and still central entrance into the belonging together of being and man, of presence and opening, of the clearing, is in his discussion in *Being and Time* of the temporal extendedness of human beings.

Why has this dimension of temporality been missed by others? Why have thinkers not seen that being is always implicitly understood temporally and, indeed, as presence? It has been missed because all thinkers took temporality for granted or see human time as identical to the time by which we measure things. We consider time to be a series of passing "nows," and we overlook the time span of the everyday world, and the extension, the stretching forward and backward, of human time.

Temporality has been missed as well because the philosophers interpreted being as what Heidegger later called beingness. When Plato, Aristotle, and the thinkers who followed them sought the true being of things, they overlooked the dimension that Heidegger is discussing. Being for them is the most fully present, the permanent or eternal, the never-ending, the standing now, the most fully accomplished "product" (those natures that arise and stand on their own in their own limits), what is always there. Their question is what constitutes this permanent presence—a Platonic idea, an Aristotelian actuality, a Cartesian subject, and so on. But what they took for granted, according to Heidegger, was presence

---

[16]These works are now available, and have been analyzed by, among others, Theodore Kisiel in *The Genesis of Heidegger's* Being and Time, University of California Press, 1995. Various additional documents are available in Theodore Kisiel and Thomas Sheehan, *Becoming Heidegger*, Northwestern University Press, 2007.

itself, as the horizon for interpreting being. More broadly, philosophers overlooked temporality in its full dimensions. So what seems to them to be the most original dimension or location, namely, the realm populated with the objects of the philosophers, their ideas and subjects, is in fact secondary. They miss the primary temporal dimensions, and our human opening of and standing within temporality's horizons. This realm is where everything that is, including philosophers' basic concepts, can first present itself. Temporality allows or indeed is not different from authentic human temporality. From this standpoint, what the philosophers discuss, Plato's ideas, say, is in fact not being as such, but only particular beings. Anything 'eternal' is discoverable and meaningful only within temporal horizons. What the philosophers call being is in fact only the highest and most general entities.

Some of what I have just discussed follows later formulations that are more crisp and direct than what one finds in *Being and Time*, but all of these points characterize *Being and Time* as well as later works. Many of the difficulties people faced with *Being and Time* were due to the necessary ambiguity of the distinction between being and beings when one has not yet clarified what being means. For Heidegger himself, the difficulties with *Being and Time* were apparently threefold. The belonging together of being and man (with which I opened this discussion) and the link between temporality and being (which Heidegger failed to elaborate in his unpublished third part) are always central to him. This link allows being's "meaning" (in *Being and Time*), or, later, what he calls being's truth or place (its "clearing"). But after *Being and Time* Heidegger newly experiences and examines this belonging together. The discussion planned for *Being and Time* may have seemed to him to follow too much from his already thought-out concepts rather than arising from a fresh experience of its realm.[17] This is the first difficulty. Heidegger may also have thought that his intended analysis would

---

[17]One could also say that just why temporality should have been missed by everyone else and being or even the philosophers' beingness be forgotten or unseen by everyone today was insufficiently clarified. Consider Martin Heidegger, *Four Seminars*, translated by Andrew Mitchell and Francois Raffoul, Indiana University Press, p. 68, first published in French in 1977. The seminars took place from 1966 to 1973.

make temporality look too much like a traditional cause or condition, and would fail to bring out its novel function. Finally, our standing within a given clearing (and not, as it were, "projecting" an understanding of being with complete independence) seems downplayed in the discussion of man in *Being and Time*, giving the appearance of making our understanding of being too subjective.

That said, much of what I have just written about the limits of *Being and Time* is connected to statements that Heidegger made in the years following its publication, and is not as obvious as my remarks may have made it seem. Moreover, although Heidegger came to focus on the belonging together of being, man, and temporality, and on what is "sent" to the philosophers in the extended open, he does not change his central view: the human characteristics are as he describes them in *Being and Time*; temporality is the ground of human beings who are essentially historical; being fundamentally means and has meant presence; the first way to begin to grasp all of this is to attend to our everyday world; and some version of the phenomenologists' attempt to see things just as they are, and not see them in alien conceptual terms, is the proper way to understand.[18]

Thinkers

As I said, Heidegger had planned a second part of *Being and Time*, in which he intended to consider Kant's, Descartes', and Aristotle's understanding of time and deconstruct their thought until we could see the primordial experiences on which their understanding is based. Because we are finite we always experience being and ourselves through possibilities that have been, that are understood (but also covered over) traditionally. The history of philosophy is therefore not ancillary to the direct examination of phenomena but is central to understanding being and our possibilities.

Heidegger's understanding of how philosophers' thoughts originate in something hidden from them changed somewhat as his understanding of this origin changed. Moreover, his close, pathbreaking examinations of Aristotle in the 1920s were primarily

---

[18]See, for example, Heidegger's late discussions in the *Zollikon Seminars*, which include letters, conversations, and seminars from 1947 to 1972, and the material from 1962 to 1964 included in *On Time and Being*.

aids to help him to think through the importance of everyday practical life, the breadth of what we can reveal as true, the irreducibility of various modes of being to each other, the centrality of what is accomplished and available in our understanding of being, and the significance of presence and the present. He also, however, tried to show how Aristotle ignored much of this in his formal view of time, and he "deconstructed" Aristotle and other thinkers by showing the hidden origin of their thought in *Dasein*'s characteristics and in temporality.

After *Being and Time* Heidegger considers earlier thinkers not so much by dismantling them to the origin of their thought in *Dasein*'s characteristics and temporality, but by displaying them in terms of the "sending" of presence, and by clarifying their relation to each other as progressively ignoring being. Moreover, Heidegger increasingly treats eras or generations as somehow controlled by the philosophical understanding of being that forms them. This notion comes to a head in what Heidegger understands to be the power of technology in contemporary life, where "technology" means not devices but the first and decisive presence of everything, including humans, as a standing reserve of resources to be used for the procurement of still more resources. Everything thereby loses its independent form. Indeed, it is this complete obscuring of being and non-technological modes of being that, as being's negation, helps to permit Heidegger to grasp the radical otherness of being as he does. The understanding of technology in this way is a new step from *Being and Time*. He also develops his radical view of language and truth as revealing and establishing beings and being rather than only offering statements about things that are already revealed; his understanding of artworks and, especially, the most profound poetry, connected to the deepest moods, as helping to establish being and peoples; and his discussion of the existence of simple "things" that are neither means to ends nor objects of science, and that we cannot grasp metaphysically.[19] Heidegger develops his final discussion of the clearing, of

[19]Consider in this regard his essays *The Thing* and *Building, Dwelling, Thinking*. Both are available in Martin Heidegger, *Poetry, Language, Thought*, translated by Albert Hofstadter, Harper & Row, 1971.

opening and presence, and of *Ereignis* in conjunction with these thoughts.[20]

Heidegger's concern about the oblivion of so much of being and its modes furnishes the 'practical' motivation for his work. He always debunked the thought that philosophy could provide a worldview, but he nonetheless intended to reawaken our awareness of being not merely to understand it but to save it, and us. Authentic existence may not be morally superior to inauthentic existence, but every serious reader of Heidegger would prefer to be authentic, at least at first. No mode of being may be superior to another, but every serious reader of Heidegger would prefer to participate in being and man's true richness, at least at first. The cause of a more considered hesitancy should be the connection of Heidegger's thought to his political understanding, to which I now turn.

Politics in Being and Time

Where, then, is politics in this account, and how is it grasped? There are several sources in *Being and Time* for understanding Heidegger's view of politics. I begin with his argument that part of our being is being-with others. This means that an element of being who we are is to disclose others in the world with us. To be with others authentically is to set them free into their own possibilities. Our own authenticity, indeed, is marked by seizing our being rather than being captured by particular activities of our everyday world. Being-with, however, is not directed primarily to politics. The second source concerns the public, in the sense of the utilities, laws, functions, and functionaries that our activities show us are used by all. We usually see the public merely as a tool, but we can also grasp our belonging to and opening a public authentically: we then belong to a *Volk*, a people. The third source concerns what Heidegger calls "*Das Man*," the "they," or "one," as

---

[20]In my book I mention several areas where Heidegger's analyses could be developed and clarified, in his own terms. To these areas one might well add still more, centering on these newer discussions. The connections among man, the extending of time, being as presence, the modes of being discussed in *Being and Time*, the world of simple things, the meaning of the 'gods,' and the 'beingness' that is the object of the philosophers—the connections among these elements, and in some cases the elements themselves, remain ambiguous in various ways.

when we say that "everyone" is wearing this fashion this year, or that this is how "one" behaves in this circumstance, or that "they" dislike this kind of architecture. This "they-self" is who each of us is almost all the time, the definer of our aspirations, comparisons, and possibilities. In this sense, we are essentially public, because it is not as our unique selves but rather as the one who is the same as the others that we first, and usually, experience, interpret, and develop our possibilities. We even unwittingly conceive our individuality and shrink from the "they" just as everyone else does. These possibilities of the they-self, moreover, are handed down to us in our tradition. One becomes authentic only by transforming this they-self; one can do so by experiencing the nullity at the heart of our being, the impossibility, ultimately, of securing ourselves through any entity, because beings cannot stand in their meaning, their being, without us. Any direction or involvement that guides us can slip away in boredom or be lost in anxiety, for we are co-responsible for the meaning of the possibilities in which we find ourselves and that we activate and follow. Moreover, any decision means that other possibilities are closed or unfulfilled, which is still another element in our nullity. Furthermore, what links our possibilities is their own possible nullity, the possible impossibility of all our possibilities, our dying. Recognizing our nullity, recognizing our co-responsibility for meaning and for the full or developed presence of being, can allow us to resolve upon or seize this responsibility for holding the clearing open in which beings can be present in their being: we can resolve upon our own finitude and temporality. In doing so one must also be transforming the merely public interpretation; one is transforming the public into a people, where possibilities for authentic understanding are set free, at least for one's generation, in discussion, in communication, and in struggle. A people is the authentic analogue to the public as the home for *Dasein*.

Heidegger and the Nazis

The chapter on Heideggerian politics in the book indicates how these notions make possible Heidegger's support of the Nazis: the totalizing of the "people" leaves no room for the separate realms and cosmopolitan engagements that allow one to stand away and apart from the political community of the moment. Without such a possible separateness, one expects too much from the political community and overestimates one's ability to affect it, as if all could be equally transformed or coordinated. Or one expects too little from one's ability to affect it, as if one is trapped in the dominant way in which beings are meaningful during one's time. The choices are either total action or passivity. The arguments through which one might defend an inviolable distance between individuals and their state; the standpoints through which one might keep modes of work, study, thought, and art reasonably separate from each other and not equally and fully oriented to their "fatherland"; the ways through which government might check and limit itself internally—each of these seems unavailable in Heidegger's thought, or undesirable to him. Where would one find the grounds in his work for (the desirability of) individual rights, cosmopolitan distance, and separate, checking powers? Combine this absence with Heidegger's questions about technology, his attack on liberalism as subjectivist and technological, and his views of Jews as rootlessly nomadic calculators who are grounded in the 'gigantic' and in 'machinations,' and one sees the possibility or, indeed, likelihood of his support of the Nazis.[21] The totalizing or encompassing nature of a people as he understood it, or the overwhelming dominance of our current technological (or any other metaphysically-dominated) age makes it difficult to see how Heidegger could uncover the desirability of these liberally democratic practices. America and Russia always struck Heidegger as essentially similar. Either he is wrong, or this metaphysical similarity disguises vast differences that should guide political judgment: the metaphysical similarity would be politically irrelevant or misleading. But how in Heidegger would a choice one way or the other between these regimes be anything but (philosophically) arbitrary? To these factors, moreover, I would add Heidegger's notion of struggle among or within peoples and the ambiguity of the entity that any people as an authentic public is, which leaves the

---

[21]The 'gigantic' and 'machination' are formulations of elements of what is discussed most fully as the domination of the technological. For the claims about Jews and world Jewry, see the quotations below and the Black Notebooks.

people's boundaries open and, therefore, justifies the possibility of German expansion.

Heidegger's illiberalism and his concern about ultra-technological and bourgeois America are features of his thought and rhetoric from beginning to end. This illiberalism need not always issue in Nazism, and Heidegger later became a friend of Germany's student left and a figure admired by some German environmentalists. But it can indeed issue in Nazism, as it did in his case. In fact, the seminars and lectures from 1933 to 1935 make the grounds of the affinity between Heidegger and the Nazis unmistakable. Heidegger discusses the people and community more expansively than but not differently from what he says in *Being and Time*.

The basic intellectual question in the view of politics that governs Heidegger in *Being and Time* concerns the status of the "people." (The more direct political question stemming from *Being and Time* and the speeches of 1933–1934 concerns his extreme illiberalism.) As I said, as authenticity is to everydayness, so the people is to the public. But while it is clear that *Dasein* is the being of individual human beings, who exactly is a "people"? The newly published course material from 1933 to 1935 helps us to see what Heidegger meant by the "people." Overall, it confirms and indeed makes evident the link between Heidegger's thought and his support of the Nazis, which I believed was already clear in *Being and Time* and in his rector's address and other messages from that period.

Of the several things Heidegger teaches about the people and the state in 1933–1935, the most revealing are the reports or protocols of his course from 1933 to 1934, *On the Essence and Concept of Nature, History, and State*. These may not always be verbatim transcriptions, but they were read and corrected by him. "The being of the state," he says, "is anchored in the political being of the human beings, who, as a people, support this state—who decide for it."[22] This decision is an "historically fateful" one. "The political as the fundamental possibility and distinctive way of being of human beings" is "what makes states possible."

[22]All quotations in this section are from Sessions 7–10, pp. 45–64, in *Nature, History, State*.

Each of us needs to know "the essence of the state and people." But we also require "a band of guardians in the people" to help "bear responsibility" for the state. This knowledge does not pertain to the leader, however, who "does not need to be educated politically," for "the origin of all state action and leadership" "lies in being," not in knowledge. "Every leader *is* a leader . . . and brings about what people and state are, in the living development of his own essence." When a people authentically decides for its fate as a people, i.e., is political, it also, or consequently, decides for a state. Each people has the 'urge' for a state, but if it is stateless it has "not found the gathering of its essence" and "still lacks the composure and force to be committed to its fate as a people." The people is the entity whose being is the state. That is: it is only as the people's being, and not as a concept or alien imposition, that the state can endure. "Every state and all knowledge about the state grows within a political tradition. Where this nourishing, securing soil is lacking, even the best idea for a state cannot take root, grow from the sustaining womb of the people, and develop." "Just as human beings" "are concerned with "their being-human," "in the same way, the people as a being has a knowing fundamental relation to its state." "Just as every human being" wills, "loves," and holds on to "his *Dasein* in the world," "the people wills the state as its way to be a people."

The people's *eros* for the state is different from anything animal or instinctual, the sociality of bees, for example. It includes "concern for the essence and form of the state," "rejection, dedication" and "taking a position." This means that "the form or constitution of the state is . . . an essential expression of what the people takes to be the meaning of its own being." This is not an anodyne statement, for it suggests that "the constitution is not a rational contract, a legal order . . . or anything else arbitrary and absolute." "Constitution and law are the actualization of our decision for the state . . . attestations of what we take to be our historical task as a people." Each of us takes "upon himself the struggle and responsibility for his people."

Such responsibility "also includes commitment to the order of the state." This order is not organic, but "spiritual and human" and therefore voluntary, and is expressed in the tasks of groups and individuals, "the relations of human beings in ruling and serving each other." True order in a state arises only where "the leader and the led bind themselves together to *one* fate and fight to actualize *one* idea." "Then spiritual superiority and freedom develop as a dedication of all forces to the people, the state, as the most rigorous breeding . . . and love. Then the existence and superiority of the leader sinks into the being, the soul of the people, and binds it in this way with originality and passion to the task . . ."

As I indicated, Heidegger explicitly distinguishes this notion of the state as the way of being of a people from a state based on a social contract that serves individual welfare. Such a liberal state is not the state in the sense of the political "as the fundamental character of Western man who exists on the basis of philosophy," but is only a means to an end, "in service to the development of personality in the liberal sense, one domain among many."

What is Heidegger's view of the range and extent of a people? He wants to connect but not limit the people to the land, and to differentiate a people's land and being on it from mere geography or the animal environment. He seeks to elevate a people's land to *Dasein*'s being, just as his notion of race is not simply biological. In both cases he is presenting expansion and exclusivity as essential to our being.[23]

We should not identify a people with a particular land and rootedness: rootedness in the people does not only mean rootedness in a particular soil. It also does not mean standing on some spatial coordinates, nor is it identical to how animals have an environment. A people's space is neither "an indifferent container" nor its surroundings. Rather, Heidegger claims, every people has its own space—"persons who live by the sea, in the mountains, and on the plains are different . . . nomads have not only been made nomadic by the desolation of wastelands and steppes, but they have often left wastelands behind them where they found fruitful and cultivated lands." Mastering and becoming marked by space "belong together with the essence and kind of being of

[23]In what way is this rooting of race and expansion in *Dasein* superior to the mere biologism the eschewing of which is sometimes said to be to Heidegger's credit? Is it not, rather, even more dangerous, because it connects race to what is most distinctive about man, and not to our animality?

AFTERWORD

a people." In fact, humans rooted in the soil "can make a home for themselves even in the wilderness." So, "the sole ideal of a people" is not in the attachment, settledness and cultivation of rootedness in the soil. Rather, it is also necessary "to work outwards into the wider expanse, to interact with the outside world." The homeland's rootedness in the soil becomes a natural rootedness and boundness to the earth only when the homeland becomes expansive and becomes or is becoming a state. A people is in danger of losing its peoplehood if it fails to step beyond the homeland "into their authentic way of being—into the state." Germans "who live outside the borders of the Reich" have a German homeland but not the state, "so they are deprived of their authentic way of being." From how a people knows the nature of its space, moreover, "we first experience how nature is revealed in this people." "Our German space" would be revealed differently to Slavs than for "us"; "to Semitic nomads, it will perhaps never be revealed at all." What is central is the "specific people in its historical being."

This discussion helps to answer what Heidegger has in mind with a "people," and it helps us understand further the being of the state. The state's order is one of mastery or power where "the will of one gets implemented in the will of others," the ruled. This is not mastery over the people or the people's sovereignty, however, which is absolutism. The coincidence of will of the ruled and ruler is central. The origin of the power and force, the mastery, that guarantees implementation of will "can always be raised only on the basis of a particular way in which the people has its being in a state."

The powerful will directed at the whole implements itself primarily through persuasion, not coercion. Persuasion occurs through speech and through acts—the "*Führer*'s" speeches and especially the acts of the "great effective actor" "whose *Dasein* and will become determinative through persuasion, that is, when one knows and recognizes the soaring will of the leader." "The true implantation of the will" is therefore "based on" "awakening the same will in another, that is, the same goal and engagement or accomplishment." "The will of the leader first transforms the others into a following, and from the following arises a community," "sacrifice and service": the implementation of will may include education, administration "and the justice system." "The highest actualization of human being happens in the state." "The *Führer* state" completes the historical development of the Prussian state and nobility, and the tradition of "leadership . . . knowing that it is an affair of the people" that stems from Luther.

Other courses from 1933 to 1935 further illuminate Heidegger's view of the state. I should especially mention *Logic as the Question Concerning the Essence of Language*, which clarifies Heidegger's understanding of the connection between leader, state, and people and his grasp of temporality as the ground of human being. Temporality is unified, but its heart is the future. The future comes toward us only when what has been, the tradition, is carried over. This reaching over as reaching back also allows a present. Politically for the Germans this means that their "mandate," their self-determined future, is "predetermined" by the "mission" that empowers and "bequeaths" their origin—it is not arbitrary; their future clarifies what has been obstructed in their mission. What preserves yet also creates this determination is the "labor," the setting to work, that fits together "our entire comportment and our bearing from that which is mission and mandate for us."[24] Labor "transposes our being in the binding appropriate to work, in the liberation of beings themselves. . . . In labor . . . beings first become manifest to us in their determinate regions . . ." Such labor is our "historical moment," our human present. In addition to this, and even more original, is the people's "fundamental mood." Great works and great art are possible only from a fundamental mood; "moods are that by virtue of which we open or also lock ourselves to beings in the deepest and broadest and most original manner from out of our essence." Time is the "joint" of our historical being. It lets us experience "the historical singularity of our self." Time is the unity of man-

---

[24]All quotations are from Martin Heidegger, *Logic as the Question Concerning the Essence of Language*, translated by Wanda Torres Gregory and Yvonne Unna, State University Press of New York, 2009. The German original was published in 1998, and the lecture course was delivered in the summer semester of 1934. Quotations are from pp. 106–107, 127, and 108.

date, mission, labor, and mood, "the fountain of the historical *Volk* and of the individuals in the *Volk*."

Although the precise political analogue to the "dying" that allows each of my possibilities to be mine is obscure, authentic totality is possible for the people's founding statesmen, poets, and philosophers, as is the experience of a fundamental mood: perhaps, indeed, such a mood, and the struggle that shows the nullity at the heart of our possibilities, can be raised by them in their people. Heidegger's discussion of Hölderlin in 1934 suggests this. Hölderlin gives and has given to him the language that preserves the German vocation. Central in Hölderlin is "the fundamental attunement (mood) of a holy mourning, yet in readied distress," which "alone places us at once before the fleeing, the remaining absent, and the arriving of the gods."[25]

Overall, the "state is essentially necessary" because our being is grounded in care or temporality. The state is not abstract or "derived from a right [that is] invented, and relative to a timeless human nature that is in itself," but, rather, "the state [is] the law of essence of historical being by virtue of whose decree the *Volk* first secures for itself historical duration, that is, the preservation of their mission and struggle over its mandate."[26]

This discussion in *Logic as the Question Concerning the Essence of Language* brings the arguments in *Nature, History, State* into Heidegger's full temporal understanding. Heidegger's state is obviously different from states based on natural justice and natural rights, whose "people" are the people of Locke's natural state, the 'we the people' of our Constitution. Lest one be uncertain what the *Volk* requires, lest one be uncertain about the implication of the thinly veiled suggestion that the nomadic nature of the Semites shows their unsuitability to be members of the German *Volk*, we close our exposition with Heidegger's statement, from 1933's "The Fundamental Question of Philosophy":

[25]Martin Heidegger, *Hölderlin's Hymns, "Germania" and "The Rhine,"* translated by William McNeil and Julia Ireland, Indiana University Press, 2014, pp. 122 and 123. The German original was published in 1980. See too *Logic*, p. 140.

[26]*Logic*, p. 136. *Volk*, state, human being, being, time, and history are not "abstracted concepts": the essential relationship is always historical, i.e., "self-deciding that futurally has been." *Logic*, p. 136.

An enemy is each and every person who poses an essential threat to the *Dasein* of the people and its individual members. The enemy does not have to be external, and the external enemy is not always the most dangerous one. And it can seem as if there were no enemy. Then it is a fundamental requirement to find the enemy, to expose the enemy to the light, or even first to make the enemy, so that this standing against the enemy may happen and so that *Dasein* may not lose its edge.

The enemy can have attached itself to the innermost roots of the *Dasein* of a people and can set itself against this people's own essence and act against it. The struggle is all the fiercer and harder and tougher, for the least of it consists in coming to blows with one another; it is often far more difficult and wearisome to catch sight of the enemy as such, to bring the enemy into the open, to harbor no illusions about the enemy, to keep oneself ready for attack, to cultivate and intensify a constant readiness and to prepare to attack looking far ahead with the goal of total annihilation.

Indeed, "Struggle . . . determines beings as a whole and determines them in a crucial way."[27]

The seminars that Heidegger gave from 1933 to 1935 clarify his political understanding but do not depart from what was visible in *Being and Time* and his rector's address. The link between his understanding and Nazi rhetoric and action is manifest. A people is connected to but not simply rooted in the soil, and the German people may experience its proper destiny in expansion. Nomadic peoples cannot set roots, wherever they happen to be. The people's being is its state, the "philosophical" state that should be distinguished from the liberal state that is merely one unit among many. The state requires political knowledge from each citizen, and a deeper knowledge and responsibility from some, but it is primarily formed by the leader's existence. Today's German state has a mandate and mission that it experiences in labor, and that properly brings forth its tradition and future. To be and become what it is, the state must recognize and perhaps annihilate

[27]Martin Heidegger, *Being and Truth*, translated by Gregory Fried and Richard Polt, Indiana University Press, 2010, p. 73. This compiles "The Fundamental Question of Philosophy," a course given in the summer of 1933, and "On the Essence of Truth," a course given in the winter of 1933–1934. The original German was published in 2001.

its enemies. Heidegger's discussion of the state and people in his temporal terms is not an intellectual accident, ephemeral manipulation of his basic concepts, or a misguided attempt at prudence. Rather, it displays his attempt to unify his political and philosophical understanding and to unify his political and philosophical existence.

Conclusion

Heidegger's understanding of politics is connected essentially to his understanding of a people's state and destiny as historical. As I said, one reason I chose to study Heidegger was to explore the question of history and historicism, and the relativism and arbitrariness connected to them. Heidegger discusses *Dasein*'s being-historical at length in *Being and Time*. He also claims that his work is not relativistic. As he says in the lectures on *"Logic"* from which I have just quoted, the fact that "we have disavowed an absolute truth . . . does not mean . . . that we advocate the thesis of an only relative truth; relativity is merely arbitrariness. The rejection of the standpoint of the absolute truth means, at the same time, the rejection of all relations between absolute and relative. If one cannot speak in this sense of an absolute truth, neither can one speak of relative truth. The whole relation is askew." Should this be a cause for concern? No, for "it is time we cure ourselves of the consternation over this and finally take seriously that we are for the time being still human beings and no(t) gods." Indeed, "from the fact that there is no absolute truth for us . . . we may not infer that there is in general no truth for us. By truth we understand the manifestness of beings which manifestness fits and binds us into the being of beings—in each case, according to the kind of being of the beings that enter here into manifestness. What for us is true in this sense of truth is quite enough for human life." Moreover, the statement that there is no absolute truth is not itself absolutely true, but is true only for us. We humans stand "always in the truth of certain regions and states." Furthermore, concealedness, disguise, suppression, and "untruth" "constantly rules our standing in truth." Philosophy cannot be free from a standpoint; the standpoint is to be "gained by struggle"; it is "a decision of standpoint."[28] Indeed, it is not clear why an "eternal" truth, which is the congealing into presence, is the most pervasive, prevailing, or powerful truth. Rather, compared to what prevails in emerging, the preservation of essence, it is perhaps a non-essence.[29] In fact, what is "true for everyone" is "binding" for no one. One individual "can stand in the truth, in which others do not stand because they are not ripe for that." Universal agreement is not a sign of truth, any more than truths that are not absolute are therefore untrue. The true depends on or belongs together only with its time, the duration and perdurance that are appropriate for each entity.

Whether Heidegger's statement here about the temporality of truth offers good grounds on which to choose a "standpoint" properly, deals adequately with the issue of beings that limit our actions because they exist prior to man and being, or comes to grips with the issues that lead to our concern with eternal truth is another matter.[30] I discuss these questions in the book. Heidegger himself outlines structures of our being—we are always already thrown, we are by being open to being, only possibilities that we understand in terms of dying can make us whole—that are as long as we are. And he outlines a connection between truth and untruth, understanding and forgetting, that is as long as man is. Nonetheless, these structures cannot be apart from how we decide upon and develop them.

I also outlined in the book several areas where Heidegger's discussion provides opportunities to challenge his arguments while also capturing what one learns from him about human being and modes of being. It is through such challenge that Heidegger can best be met intellectually. Each of these areas is also connected to grounds for disputing his political choices, and for properly fighting and condemning the Nazi regime he served.

[28]All quotations are from *Logic*, pp. 74, 68, and 69.

[29]For the question of the eternal and the permanent, consider *Hölderlin's Hymns*, p. 54, and Martin Heidegger, *Basic Concepts*, translated by Gary Aylesworth, Indiana University Press, 1993, pp. 96–100. This is a lecture course from 1941, first published in German in 1981.

[30]His arguments here in *Logic as the Question Concerning the Essence of Language*, after all, belong together with the remarks about the mandate, mission and labor of the Volk that I quoted earlier.

One such area centers on the relations among entities that we discover in different modes of being and in different philosophical discussions. I concentrated in particular on the connection among entities that we free theoretically and those that we free practically, both as they might support and as they might contradict each other. This connection is difficult to account for, given Heidegger's arguments. But the justice that we seek is the same theoretically and practically, although we cannot secure it in the same manner and degree philosophically and politically. This is the teaching of Plato's *Republic*. My critical arguments further centered on the interplay that Heidegger seemingly ignored between the perfection for which we strive and the difficulty or impossibility of bringing about this perfection, politically or philosophically. I claimed and claim that this interplay, properly grasped, enables us both to understand human limits or finitude and to find guidance for our actions. These guides could not be simply historical, even in Heidegger's complex sense. Among other things, they would enable us to defend intellectually the equal liberties, responsible character, and self-government that give the lie to the stupid and brutal fascistic grounding of human life on the exclusivity of races and "people," and to the less brutal but still brutish and ignorant identity politics of the past fifty years.[31]

To understand human affairs, in articulated detail, in terms of this connection between the theoretical and the practical and the interplay between striving and perfection, to grasp the true source and limits of justice, freedom, the common good, natural rights, virtue, human happiness, practical reason, the philosophic life, and other basic political concepts and guidelines remains a fundamental task. Heidegger's understanding of man and being can illuminate our approach to this task, but only if we are neither blind to his politics nor blinded by them.

January, 2017

---

[31] I have discussed some of these questions in Mark Blitz, *Duty Bound: Responsibility and American Public Life*, Rowman and Littlefield, 2005; *Plato's Political Philosophy*, Johns Hopkins University Press, 2010; and *Conserving Liberty*, Hoover Institution Press, 2011.